Loyola Pastoral Series

Lumen Vitae Studies

Ecumenism and religious education

Le Guillou	Debauche
Roux	Corbon
Scrima	Mélia
Heyer	Elkind
Coleman	Van het Hof
Brown	Westphal
Mejia	Van Caster
Seumois	Thils
Mailleux	Giblet
Desseaux	Beauduin
Decoudun	Moeller
Gressot	

21989

Chicago 1965

Loyola University Press

Distributed in Canada by
PALM PUBLISHERS, LTD., *Montreal*

IMPRIMI POTEST John R. Connery, s.j., Provincial of the Chicago Province, September 15, 1965. NIHIL OBSTAT John B. Amberg, s.j., *Censor deputatus*, September 17, 1965. IMPRIMATUR Most Reverend Cletus F. O'Donnell, j.c.d., Vicar General, Archdiocese of Chicago, September 21, 1965. THE NIHIL OBSTAT AND THE IMPRIMATUR ARE OFFICIAL DECLARATIONS THAT A BOOK OR PAMPHLET IS FREE OF DOCTRINAL OR MORAL ERROR. NO IMPLICATION IS CONTAINED THEREIN THAT THOSE WHO HAVE GRANTED THE NIHIL OBSTAT AND IMPRIMATUR AGREE WITH THE CONTENTS, OPINIONS, OR STATEMENTS EXPRESSED.

American Preface

Following the spirit of the Council, religion teachers and educators are eager that religious education at all levels be animated by an ecumenical spirit. Students must be brought not only to understand but also to respect and to love the other confessions.

With this in mind the editors of *Lumen Vitae* devoted two issues of Volume XIX (1964) to a study of ecumenism and religious education. Cooperating in the effort were Catholic, Orthodox, and Protestant theologians, pastors, and teachers. The completed study appears here, together with two original articles that were not published in the magazine.

The first section takes up the meaning of the word *ecumenism* from the Catholic, Protestant, and Orthodox viewpoints. It also inquires into the dispositions for dialogue that one finds in each of these confessions.

The second section studies the mentalities prevalent in a number of countries. What are this country's dispositions toward ecumenism? Are there major difficulties in regard to other confessions? What evolution is in progress?

Section three studies current pastoral activities inspired by the ecumenical spirit. One article calling for special attention is "Towards an Ecumenism of Charity." It investigates an important area referred to by Cardinal Gracias, archbishop of Bombay, who had asked that the International Eucharistic Congress (November 1964) be a testimony of the Church's love for the poor.

Section four investigates psycho-sociological situations: aspects of ecumenism in the Near East, among the Orthodox, and the child's conception of his religious identity.

Section five sets down certain principles and methods for an ecumenical catechesis. How can the teacher put forward the Christian message in its integrity and with fidelity to the order of truths and the hierarchy of values?

The final section discusses the presentation of doctrinal themes in an ecumenical spirit.

Contents

1

Meaning of Ecumenism

The Meaning
of Catholic Ecumenism

by M.-J. Le Guillou, O.P.

Istina Centre, Professor at Saulchoir [1]

Anyone reflecting on the history of relations between the Christian Churches, must admit a change of mentality in our time.

The coining of a new word always indicates a new reality ; take, for example, the words sociology and socialism in the XIX century. The word « ecumenism, » the appearance of which dates from the end of last century and the beginning of this, reveals the fact that *a new point of view has arisen in the mind of Christian unity.* The Churches which, until recently, showed antagonism to one another, are discovering what they have of positive quality and are seeking fraternal unity.

Relations between the Churches are henceforth settled by an essentially religious perspective. Until the end of the XVIII century, the Churches had, more or less consciously, linked their search for unity with political dealings with the civil powers. The book by Père Tabaraud, *De la réunion des communions chrétiennes* (1808), shows the change which was already at work in Christian consciences at the beginning of last century. The first signs of a

---

1. Father M.-J. le Guillou was born at Servel (Côtes du Nord) in 1920. He obtained a Licenciate in Philosophy and Letters, and a Doctorate in Theology. He taught moral theology at Saulchoir and the Institut Catholique de Paris, 1949-1954. Since 1958 he has held the chair of Oriental theology at Saulchoir, and is Director of the Seminary of Ecumenical research in Paris (1963). He is a member of the « Istina » Centre for Ecumenical Studies at Boulogne-sur-Seine. He has published several works of outstanding importance: *Mission et Unité. Les exigences de la communion.* Paris, Le Cerf, 1960, 2 vol. *L'esprit de l'orthodoxie grecque et russe.* Paris, Fayard, 1961; *Le Christ et l'Eglise. Théologie du Mystère.* Paris, Centurion, 1963; *Le mystère d'Unité.* Paris, Desclée de Brouwer, 1962, 2 vol., collaborated. *Dialogue œcuménique.* Paris, Fleurus, 1962, in coll. ; *Le Christ et les Eglises.* Paris, Ed. Univ., 1960, in coll. Address : Centre Istina, 25, Bld. d'Auteuil, Boulogne-s./Seine, France. (Editor's note).

change of climate date from the end of the XVIII and beginning of
the XIX centuries; the Churches, at grips with the whole world in
the totality of the historical and social future, came *existentially* face
to face with one another. With time, the era has dawned for a
serious, difficult meeting of Christian communions, at the level of
integral experience in a truly spiritual emulation.

EVOLUTION OF THE ECUMENICAL REALITY

1. *The Protestant Churches.*

The call to unity rang out across Europe in the XIX century,
but it was chiefly in North America, in English-speaking Protestantism in the second half of that century, that the great urge became
apparent and which led to the present Ecumenical movement.
Through the two movements, *Foi et Constitution* and *Vie et Action*,
emerged an organization for dialogue between Christian Churches,
the World Council of Churches, set up at Amsterdam in 1948.
It has led Christians of different creeds — *in* these not *in spite*
of them — to reflect on each other in a positive fashion.

2. *The Orthodox Church.*

Very ready to quit her isolation, the Orthodox Church quickly
joined first the Ecumenical movement, then the World Council
of Churches. In 1905, the Ecumenical patriarchate had organized
an enquiry into the interest in meeting the other Churches, and
in 1920 published an encyclical suggesting a League of Churches
similar to the League of Nations. This shows that from the outset,
the patriarchate was in perfect agreement with the big organizations
of the Ecumenical movement. Even if, through the force of circumstances, the share of the Orthodox Churches only became complete in 1961 at the Meeting in New Delhi (the Churches behind
the Iron Curtain joined the W.C.C. at the same time), they have
played an active part in the Ecumenical movement from its
beginnings.

3. The Catholic Church.

At first the Catholic Church eyed this movement with caution. Groups of theologians followed it with interest, so much so that the secretary of the W.C.C., Dr. Visser 't Hooft, said that the best studies on the Ecumenical movement were often written by Catholics, but the Catholic Church as such did not take part in real dialogue.

In giving Christian Unity as the final but real aim of the Council, Pope John XXIII brought the Ecumenical problem into the forefront of Catholic consciousness. The setting up of the Secretariate for the Unity of Christians, as an organization for dialogue, the invitation of Protestant and Orthodox observers to the Council, and their presence at it, has enabled the Catholic Church to create new conditions of encounter among Christians. By his acts, attitudes and declarations, John XXIII put an end to an age-long attitude of ignorance. He inaugurated the era of direct relations with the Orthodox and Protestant communities as such (sending Mgr. Testa to Constantinople, receiving Mgr. Fisher, etc.). His Holiness Pope Paul VI emphasized this new position by announcing his election to all the Christian Churches from the second day of his pontificate, by sending representatives to the Jubilee Celebrations of the Patriarch Alexis, by writing directly to the Patriarch of Constantinople making use of his full title : « To His Holiness Athenagoras, archbishop of Constantinople, Ecumenical Patriarch. » He set a seal on this orientation of the Catholic by his pilgrimage of prayer, penance, renewal in the Holy Spirit, to Jerusalem, and by meeting the Patriarch of Constantinople there. The Council, moreover, has allowed the whole Church to measure the new importance of Ecumenism, and some major declarations of Catholic consciousness seem to be appearing already.

A. *Ecumenism, Search for the Plenitude of the Mystery of Christ, in Communion with the Christian Communities.*

I would describe Ecumenism as the search for the plenitude of the Mystery of Christ in an ever deepening communion with all Christian communities.

a) *The Search for the Plenitude of the Mystery of Christ.* Within the Mystery of Christ, the Church is defined wholly in relation to

Christ, as the Epiphany of God's Mystery. Strictly speaking, this Mystery is the reality of Christ as God and as Man risen and glorified beside the Father, Bearer of the dynamism drawing all mankind into Himself until « God may be all in all » (*I Cor.*, XV, 28). It is the personal reality of a divine Presence, that of Christ, drawing together and reconciling the whole world in Himself, in His Body on the Cross, and in the Body of the Church : « Which is Christ in you, the hope of glory » (*Col.*, I, 27). It is the Church in course of construction and the constitution of this « perfect man, unto the measure of the age of the fulness of Christ » (*Eph.*, IV, 13), the true « fulness of him who is filled all in all » (*Eph.*, I, 23).

As Pope Paul VI stated emphatically in his address at the opening of the Council's second session, Christ is our Principal, our guide, our aim, and the Church must show up transparently in her life the mystery of Christ her Founder. Thus could the words of Saint Paul frame the dominant aim of ecumenism, « that you may be filled unto all the fulness of God » (*Eph.*, III, 19).

We are therefore summoned to a determination to surpass ourselves in order to discover and manifest more clearly the plenitude that is in Jesus Christ, and Catholic Ecumenism lives by the search, both in time and space, of Catholic plenitude. Is not Catholicity the gift of Christ Himself, enabling the Church to aspire effectively and without ceasing at universality, both in quality and extension, in the unity of the Spirit of Christ, which finds expression in the unity of faith, community of sacraments and of government.

In this search we need all our brother Christians because their communities — which also share in the Mystery of Christ — set the question of her fidelity to this mystery before the Catholic Church. She certainly does declare that she is the one and only Church intended by Christ, but she eagerly insists that Catholics who are her members must be more and more converted to Christ. It is our duty to bear witness more and more daily to this catholicity of the Mystery of Christ. It is in this ever-deepening renewal of herself, concerning also her collective dimension (worship, institutions, presentation of doctrine), that the Catholic Church goes to meet the Protestant and Orthodox Churches, in order to manifest *to the world* the authenticity of the Gospel.

Ecumenism is thus founded on the most dogmatic truth possible : the Mystery of Christ working within the Catholic Church and our brother Christians, and demanding the renewal of the Church in order to reveal more clearly the very Countenance of Christ. It rests on *divine truth* — never on some kind of relativism — which must be unceasingly deepened in order to know it better and live it more fully. In the words of Pope Paul VI : « A real Christian never remains stationary. »

b) *In Communion with Other Christian Communities.* Our brothers, Orthodox or Protestant, who are baptized in Christ, live by the Holy Spirit, in the essential of the Catholic faith, and share the Mystery of Christ in an unequal manner, according to the different communions. They hold implicitly all that is lacking to the fulness of belonging to the Church, through their earnest desire to adhere to the Divine Will, even while, in good faith, they reject some of the demands of this Divine Will.

The era of polemics having passed, the Catholic Church is attentive to what is positive in the Christian communities, considered for themselves henceforward, in a relation to Christ and the Church, which must be analysed. That is why she asks for the greatest attention to their Christian patrimony, their Christian life, the positive values which form the life of these communities. We must not only consider individuals but the *communities themselves.* Mgr. Baudoux, Archbishop of St. Boniface, Canada, said recently before the Council : « When we speak of links between the Catholic Church and separated Christians, we must remember the following facts : these Christians form authentic communities, that is, communities of faith and worship. Therefore, we fall short of the truth if we consider them as merely individuals. »

Instead of simply seeing these communities from the canonical and juridical standpoint only, the Catholic Church means to put the idea of communion in the foreground, and to present Ecumenism as the effort to re-establish the entire communion of faith, discipline and sacramental life, in which the true unity of the Church consists. If, on the canonical plane, the question of a local Church in relation to the one, only, universal Church can only be answered by a definite yes or no (one is, or is not, a member of the Roman Church), the answer to the question of communion in the content of faith allows an infinitude of shades and of degrees.

The Ecumenical attitude is founded on this proximity in communion ; for the sake of truth, which is Christ, to whom these communities firmly desire to be faithful, they must be treated as *people* whom we sincerely love, and with whom we collaborate as brothers in all domains where basic convictions do not clash.

As Catholics, we must have absolute confidence in God's action expressed through the dynamism of faith and charity of each

member of the separated communities. The weight of radical transformation received in baptism, marks them of itself for Eucharistic
communion and the redeeming sacrifice. The Divine initiative of
salvation includes our brethren, and urges them to seek the fulness
of the Mystery.

Their ecumenical search is an incessant call to live the plenitude
of the Mystery better.

As a Methodist theologian said at Montreal not long ago, Catholicity should « essentially direct attention to the plenitude of God, »
the pleroma which is God Himself (*Col.*, I, 19 ; II, 9 ; *Eph.*, III,
19), « the unfathomable depths of the riches, of the wisdom and
of the knowledge of God, » and the *ta panta*, all things, which are
« of him, through him and for him » (*Rom.*, XI, 36). This means,
in its integrity the one Lord Jesus Christ in whom God has willed
that « all fulness should dwell, » in whom and through whom « all
things subsist » (*Col.*, I, 19 ; 16, 17 ; cf. *Eph.*, I, 22, 23). This
means the plenitude of God's work in Jesus Christ, the reign over
all things to Him who has ascended « to fill creation with His
presence » (*Eph.*, IV, 10), who is « above all princedoms, and
powers, and virtues and dominations » (*Eph.*, I, 21), in whose
name « every knee should bow » (*Phil.*, II, 10), and in whom God
« reconciles the world to Himself » (*II Cor.*, V, 19). It is only in
the measure in which the image of Catholicity refers us to this
totality and plenitude, and puts us in relations with it, that it can
have a meaning for the Church as body of Christ, as « plenitude
of Him » that we may be « filled with all the plenitude of God »
(*Eph.*, I, 12 ; III, 19). Only thus is there exteriorization of this
term *panta*, in the adoration of men of « all nations and tribes and
peoples and tongues » (*Apoc.*, VII, 9), or in the mission given the
apostles « to teach all nations » (Matt., XXVIII, 19), if we only
consider one extension of the meaning of this word.

B. *Ecumenism, a Perpetual Discovery.*

In the fidelity Christ asks of his Church, we must always look
in front of us, as Pope Paul VI has stated so effectively : « The
best thing is not to look back at the past, but at the present and
especially towards the future. We look towards a new birth, a dream
to be made a reality. Allow us to repeat the words of St. Paul :
forgetting what is behind, intent on what lies before, I press on
with the goal in view, eager for the prize, God's summons in Christ

Jesus. Hope is our guide, prayer our strength, charity is our method at the service of divine truth which is our faith and our salvation. »

This desire for creative discovery and fidelity will settle to a certain extent the fresh fact of relations between the Churches. The era of encounter between Christian Churches has begun. Without doubt, there will be obstacles and difficulties and windings in the path before us, but a new and irreversible fact is being firmly established : the Christian Churches have begun to have mutual esteem for each other, and to work together.

A decisive turning-point in relations between the Churches is being reached, in a much more evangelical fashion, characteristic of the new situation ; spectacular steps have been taken, which would have been unthinkable only a few years ago. Still greater ones may come, but in spite of what may appear in the press, we have not yet reached summit conferences, there is much to be done before then. Only a theological and spiritual progress in depth for each Church, will strength and direct these relations, and avoid certain misunderstandings.

A new map of Ecumenicism is taking shape. Since the beginnings of the Ecumenical movement, then of the World Council of Churches, ecumenical dialogue has been carried on practically *without* the Catholic Church. By her very absence, she was in some way included among the Protestant and Orthodox Churches in dialogue, but she took no active part in the meetings. That is why dialogue within the W.C.C. will undergo very real revision ; it cannot disregard the importance of the new fact, the entrance of the Catholic Church into the Ecumenical movement.

The W.C.C. need not fear — as some seem inclined to think — that the Catholic Church, through direct relations with the Orthodox Churches (or the Anglican or Protestant Churches), will call its future into question. It has often declared how much it desired direct contacts. The Catholic Church will be most anxious to encourage dialogue within the W.C.C. itself. For Ecumenism cannot be based on a competition unworthy of true Christians ; it is not a question of asserting that its centre is in Rome or Geneva, but of asserting whether we all wish to be more faithful to Jesus Christ. As Karl Barth says in his excellent little book *Réflexions sur le deuxième Concile du Vatican* (Labor et Fides, Geneva, 1963) : « the way towards unity of the Church, *Whether it starts from here or there*, can only be that of renewal. Renewal means conversion — not that of others but of ourselves. »

We Catholics acknowledge that our brothers are the unknown half of ourselves, whom we need in order to find in their plenitude certain exigences and evangelical qualities of Catholic realities.

Ecumenism only has a meaning as conversion of the whole Catholic Church and of Christian communities to the Mystery of Christ, the Catholic Church in order to manifest more and more the plenitude within it, and the other Churches to regain this plenitude more fully, in a mutual and brotherly assistance.

The Meaning
of Protestant Ecumenism

by Hébert ROUX

Pastor of the Reformed Church,
Delegated Observer from the World Reformed Alliance to the Council,
Paris [1]

To grasp the meaning and bearing of the Ecumenical movement, it must first be situated historically, and not confused with
a universalist ideology or a « mysticism of Unity, » the incidences
of which would have some influence for psycho-sociological or
political reasons, at the level of separated churches, some of whom
seek for « unification. »

It is significant that what is now called the « Ecumenical Movement, » [2] and which has led to the creation of the World Council
of Churches, began among Protestant Churches in settings and
under the influence of personalities chiefly faced with the demands
of the Missions and Christian Testimony in the world.

The unicity of Christ's Gospel for the world, which the many
societies and missionary movements started in the XVIII and XIX
centuries in various Protestant Churches declare, and profess to
proclaim, forced upon them the search for, and manifestation of,
the visible unity of Christians, as condition of the apostolate. It is
equally significant that the initial intentions and aims chosen by
the two movements « Life and Work » and « Faith and Order »
in which Orthodox, Anglicans and Protestants closely share, were

---

1. Born in 1902, Hébert ROUX was ordained pastor in 1928. With a Licentiate
in philosophy and theology, he exercised the ministry at Crest, Die, Bordeaux
and Paris successively. President of the Conseil Académique de l'Eglise Ré-
formée, and of the Commission for relations with Catholicism in France, and
one of the three observers from the World Reformed Alliance at the Council.
For 30 years he has been the animator of « Amitié », a group of Catholic-
Protestant teachers. See the biographical note p. 427. Address : 168, rue de Javel,
Paris, 15ᵉ, FRANCE (Editor's note).

2. On the origins of the Ecumenical Movement can be consulted : P. CONORD,
Brève histoire de l'Œcuménisme. Paris. Les Bergers et les Mages, 1958. —
R. ROUSE and St. NEILL, *Histoire du Mouvement œcuménique,* London, 1954.

finally found to be convergent, complementary and closely united in the work undertaken by the « World Council, » which the International Missions Council joined in 1961. It would certainly be inaccurate to think of such a movement as a kind of organization or re-unification of non-Roman Churches ending in the creation of a super-church. In reality, the World Council is, and intends to be, merely a means of connection and communication which the Churches belonging to it wish to have, as a mutual help in the search for and manifestation of unity, and also as an expression among themselves and at all levels of the degree of ecclesial unity which they *already* possess.

The fact of a Protestant Church belonging to this Movement entails a duty of research and dialogue, a question, in the process of dialogue, of her own authenticity as Church of Christ. This research and dialogue suppose that each Church-Member agrees to be questioned by the others, and to deepen her own nature and vocation as a Church, on the basis which was accepted in 1961 by the Meeting at New Delhi, after it had been submitted to all the Churches: « *The World Council of Churches is a fraternal association of Churches which confess the Lord Jesus Christ as Lord and Saviour according to the Scriptures, and are striving to fulfil together their common vocation for the glory of the one God, Father, Son and Holy Spirit.* »

It is not enough to deplore the pain and scandal of divisions. It is not enough to admit the faults of the past or to draw up lists of them (for the division among Christians is not simply a moral fault, it lies on the very level of faith); we must also recognize the real questions that this state of schism raises to the faith of all the Churches ; the Ecumenical dialogue of today cannot evade them. For these questions challenge, one way or another, the fidelity, authenticity, validity of every ecclesiastical institution as regards the nature and very essence of the Church. All reflection in this domain must therefore start from the very centre of the Christian faith in what it holds in common with all confessions, that is, from the organic and living relation between the Church and Jesus Christ, as described and revealed to us by the apostolic testimony itself, considered as the source and norm of all Christian truth.

The Principle of Unity.

The New Testament shows us how the Apostolic Church, from the moment it appears on the scene of history, thought of and lived her communion with Christ Our Lord. Through the event of Pentecost, the Church appears as the New Alliance, both as the fruit and the testimony, at a chosen moment in history, of the universal redemptive work of God, in and through Jesus Christ. This work was accomplished in the person of Jesus of Nazareth, true God and true Man : « God was in Christ, reconciling the world to himself » (*II Cor.*, V, 19). By his sacrifice on the cross, his resurrection and ascension, Jesus Christ fulfilled all the promises of the Ancient Alliance, reconciled Israel and the nations by reconciling them to God, and uniting « the two in himself into one new man » (*Eph.*, II, 15), prototype of the new humanity. The first Christian community formed by the apostolic preaching appears from the very first as the continuity of the unfolding of the history of salvation which the history of Israel prefigures ; at the same time it is aware that it is inaugurating a new era, it is the premises of a new creation, which in the heart of the old one, bears testimony to the realness of Christ's decisive work, while waiting for His return in glory.

The expressions used to designate the first Christian community, and those which the apostles created in any place, vigorously stress the character of their belonging to Christ and their dependence on Him. The Church is *God*'s or *Christ*'s, « the people acquired by God, » « the Israel of God, » the « Body » of which Christ is the head, « the Bride » of whom He is the spouse. It shares by faith in His Word and the action of the Holy Spirit, an intimate communion with Christ, dead and risen again, while Baptism and the Supper attest His living and sanctifying presence in expectation of His actual return.

But this Church is not only this people of believers « drawn from the whole human race, » called by God's grace to benefit by His redemptive work in the unity of faith, hope and love ; or rather, it is only thus sanctified and « consecrated, » because at the same time it is « sent » into the world as a servant to announce Christ's universal kingdom. The apostolic character of the Church is inseparable from her unity, holiness and universality. One may even say that in one sense the apostolicity of the Church determines her other characters. Proceeding from Him who was « *sent* » by the Father, She herself has apostolate to perform : « As the Father has sent me I also send you, » said Christ to his apostles. Recognizing that God sent Jesus Christ, her mission is to testify this to the world, being herself the result of this apostolate. Her task is to manifest to the world that Christ's mission has been accomplished, and that God's plan is now in its decisive phase. The Church, therefore, is apostolic, not only because historically it was founded by the apostles, who bear witness that Jesus is the Christ, but also because in her very nature she is the people-Body of Christ Whose mission it is to exercise the ministry of reconciliation throughout the world. According to the first Epistle of St. Peter, the Christians scattered throughout the world form through their union with Christ, « a royal priesthood, a holy nation, a purchased people, that may declare his virtues who has called you out of darkness into his marvellous light » (*I Peter*, II, 9).

The evangelization of the world consists in the proclamation of this decisive event to which every believer testifies, and in which every creature is called to discover the secret of his reconciliation to his Creator. The proclamation of this Good News which is « the Word of faith » becomes creative of a new life in those who receive it. St. Paul defines the apostolate thus : « By him (Jesus Christ) we have received grace and apostleship for obedience to the faith in all nations » (*Rom.*, I, 5). The Gospel, by which the Church lives by proclaiming it, is not a philosophical or moral doctrine, or even a « religion. » It is not a mere « message, » but the living and lasting Word of God, a power generating life. That is why the proclamation of Christ's God is accompanied by baptism : « Go ye and teach all nations, baptizing them in the name of the Father and of the Son and of the Holy Ghost. » The baptismal act is inseparable from the Word preached, creating faith, powerful and active in the man who receives it, to make him a new creature. But this power resides wholly in the secret action of the Holy Spirit, sent also by God to attest the reality of his presence, to render his Word efficacious, and to seal it within men's hearts, when it is spoken and transmitted through human means.

For this people of God is made up of men, it is destined to live a concrete existence on earth, to be set down in the history of humanity. As such, this people is organized, ordered and governed with a view to accomplish its mission. Our Lord himself chose out and appointed men to be apostles. By giving His Church ministers, He makes her able to exercise her apostolic ministry, and thus to fulfil her mission faithfully (cf. *Eph.*, IV, 6-11).

The Guarantee of Unity.

This brings up the great debate which has divided the Church in the course of centuries. It exists among the non-Roman Churches, culminating in opposition to the Roman doctrine of unity. It concerns the interpretation of the role and nature of the ministers of the Church ; it vitally concerns the way in which faithful transmission of Christ's Word, the deposit of faith received from the apostles, is to be assured and guaranteed in the Church.

Throughout the centuries the Roman Catholic Church has settled this guarantee and continuity by the doctrine of the apostolic succession and the privileged assistance accorded and recognized of its infallible magisterium, under the authority of the sovereign pontiff, successor of Peter and vicar of Christ. The result has been that this Church has been irresistibly led by the interior logic of her historic and dogmatic evolution, to refuse the title and quality of Church to communities other than her own, since in her eyes, full communion with Christ can only be assured by submission to the Roman institution herself, the guarantee of that communion.

The Churches of the Reform, which refer explicitly in their confession of faith to the great Ecumenical creeds of the first three centuries, have been led into forming separate Churches after the failure of the Reformation, whose original aim had been to reform the entire Catholic Church. In refusing the authority of the See of Rome, they never intended to break with the tradition of the ancient Church in what it has in conformity with the teaching of Christ and the apostles. By asserting the sovereign authority of God's Word, received and heard in Holy Scripture, they intended, on the contrary, to remain in the communion of the universal Church. One of the oldest documents of the Reform states, in 1528 : « The Holy Christian Church, whose only head is Jesus Christ is born of God's Word, cleaves to it, and hears not the voice of a stranger. »

For these Churches, then, the guarantee of continuity and fidelity in exercising the ministry of the Church, does not lie in the existence of an historical succession and structures of the Church, whatever they may be, but in the permanent action of God's Word itself, generating the Church, and to which everything, institution included, submits. Churches of the Reform in no way question divine institution and the necessity for particular ministries, they question the juridical and normative character and sacramental power.

Between these two views, which obviously need fuller and more detailed explanation, there is contradiction, aggravated by the weight of time-honoured tradition. Can dialogue on the nature of the Church and her relations to Jesus Christ overcome the obstacles and impediments ?

The Apostolate, Hope of Unity.

One thing is certain, a return to Unity cannot be conceived as a mere grouping, a rally, a re-unification resulting from compromises or pious endeavour. *All* the Churches eager for dialogue must define the manner in which they themselves live and express the full reality of the Holy, Catholic and apostolic Church.

As we have seen, the unity of the Church proceeds from Jesus Christ Himself, One Lord and Saviour whom we all confess and in whom we receive divine Revelation through the Gospel. This unity is inseparable from the fidelity of the Church to her sacred vocation and the fulfilment of her universal mission : to preach the Gospel to every creature. The problem of unity, therefore, sets before each Church the problem of her own fidelity to this vocation and this mission. It is in the measure that authentic signs of return to the original vocation of the apostolic *Church* appear *within the Churches* that the way to unity opens. It cannot be otherwise if we believe with the apostles themselves that this God's Gospel « is at work in the whole world, » and that it is « the power of God for the salvation of every believer » (*Col.*, I, 6 ; *Rom.*, I, 16). It is this power of the Gospel which is alone able to authenticate, legitimize, and render fully valid and efficacious, institutions and their structures. It is the Gospel that confers on every Church, ministry and ecclesiastical organization, and finally on the Christian people, its authentic apostolic character and not the other way round.

It is this advance, this progress within the Churches towards the plenitude of faith in Jesus Christ, the discovery in real depth of all its demands and all its promises, which is the surest guarantee and the token of unity which the Lord desires for his Church. And that is why through our searching and our human gropings, in the very ignorance of the means at God's disposal, we know that this progress towards unity is not a vain hope nor an illusion, but the fulfilment of God's work, who is leading his people towards the light of his Kingdom.

An Orthodox Glance
at the Meaning of Ecumenism

by André SCRIMA

Archimandrite of the Ecumenical Patriarchate[1]

If ecumenical interest today is tending to become a factor associated with Christian consciousness, it means that it expresses an essential demand. To believe in Christ is also to declare adherence to a plan of unity whose origin lies in the very mystery of the living God and whose final end is the restoration in Him of a world forever marked by His saving act.

Should we be surprised, therefore, if ecumenism spontaneously arouses in us, beyond its immediate object, a united search for unity — a renewal of our whole life as « Christians » ? Unity was the goal of the Passion of Christ, and since then has been the aspiration par excellence of all men. To mention this now is certainly not to abandon ecumenical terrain, but rather to underscore it.

Reviewing the great events of these last years, we see that it is this plan of God that we are urged to penetrate, accept, and fulfill. In our « separated brother » we are to see an authentic presence, enabling us to deepen our own understanding of the Church and to purify our fidelity to it. This is by no means easy. In a way it is the total vocation of the Church — the « place » where the plan of God is manifested, inseparable from the creative and concrete existence of man — which is drawn toward the word « ecumenism. » The rapid progress of ecumenism in our time somewhat proves that it is fully in line with accepted Christian truth.

1. Reverend Father André Scrima, Archimandrite of the Ecumenical Patriarchate, licentiate in letters and doctor in philosophy and theology, was born in Rumania, December 1926. A specialist in dogmatic theology and comparative spirituality (studies and writings at the Hindu University, Benares), he has published several studies and articles under a pen name. Since his arrival in the West (1960), Father Srima has devoted himself to ecumenism. He was present at the third session of Vatican Council II as personal representative of the Patriarch Athenagoras. — Address: « Istina, » 25 Boulevard d'Auteuil, Boulogne, S. Seine, France.

This « simplicity, » perceived by the eye of faith, it must be added, is caught up into the complex, and very often dramatic, tapestry of history. Mysteriously adjusted to the conscious response of man, the action of grace matures, one might say, within a plan of distress and of mercy, of patience and of hope. Vatican Council II, a great « educational » force, demonstrates to us the laborious journey of an ecumenical consciousness in close solidarity with the deepening and purification of the ecclesial conscience. This is a fact of utmost importance, at least for the Orthodox East for whom the ecumenical problem is based entirely upon the reality of the Church. If today we are seeking its full manifestation, if we aspire to the consummation of its visible unity in order to bear complete witness to this ultimate mystery which attaches it to the inscrutable unity of God (John, XVII, 21), it is only because this unity has been *instituted* by Christ, sealed by His Spirit, lived and transmitted by His apostles and disciples. It has been achieved in history ; it is being expressed now at different levels, bringing our divisions into question and demanding that we all get beyond ourselves, which St. Paul saw as the condition of our stability in Christ (Philippians, III, 3-5). It is but right to place the reality and truth of the Church at the beginning of all reflection on the meaning of our ecumenical effort.

I. THE CHURCH, THEOCENTRIC « PLACE » OF THE MYSTERY OF SALVATION

One need only go into an Orthodox church during the Eucharistic Liturgy or an Office to hear the untiring supplication of the priest or deacon « for the unity of the holy Churches of God, » « for unity of faith and communion with the Holy Spirit, » « for peace and union of all men. » The people thus become penetrated, as by undeniable evidence, with the fact that the Church must watch over the preservation of unity, the supreme sign of God's work. This liturgical approach makes us relive every day the journey toward Christ. Through significant events, special interventions, prophetic divisions, violent disagreement, man has been led from his stagnancy and from his repeated rejecctions of God towards Christ, in whom « dwells all the fullness of the Godhead corporeally » (*Colossians*, II, 9). and toward the effusion of the Holy Spirit, the principle of life in the new Christian creation. In the midst of, and in the service of humanity, the Church is the « place » where the plan of salvation is to be seen ; it is a paradoxical institution having its unique center in God, called upon to show by her life and fidelity « the breadth and length and height and depth... of Christ... that you may be filled unto all the fullness of God » (*Ephesians*, III, 18-19). We will not insist further on these basic aspects of the Church, in which dogmatic truth and the lived mystery are ultimately united. But they will allow us to understand both the essential reason for our vigorous protest over the scandal of disunion and how, by becoming more aware of it, we can squarely face our divisions today in an « ecumenical » plan of research, patience, hope, and creative effort. [1]

1. *Sacrament and Eschatology.*

To say that the Church is the « place » in which the divine plan is fulfilled, is to say that she is God's sacrament. The special function of a sacrament is to unite the two orders, distinct but made inseparable by the Incarnation, the human and the divine, the visible and the invisible, time and the living eternity of God. It is precisely as a whole that the Church is a sacrament, a worshipping people, leading the world to God in virtue of her sacramental transcendency, and considering herself as an end. The « signs » of the seven classic sacraments — here lies an important element in our present ecumenical thought — are thus set within a wider sacramentality, which finds its supreme expression in the Eucharist, the sacrament above all others of reconciliation and unity. It is as if the Church goes beyond her own visibility to draw strength increasingly from the risen Christ, thus making progress in this eschatological movement in which our ecumenical effort unfolds and labors.

2. *Spirit and Tradition.*

God's constant work, the Church, is in fact the presence and actuality of the paschal Christ, who died and rose again, a mystery which is accomplished only through the Holy Spirit. Just as He was responsible for Our Lord's body in time, so the Spirit is always the principle of His Mystical Body which is the Church, continually coming together in plurality of persons, peoples, and human « types, » communicating in unity. Institution and inspiration, sacrament and charism, are reciprocally implied in the life of God's people since His coming at Pentecost. « In one Spirit we have all

---

1. We have treated this aspect of the ecumenical effort in *Dialogue Œcuménique*. Paris, Ed. Fleurus, 1962, pp. 27-29.

beenmade to drink, » says St. Paul (*I Corinthians*, XII, 13). Since, then, the Church manifests her communion of life and truth through the « tradition » of the Spirit in the sacrament of the episcopate, which is a sign of fidelity linking through the ages the fullness bestowed at Pentecost with that promised at the Parousia.

3. *Truth and Prayer.*

There is no doubt that the *reality* of the Church, as seen by the ecumenical movement, at the same time raises the question of *truth*, just as responsible thinking and ecumenical fidelity would require. At the beginning of the modern ecumenical movement one sometimes heard the rather brutal and sometimes bitter remark, « Truth separates, charity (or activity) draws together. » If it is true that such a statement echoes sad events in the past, an objective and clearsighted historical research would have allowed us, meanwhile, to evaluate these regrettable happenings in a better manner, reminding us of our common responsibility for these happenings and inviting us to make up for them. But more especially, ecumenical evaluation would have helped us to grasp more clearly the existential relationship between theological truth and the full reality of the Church. Ecumenical activity does not challenge theology ; on the contrary, it implies it as a precious element of research and of unity. If, as we have said, ecclesial unity presupposes unity of sacramental life and hierarchical communion, it is because it is primordially a unity of faith, a conscious adherence to the saving truth. Here again, the ecumenical movement occasioned an experienced deepening of our relationship with theological truth, both in the act of grasping it and of expressing it. For example, we realize better that the truth of Christ is not, in itself, an object reached by speculative thought, but the manifestation of the mystery of God. Before this mystery theological knowledge, both more lowly and more receptive, admits that it is part of the mass of the Church's riches : Scripture, Liturgy, the spiritual life of the people of God. We also begin to perceive how far communion of faith allows a *pluralism* of formulation, even, if we may say so, of theological perception — a fact which, if not decisive, is at least full of promise for the future of the ecumenical movement. *Truth* itself thus invites us to welcome it in a manner more suited to its fullness and to share it with our brothers.

All this presupposes in us a lasting disposition, probably the most intimate demand of Christian truth, borne out many times in ecumenical experience. The personal attitude of the theologian — who is also a member of God's people at the service of their questionings and their hope (*I Peter*, III, 15) — and the objective relationship between doctrinal truth and the transcendence of God — which is the final object in view — are both at stake. Can anyone question the obligation to become aware of this at the level of the Churches as well, in a spirit similar to the act of *prayer* ? In this action we express our acceptance of the « tearing down » and « building up » by the Holy Spirit. For the truth of union in faith cannot lie in the triumph of one Church over another, and still less in a doctrinal compromise. It can rather be foreseen as the end of a journey leading beyond the positions now marked by differences, as the very truth of the Church of Christ and the apostles, restored in a more perfect and more evident fidelity.

II. ECUMENISM,
ACTUALIZATION OF THE CHURCH'S FULLNESS

We have been obliged to glance rapidly at the ecclesial basis of ecumenical research in order to bring out the status of ecumenism itself. In spite of what some thought at the outset, ecumenism is not some outer domain or an incident in the life of the Church. Quite to the contrary, it returns to and makes actual our first vocation, which is always to hasten the coming of the fullness of God's « dwelling with men » (*Apocalypse*, XXI, 3). To this end God now is allowing us not only to reverse as it were the current of history which has tended to multiply and perpetuate divisions almost since the beginnings of the Church, but even to give these divisions a new meaning. They are revealing in another way ; God is speaking to us through our differences of opinion, and that is our ultimate reason for hoping to overcome them.

It is evident also (and we need not therefore linger over it) that this ecumenical awareness is interdependent on ecumenical practice or activity, which includes both application and a continuous source of discovery. We have begun by regaining fraternal charity (sometimes under its more acceptable name of courtesy), the first step beyond polemics and towering antagonism. Once the « other man's » presence was admitted, it became possible to appreciate his positions « from within, » as the deep truth of dialogue demands, while listening with the elementary objectivity required by the technique of dialogue.

This forms the fundamental presupposition of ecumenical work. On condition that it is not taken up in a state of vexatious lack of preparation, it does not lead to indifference or confusion, but to renewal. In other words, each one becomes a better member of his own Church through vitality of conviction, readiness to serve, consciousness of principles. One can also catch sight of the path which leads to a more perfect manifestation of the mystery of the Church. Taking into account the present ecumenical situation, we would like to mention three distinctive features.

1. *Conversion.*

Much more than a concern for specialists, it has been said, ecumenism is a certain quality of the whole activity of the Church, even of every Christian existence. The term *conversion* supplies both the individual and ecclesial dimension. In its New Testament sense (*metanoia*) it means advancement in the fullness of Christ already bestowed and yet to come. We must indeed stress « fullness bestowed » because it is not a journey into the unknown and in darkness, but in the light of the Church, an historical reality founded by Christ. Yet conversion means this anxiety for catholicity fully regained, which cannot be efficaciously strengthened without the resolution to get beyond our present separation, without love for others, without longstanding yearning. [1]

2. *Loyalty.*

We are imperiously bound also to loyalty toward God and to our own Church. If this is lacking, our ecumenical labors would lose all content, and our spiritual dedication would lose its momentum which is a condition for success. For a faithful Orthodox, for example, future unity is to be found in the meeting of his Church's fidelity with that of the Church of Christ, the apostles, and the Fathers. He will feel nonetheless obliged, precisely in virtue of this loyalty, to follow God's call to His Church « where He wishes to lead it. ».

3. *Creation.*

The ecumenical attitude, then, is above all a creative attitude. This requirement is not at all theoretical, since it is inherent to an existential confrontation which places us before the great queries of faith, obliging us to tackle and fathom them. So much so that it involves theological discovery strictly speaking, « old and new » (Matthew, XIII, 52), and our spiritual responsibility as God's

---

1. Cf. *Dialogue Œcuménique*, p. 111.

coadjutors (*I Corinthians*, III, 9) in creating new *situations* in which men can recognize signs of the times, the seal of the Holy Spirit, « the change of the right hand of the Most High » (Psalm LXXVI, 11).

III. HISTORICAL FORMS AND STAGES

The ecumenical problem has been (and still is) that of becoming conscious, through the shocks of « exterior » history and also interiorly, of an essentially religious discovery of the presence of others. What we now call the « ecumenical reality » has been formed of this twofold and convergent urge, often unpredictable and sometimes disconcerting, yet whose final tendency remains an irrepressible advance forward. The few stages we are going to speak of now, and which concern more particularly the Orthodox Church, will show the length of the road behind us so far and the extent of the one on which we are only just beginning to set out.

1. « *East and West.* »

For Eastern Orthodoxy the distinction East-West dominates the first perception of the ecumenical factor, both concerning its value of spiritual complementing, and its fate of historical opposition. Better informed, if not better disposed now, we know that the great break (in a way the archetype) between the Orthodox Church and the Catholic Church hardly had the character of a strictly definitive gesture in the beginning. (The excommunication of Caerularius, Patriarch of Constantinople, pronounced by Cardinal Humber on July 16, 1054, marks a symbolic rather than a chronological date.) The rupture grew in the course of a complex history which, for reasons partly theological but partly quite outside the faith, saw the two Christianities evolve in divergent ways, in spite of the basic truth of the apostolic variety of the universal Church, a truth recognized by both sides until then. It is true, also, that consciousness of the common reality of mystery for the two Churches remained more or less alive until the fifteenth century in both East and West. This did not prevent the Latin tradition from becoming powerful in the West after the thirteenth century. The tradition of the first thousand years, with its ecclesiological pluralism and specific potentialities, which were continued and later developed in the Orthodox Church, was thus overshadowed. Henceforth the latter would see in this living tradition a universally valuable reference to that apostolic fullness in which all Christians could find a starting point of common faith and its ecclesial mediation.

2. *Modern Times : Divergence and Expectation.*

In the sixteenth century the Reform movement set up a new state within the Western Church and ended by questioning the universal Christian conscience. Nevertheless, and in spite of contacts sought by the first Protestant reformers with the ancient Eastern Churches, we can hardly speak of encounter between the reformers and the Orthodox Church before our own century. Besides, the eddies of the Counter-Reformation and the hardening of positions which ensued, only increased the gulf between Catholicism and Orthodoxy in the centuries that followed. And yet the Orthodox theological renaissance of the nineteenth century, notably in Russia, did not fail to put forward, often with much feeling, the problem of Christian unity. At the same time Orthodoxy was striving to point out, not without a keenly refined intuition in a century dominated by the Hegel problematics, the spiritual, cultural, and social dimensions of Christian « Catholicity. »

3. *Our Own Day : Dialogue and Convergence.*

In 1920 the Ecumenical Patriarchate of Constantinople addressed an encyclical letter to the « Heads of Churches and Leaders of Christianity, » exhorting them to try to bring Christians more closely together by establishing continuing relations, mutual help, social cooperation, without forgetting to prepare the way for an impartial examination of dogmatic controversies. The gesture and the document stand among the first signs of an ecumenical movement in our century. These led to the foundation of the World Council of Churches, at which the Orthodox Church has been represented since the beginning. Eventually one could wish for more consistency and effectiveness from this presence, but at least it has the undeniable merit of recalling the ecumenical potentiality of the « Catholic » tradition within an organization due to a largely Protestant inspiration.

Meanwhile a silent development, which was preparing for the ecumenical trend of more recent years, had been going on in the West, more particularly in the Catholic Church. Thanks to successive and convergent « returns to sources » — biblical, liturgical, patristic — the living theological tradition of the East, a tradition formerly obscured or studied in notional fashion, had once more become a presence in the order of *realities* of the Church. A common language, signified by ecclesial realities before being made articulate in systematic dialogue, is being formed anew between East and West. The « other » is being discovered now from within ourselves, like a presence which completes us. There is an otherness of love and of dialogue, not just a negative otherness, a situation realized up to a certain point by the work of Vatican Council II. At the same time « unexpected » events — such as the meeting at Jerusalem of Pope Paul VI and the Patriarch Athenagoras I, and the restoration of the relics of St. Andrew — seem intent on reminding us of the value of drawing closer together « via facti, » as the Patriarch Athenagoras never ceases to recommend, were it only as gradual education toward full unity. The Third Pan-orthodox Conference at Rhodes, which met from November 1 to 15, 1964, to study the question of dialogue with the Catholic Church, recorded in its decisions this double methodological aspect of an indivisible ecumenical research to be carried on henceforward as « ministers of Christ and dispensers of the mysteries of God » (*I Corinthians*, IV, 1).

2

Present Mentalities and Ecumenism

Dialogue with Roman Catholicism from within French Protestantism [1]

by Hébert Roux

Pastor of the Reformed Church,
Delegated Observer from the World Reformed Alliance to the Council,
Paris [2]

The invitation made to an Observer to send this communication is a sign in itself of the ecumenical attitude within the Council, especially when the schema *De Oecumenismo* is under debate.

The study of this schema marks an important moment of this session, and the conclusions it reaches will have decisive weight in future inter-confessional relations, and on the way dialogue will be begun or continued.

Therefore it is natural that in all the non-Roman Churches, hope and anxiety await the issue of this debate, and people are wondering how the Catholic Church will formulate the principles of Catholic Ecumenism, what is to be understood by the phrase, and its practical content in concrete application.

It must not be forgotten that the problem raised by dialogue between the Catholic Church and the other Churches or communities which have existed for centuries outside her, exists now on

---

1. Communication presented at the weekly meeting of French bishops at Saint-Louis des Français, 20 November 1963. It was printed in January 1964 in *Feuilles aux vents, Feuillets des Avents,* two-monthly pamphlets, « Les Avents » by Lautrec (Tarn). This pamphlet was called *Œcuménisme spirituel.* We reproduce this suggestive article with the author's permission, and the kindly consent of M. l'abbé André Fabre, director of the review, who has supplied the notes.

2. See the biographical note p. 421. Among the works published by Pastor H. Roux, we mention: *L'Evangile du Royaume.* Commentary on the Gospel according to St. Matthew, Geneva, Labor et Fides, 1959, 2nd. ed. ; Commentary on the *Epîtres Pastorales,* ibidem, 1959 ; *Eglise et Mission.* Paris, Société des Missions Evangéliques ; Collaboration à la revue « Foi et Vie » ; *Bilan de l'Ecriture du point de vue protestant,* dans « Mariologie et œcuménisme », Bulletin de la Société Française d'Etudes Mariales, Paris, Lethielleux, 1963 ; *Recommandations et conseils en vue du dialogue avec le catholicisme romain.* Paris, Féd. Prot. de France, 1963 (Editor's note).

a world scale, and must be thought of at the Universal Church
level. That goes without saying from the Catholic point of view ;
but it is equally true for the Reformed Churches, since they have
established bonds of « communion » between themselves all over
the world (World Council of Churches, World Alliances or
Federations), and also because they recognize themselves, within
their respective confessions of faith, as « in the communion of the
Holy Universal Church. »

This essential point must be borne in mind while considering
here the French situation. What exists or what is happening in
France as to the conditions of dialogue with Catholicism cannot
be *isolated* from what is happening in other parts of the world
(ex. : French Protestants are in solidarity with those in other
countries who live under conditions different from ours). Neither
should we *generalize* experiences proper to France in the domain
of dialogue, the conditions and perspectives of which are, in some
ways, privileged as regards other countries.

The one aim of this article is to try and explain, or shed light
upon, the various reactions within French Protestantism towards
the *ecumenical problem*, and particularly on the perspectives of
a dialogue with the Roman Church.

Impression of Novelty.

The dominant impression is one of *novelty*, which the study of
the « ecumenical » problem has within the Catholic Church herself. Novelty in the spirit in which this problem is approached,
novelty as to the methods of approaching it. This was clearly
stressed in the *relatio* by Mgr. Martin at the opening of the debate.

For the first time in her history, the Roman Catholic Church
is studying, under the title « ecumenism, » the principles and
manner of her relations with, and attitude towards, « Churches »
or communities separated from her, and re-considering the unity
of Christ's Church and its visible manifestation, taking their existence
into account.

This raises enormous questions for the Catholic Church, in her
demeanor and traditional habits as well as in her doctrinal statements and theological reflection on the Church... It will be understood that this « ecumenical advance » from the Council stirs
complex and varied reactions on the Protestant side. For it must
be admitted that we are faced with a fairly radical change, not
only of the *attitude* of the Catholic Church towards the « *disjuncti*, »

but also of the way of thinking and speaking of the *doctrine* of Christian *unity*... This is one of the most striking and moving aspects of the immense effort at interior renewal which the Council has undertaken...

Two Currents.

How should Protestant reactions to this event and its possible results be described ? They range from interest and even unqualified enthusiasm to systematic and flat refusal of all dialogue. While mentioning them, we must try and discern what *each one* contains of positive and negative.

Of the Interested Groups.

a) For some Protestants, Catholicism is changing so much that they speak of a « reform. » They think this so far-reaching that reasons for separation will soon no longer exist (cf. the serious questions asked by Karl Barth to Protestants in his last conference [1]). But such a reaction cannot diminish either the permanence of the doctrinal causes of our separation (notably in the domain of ecclesiology), or the permanence and still existing weight of the conservative and canonical forces of the Roman Church.

b) Others think that old separations and their causes have little importance as regards present demands of the mission of the Christian Church in the modern world, and that it is urgent for Christians to unite, either against dominating powers or pernicious ideologies, or in the service of humanity and its spiritual and social welfare. On the whole, this attitude is found under various forms (among Catholics too) in settings or movements keen on « presence in the world, » efficacity, and practical Christianism.

c) Other Protestants are alive to the spiritual, liturgical and Biblical renewal within Catholicism. They rightly insist on the importance of sacramental and community life. But they usually pay more attention to concrete expressions of Christian spirituality as factor of unity, than to its doctrinal tenets and ecclesiological conditioning.

---

1. *Réflexions sur le 2ᵉ Concile.* Geneva, Labor et Fides, or « Ecumenical Review » July, 1963. (Editor's note).

Of the Cautious Groups.

On the other hand, within French Protestantism we find currents of extreme caution, even open hostility, to the idea of dialogue with the Roman Church. Besides some reactions prompted by passions or sociology, which are understandable as regards an historical past sometimes quite recent, the following motivations can be noted :

a) A basic scepticism towards any possibility of a really « *evangelical* » renewal within Catholicism, essentially considered from its unreformable dogmatic definitions, its juridical and institutional monolithism, and historic immobilism. It is probably true to say that Roman conservatism feeds and in some way justifies a certain Protestant conservatism which will only abandon its anti-Catholicism in the measure that the spirit of the Counter-Reformation dies away.

b) Anxiety to safeguard the doctrinal and spiritual heritage of the Reformation, in *faith* and *liberty*. Any approach, even for dialogue, with the Catholic Church, looks like a surrender, even a betrayal, of the principles underlying the historical constitution of the Reformed Churches, and which correspond to their spiritual vocation to defend basic liberties of conscience and rights of the individual, too often disregarded in practice by the Roman Church. On this matter, the importance of a clear statement from the Council about « religious liberty » can hardly be over-rated.

c) Protestantism's innate distrust of the visible *institution* and the uniformity it implies, especially as it appears in the Roman Church under its juridical aspect. This reaction is largely explained by ecclesiological motives : Protestantism laying much greater stress on the unity of the local Church, grouped round the Word of God and the sacraments, in faith in Christ present through the Holy Spirit, than on institutional unity guaranteed by a magisterium...

d) The fear that by a certain « mysticism of Unity » the way is being laid open to an enterprise of « *proselytism,* » more or less under disguise (to be noticed in some cases of « mixed » marriages)...

e) Finally, and perhaps chiefly, there is fear of what might be called *ecumenical ambiguity*. This is denounced on the Catholic side, but it also dreaded in the opposite sense by Protestants...

In so far as the Catholic doctrine of unity and the Oneness of the Church asserts that the only way to unity is the « *return* » of the separated brethren, the latter feel justified in refusing any form of Catholic ecumenism which might simply tend to the reintegration or absorption of non-Catholics into the only true Church, the Church of Rome.

At present it is certain that in the debate on ecumenism there are two conceptions of return to unity : one which considers the Roman Church as « centre, » around which gravitate non-integrated Christians or disjoined factions to be joined to the centre ; and another, which sees the non-Roman communities in their own value or strictly ecclesial character, and seeks to establish with them all, and at differing degrees, the measure of « *communion* » which will only increase through a renewal and deepening of faith in Jesus Christ, the only true Centre of unity...

The mention of these reactions allows us to estimate the level of the problems raised by dialogue. Far from closing the door to it, Protestant reactions may mean questions for the Roman Church, just as what is happening at the Council today raises questions for Protestants.

Towards a Loyal and Positive Dialogue.

Some obvious signs of Protestant readiness for a loyal and positive dialogue must now be set forth :

a) First of all, there is the persevering labour carried on for some years by *theologians*. Orientated not towards a hardening of traditional positions, but towards a common research, a re-evaluation of data biblical, patristic and theological of the basic doctrines over which separations have arisen, theological dialogue, conducted in all respective fidelity to each Church, will permit a new approach to points under discussion. This is particularly felt over exegesis on one side and over ecclesiology on the other. This will allow a deepening on both sides of research in co-operation and emulation, and the settling of a positive method of dialogue, real intellectual ascesis and « *ethics of spiritual intelligence,* » by which the expression of truth has everything to gain.

b) It must be pointed out also, that since the opening of the Council, ecclesiastical authorities in France have felt the need of arranging and determining the conditions for dialogue between Protestants and Catholics, which has begun in recent years, either following private initiatives, or spasmodically in specialized groups.

Thus it was that the National Synod of the Reformed Church of France (followed by that of Alsace-Lorraine) appointed one of its pastors in 1962 to follow up the development and conditions of dialogue. In January 1963, the Protestant Federation of France created a « *Commission des Relations avec le Catholicisme* » which included representatives from the four Reformed and Lutheran Churches of France, and from movements and communities concerned by Ecumenism. The essential role of this Commission is to co-ordinate and encourage information and research, to help pastors and parishes in their relations with Catholicism, especially by the activities of groups of regional contact agents, designated by the Church councils, and finally to promote a real « pedagogy » of dialogue at the level of the Christian people. [1]

c) Let us say in conclusion that both Protestants and Catholics are keenly aware how much the search for Christian unity is inseparable from spiritual *renewal*, and the realization by the Churches of their responsibility in testimony and service. « *No unity without renewal in the Church*, » declared the Message from the recent Assembly of French Protestantism at Aix-en-Provence. [2] And we all know well that it is in and through Jesus Christ, Lord and Saviour of the world, Author of the « new creation, » that the vocation of the Church to her mission of Servant of Christ can be renewed and strengthened, until we have all reached the unity of faith.

---

1. Pastor Hébert Roux is President of the Commission of the Protestant Federation of France for relations with Catholicism.

Two « directories » for ecumenical relations have recently been issued in France :

— from the Catholics, by Mgr. Martin, in charge for the French Episcopate of the « National Secretariat for Christian Unity » (2, rue des Bonnetiers, Rouen) : « *Pastorale des Rencontres Œcuméniques* » by T.R.P. Dumont.

— from the Protestants, by M. H. Roux : « Recommendations and practical advice concerning dialogue with Roman Catholicism », introduced by a « Letter to the Churches » by the President of the Federation and the Presidents of the four chief branches (Bulletin of Information from the E.R.F., 47, rue de Clichy, Paris). Pamphlet issue obtainable from the same address.

2. The *Exposé sur le Concile*, presented by Pastor Hébert Roux to the General Assembly of French Protestantism, November 2, 1963 at Aix-en-Provence, was published in the *Documentation Catholique*, 1-12-63.

The Ecumenical Mentality
of the German Evangelical Church

by Friedrich HEYER

President of the « Evangelische Akademie, » Schleswig-Holstein, Schleswig [1]

I. WEAKENING
OF CIVIC ANTI-CATHOLIC PREJUDICES

The great event in Germany in 1945 was the re-appearance of Churches of different creeds from other countries, just when the history of Germany seemed to have come to an end and the survivors of the huge catastrophe stood dishonoured before the whole world. The first pre-occupation of these Churches was to welcome as fellow-creatures the inhabitants of devastated Germany, and to create an atmosphere of confidence. Big bundles of clothes arrived from Swiss Churches of the Reform. In Evangelical presbyteries, herrings, sent by the Scandinavian Churches, were distributed among the starving. Sacks of dried beans arrived, labelled : a gift from the « brethren » of Middle West America. The Lutheran synod of Missouri accompanied material gifts with a spiritual one, inviting German Lutherans to Hermannsburg at their expense for an exchange of views on theological subjects.

Men of truly Christian spirit who came to Germany in the service of the allied military command saw in the Evangelical Church the only value worthy of confidence in German life. Had it not defended its beliefs against the National-Socialist ideology during the Third Reich ? On this point, the « Stuttgarter Schulderklärung » (acknow-

---

1. Professor Doctor Friedrich HEYER born at Darmstadt, 24-1-1908, is now President of the « Evangelische Akademie, » Schleswig-Holstein, and professor of modern Church History at the university of Kiel. The subject of his Doctorate's thesis was *Die Kirche der Schwärmer*, which he presented in 1938. After world war II, during which he was with the forces, he took part in the foundation of the « Evangelische Akademie. » In 1951, the University of Kiel conferred upon him the diploma of Aggregate for a work he presented on : *Die Orthodoxe Kirche in der Ukraine 1917-1945*. In 1963 he published : *Die Katholische Kirche 1648-1780*. Address : Friedrichstrasse, 75, Schleswig, GERMANY. (Editor's note).

ledgement of guilt published at Stuttgart) by the EKD (German Evangelical Church) should be read. Addressed to Christians in other countries, this statement acknowledged that because they had not loved, professed their faith and suffered more generously, they were partly to blame for the horrors perpetrated. The words of forgiveness, received in answer, made a starting-point for the development of a new life in Germany.

It meant the definitive elimination of the narrow nationalism which had set its seal on the life of the Evangelical Churches, a nationalism inevitably introduced into an ecclesiastical régime dependent on « Princes. » The idea of nationalism, over-enlarged in the Third Reich seemed absurd after the catastrophe it had brought to our country. The readiness manifested by the German people for supra-national political and economic relations, was accompanied by a readiness among evangelicals for a Christian life with an ecumenical range. The argument which German Protestants had used for being distant towards the Catholic Church lost its weight. They had been accustomed to consider their Catholic neighbours as less reliable than Evangelicals, because they were bound by extra-national obligations. Bismarck himself said this in his speech before the Prussian Landtag, on the 16 April 1875, when the Kulturkampf was at its height : « At the head (of the Catholic Church) of this State within the State, stands the Pope with an autocratic power. This monarch is at the head of a closed party among us, who chooses and votes as he wishes. Thanks to (his) officious press, the Pope can promulgate his decrees officially in Prussia, and declare the laws of our State to be null ! Besides that, on our own soil he has an army of priests, he levies taxes, he has set up a network of associations and congregations which exercise great influence. In short, there is hardly anyone, since we have been a constitutional State, who is as powerful as this lofty Italian prelate. Such a situation would be very dangerous and almost intolerable for the State, if it were accorded and guaranteed to one of our own people. And it is held by a stranger. » In extreme terms, these words describe the Evangelical attitude towards the Catholics. Full of these ideas, zealous Evangelicals, for whom the end of the Kulturkampf was a kind of capitulation before Rome, founded the « Evangelischer Bund » (Evangelical Association) as the organ of their debates with the Catholic Church. It counted about half a million members when World War I broke out. After 1945, antipathy against Rome grew less and less. The German Evangelicals began to fit into the structures of the World Churches, as the Roman Catholics had already done.

II. THE EVANGELICAL CHURCH
INSTITUTIONALIZES ITS ECUMENICAL ACTIVITIES

When the German Evangelical Church as such joined the Ecumenical movement in 1945, it put an end to a period of twelve years during which it had been forced to break off ecumenical relations. Some well known Evangelicals from the Reich had certainly contributed to the beginnings of Ecumenism at Constance in 1914, and at Stockholm in 1925. Siegmund-Schultze had done some advance-guard work in Berlin, and published a set of studies written by and about the different Churches in the world. Pastor Rambaud of the Reformed Church in the South of France, had met the German Pastor in a charismatic attempt to bridge over the separation of the German and French nations. But National-Socialism forbade representatives of the German Church to attend ecumenical conferences, as, for example, the World Conference at Edinburgh in 1938, and made ecumenist efforts illegal.

The revival of ecumenical life in Germany coincided with the efforts of the unity movement intending to put an end to the epoch of isolated enthusiasts and adventurers in ecumenical questions, setting up instead a system of official representations in the name of the Church. No one in Germany protested when the « World Council of Churches » was founded in 1948 at Amsterdam. Such an evolution would have been unthinkable except for the theological maturation of ecclesiology within the German Evangelical Church. If during the Protestant XIX century, the Church was still considered as an « invisible » reality and her earthly institutional form destined to disappear, the struggle of the faithful Church under the Third Reich had proved how much believers needed a visible assembly, how necessary was the struggle for the rights of the Church, in the name of the ministerium of sacraments and the word. At Lund, the Lutheran formula was soon accepted : the Church which is already one in God's sight, should also become visibly One through us in time. The Christian tasks of mission work, Caritas and home missions among the people, hitherto entrusted to « associations, » were declared to be « the business of the Church, as necessary manifestation of her nature. » The participation of the German Evangelical Church in the ecumenical movement was understood in this way. Thus was the way prepared for Churches of the Reform, to consider themselves as particular Churches. But henceforward, instead of setting up our own Church as an absolute, we reflected on the special charism granted us by God and which we should contribute to ecumenical life, and on our task within the mass of Christianity.

Ecumenical activity was then clericalized and institutionalized. Only official mandates were permitted. Bishops and Church leaders were appointed for big ecumenical meetings in other countries. Institutions were accredited for relations with the Catholic Church, such as : the « Konfessionskundliches Institut » (Institute for Inter-confessional Studies) of Bensheim, founded by the « Evangelischer Bund » (Evangelical Association); the « Dietzfelbinger-Ausschuss » (the Dietzfelbinger Commission) appointed by the conference of Lutheran bishops. Next, these ideas had to be made general among the communities. Response was not great. There was no place for ecumenical adventurers, independent lay circles, for exaggeration and rashness. These kinds of enthusiasts fell under suspicion. Many got lost in a « no man's land » between the creeds. Church leaders, instructed to lead their people towards the new aim (without essential changes, as far as possible !) were advised to be very prudent. That is the weak side of our ecumenical work.

III. THE THREE STAGES OF DEVELOPMENT OF THE ECUMENICAL MENTALITY

Development of the ecumenical mentality in post-war Germany went through three stages, the good work of which is still active.

1. *World Associations.*

Opposition between active believers and the National-Socialist ideology had proved that dogma is the back-bone of the Church's life. Realization of this fact was the basis of the development of the world associations formed by Lutheran and the Reformed Churches. The first director of the « Œkumenische Zentrale » (Ecumenical Centre) of Frankfurt was Dr. Menn. From personal experience he was well versed in the ideas and dispositions of American Protestant Churches ; exchanges with these Institutions were the first to produce important results.

2. *Relations with Orthodoxy.*

Relations with the Eastern Orthodox Churches had been confined to the opinion of the great Evangelical scholars, Adolf von Harnack and Karl Holl, just before World War I, when middle-class culture prevailed. In 1913 Harnack chose as subject for his discourse at the opening of the Academy of Sciences : the spirit of the Eastern Church, and Holl published an article on the religious foundations of Russian culture. The two professors put forward the Orthodox Church as something altogether odd, the result of set traditionalism. With his usual intuition, Holl wrote : « If the deep recollection of the Orthodox community forces the questioner to acknowledge that there really is a soul in the divine service, this soul is more like a phantom of the past than a living personality. » After World War II, when many Evangelicals in German uniform had been present at Russian religious services in regions under German occupation, there were some good results. Protestants were therefore very willing when the « Kirchliches Aussenamt » (Ecclesiastical Office for External Relations) of Frankfurt opened official relations with the Eastern Churches, and the « evangelical academies » proposed Orthodox and Lutheran encounters. Russian and Balkan emigrants attended these, Copt and Ethiopian students going to West Germany's universities, and even delegations from the Patriarchate of Moscow.

A twofold reaction became apparent also when the style of Eastern icons and hymns came into Evangelical piety and had a certain success. On one side, the partisans of Eastern spirituality were accused of exaggeration, of misinterpreting the oriental phenomenon and not recognizing Lutheran values. On the other hand some evangelical circles became more aware of something lacking ; they realized that when compared with the East, Christian charisms had faded from Protestantism. Since Orthodoxy had never been the adversary of evangelical Christianity like the Catholicism of the Counter-Reformation in theological controversies and civil wars, there was much less prejudice when the Orthodox expounded their beliefs than there would have been towards a Catholic. This stage of contact with Orthodoxy inclined Evangelicals to open more easily to the Catholic side also. Elements in the life of the Church, which are really Catholic in nature, became acceptable to Evangelicals on account of their expression in Orthodoxy.

We cannot forget that ecumenical relations with the Orthodox of the East have political aspects. At the height of the war in Korea, at Christmas 1950/1951, the director of « Kirchliches Aussenamt » (Ecclesiastical Office for External Relations) President Niemöller, on his own initiative, paid a visit to the Patriarchate of Moscow. He favours a peace policy with the Soviet world. Later, some Church circles with the same intention entered into relations with the Christian Meeting for peace at Prague, favouring the views of the Soviet powers on the world's political situation. All the faithful have been asking since then whether these contacts with the East are not running us into the danger of giving the Soviet government an opportunity for political influence in the West.

3. Direct Relations with the Catholic Church.

Direct encounter with the Catholic Church, third stage in the ecumenical approach, was only undertaken by the Evangelical Church with hesitation and the official courtesy of the Western German Republic ; which is surprising, given the importance of this question. A few cultured evangelical circles became interested in Père de Foucauld, the worker-priests in Paris, the discussion between the Dominicans and the existentialist Camus, the works of Catholic poets like Georges Bernanos and Reinhold Schneider. The phenomena of present-day Catholic spirituality thus crept quietly into the horizon of German Evangelical spiritual life. Churchmen themselves, occupied in watching the theological controversies, neither encouraged nor prevented this action in the literary domain, which raised conditions preliminary to any ecumenical encounter between Rome and Wittenberg.

The bonds which had come into existence between Evangelical Christians and staunch Catholics in Hitler's concentration camps and under the oppression of the Third Reich, quickly made possible the creation of a Christian party, the CDU, when the « Bundesrepublik » was formed. But the old Evangelical distrust was soon roused. The Christian governmental party, which seemed to have a Catholic majority, was surely going to pave the way for a new Counter-Reformation ? Had not key-positions been given purposely to Catholics ? When it came to nominating ministers and their officials at Bonn, the principle of confessional parity was followed. Evangelical mistrust gave rise to this joke : « Wanted at Bonn, two secretaries, a Catholic and a Protestant. One will be appointed Secretary of State, the other, Secretary to the Government. » The laws issued by the Bonn Parliament were then sifted by the Evangelical population to discover how far the guiding political ideas of Catholics, based on the natural law, had influenced the text. Was not the principle of subsidiarity, which marked the new law of social security, a result of the Catholic idea of rights ?

All this reveals our previous mentality. There are hardly any German Evangelicals today for which the events of Vatican Council II have not been a surprise, stirring them to seek a fresh orientation. The discussion on the formula of the « two sources »

of Revelation, rejection of candidates proposed by the Roman Congregations for the Council's commissions, and the proposals for
formulating the rights of bishops, came to meet evangelical ideas
in an unhoped manner.

Dr. Harms, leading pastor in Hamburg, spoke thus of the new
state of things. « Confusion reigns because we are at a moment of
transition. There was no such confusion 40 years ago. The limits
between our Churches were well determined and well kept. The
Churches were so far apart, that they did not live within earshot
of one another. Now people ask : Are the divergences between
our Churches as serious as has always been asserted ? This explains
why present Evangelical reactions are so contradictory. « Controversial theologians » apparently very anti-Catholic, are declaring
themselves delighted over the positive changes on the Roman side.
Yet former ecumenists hold back. » The words of the Catholic
Church will bear no fruit for the Evangelical Church, as long as
the unspoken idea dominates : the « separated brethren » must
« come back » while the Roman Church may stay as she is. This
Evangelical soreness is based on the historical conscience of German
Evangelicals, who do not want to either break with or repudiate
their history. However gracious the Pope's words may be, Evangelical listeners in Germany stiffen at the very sound of the word
« return. » Many hearts grow warm, however, at the idea of a
return together to Golgotha in a spirit of penance, or of journeying
forward together to meet Christ at his second coming.

The objection made to the schema on the Church by Prof.
Schlink, Evangelical Observer at the Council, reflects this state of
mind. In this schema, he says, the Evangelical aspirations after
unity are interpreted as a desire to adhere to a Church directed
by the Pope. It admits the bond of individual non-Catholic
Christians with the Roman Church but not the bond of the Churches
themselves. « It is to be understood that non-Roman Christianity feels
un-appreciated by such words, since it is not composed merely of
individuals but of Churches. » « On the Evangelical side, we do
not want the transfer of other Churches into one, but mutual
openness between Churches. »

The rejection of the mere idea of return also explains the moving
welcome given to words spoken by Pope Paul VI at the opening
of the Council's second session. The words which found so deep an
echo in Germany were : « If there is any fault of ours in the causes
of this separation, we humbly ask God's forgiveness, and we beg
the indulgence of our brethren whom we may have offended. »
Hans Asmussen, former champion of Evangelico-Catholic recon-

ciliation, then accused of « Catholicizing, » and deprived of all influence over the evangelical mentality, reacted to the Pope's words in an open letter. « Christians, » he wrote, « are very ready to listen to a request for pardon. These requests must receive a reply. To return no answer would be culpable aloofness. From my understanding of the Gospel, we Lutherans should hasten to reply to the Pope. We should say two things : first, stating how the Roman Church has offended us, and then asking the Roman Church to declare in what we Lutherans have offended them. All that does not answer this will be valueless, to be considered as without issue, or at least, as forgiven. Scripture teaches me that this is very important before God. »

The Asmussen letter provoked many replies from Evangelical bishops. Dr. Halfmann, Bishop of Holstein, always of very reserved attitude towards the Catholic Church, stated at his regional synod, a few days before he died in January 1964 : « If this attitude (in Rome) becomes a reality, we will have to abandon much of our traditional polemics. »

IV. ECUMENISM
IN THE DIFFERENT LEVELS OF SOCIETY

One of the results of our past history has been the formation of a largely laicized public ; while not appreciating the true demands of the Evangelical Church, it remains incorporated and morally linked with it. Has this « cultural Protestantism » shared the ecumenical re-orientation ? These outer zones did not accept the wave of revival which passed through the Church by means of theological dialectics or the liturgical movement. What is the position of the ecumenical problem here ?

Semi-intellectual circles unable to grasp quickly the bearing of the new state of things cling stubbornly to past anti-Catholic reflexes and resentment, more so than communities more united to parishes and their pastors. One might almost say : among people of incomplete secular training the only Evangelical trend that remains is the anti-Catholic reflex. It is quite different in humanist intellectual circles which have favoured plans for reconciliation ever since the Century of Shining Lights and the Romantic period. Cultured minds, filled with these ideas, urge us to put an end to confessional opposition, pay no attention to controversies over doctrine, « make short cuts » for those in charge of ecumenical questions in the Church.

Prof. Sucker, President of the « Evangelischer Bund » told them at Nuremberg recently : « It is an illusion to believe that the deep moat between the Evangelical and the Catholic Churches can be filled up in a twinkling. »

The Ecumenical mentality has chiefly developed where Catholic, Orthodox and Protestant Christians have met for tri-lateral talks : Byzantium - Rome - Wittenberg. Instead of discussion, they pray together. Evangelical Academies have institutionalized such meetings.

Interest in Ecumenism has grown largely among the laity of late years. In memory of Evangelical and Catholic martyrs, victims of the Third Reich, Orthodox, Catholics and Evangelicals were invited to Lubeck. Choirs from the three confessions have sung in St. Peter's Church, Hamburg. Thousands have flocked to hear them. Everyone has been surprised at this development of ecumenical mentality.

A woman of our faith revealed her own impression of Ecumenism in one sentence : « The presence of other Christians, Catholics and Orthodox, makes our prayer more perfect ; we pray more fully with them than when we are alone. »

Ecumenism
in the Anglican Communion

by F.P. Coleman

General Secretary, The Church Union, London[1]

I. CONVOCATION AND ECUMENICAL DISPOSITIONS OF THE FIRST CONFERENCE OF LAMBETH

Nearly one hundred years ago, in 1867, the Archbishop of Canterbury, Dr Longley, wrote to the Bishops of the Anglican Communion, then 144 in number, inviting them to a Conference at Lambeth Palace. He did so in response to a suggestion made in the first place by the Metropolitan and Bishops of Canada, and then submitted to the two Houses of the Convocation of Canterbury, that the Archbishop should « invite the Bishops of our Indian and Colonial Episcopate to meet... the home Bishops for brotherly communion and conference. » This was the first of the Lambeth Conferences which have now become an accepted feature in the life of the Anglican Communion. At first, the Archbishop of Canterbury was reluctant to call such a meeting of Bishops, and it is interesting to note that the initiative came not from England but from Canada. In his letter of invitation, the Archbishop made it clear that this meeting of Bishops « would not be competent to make declarations or lay down definitions on points of doctrine. » The Archbishop thought, however, that « united worship and com-

---

1. Reverend F. P. Coleman was born in Greenford, Middlesex, England in 1911 and graduated from London University in 1933. After engaging in administrative work at the university from 1933 to 1938, he prepared for ordination at St. Stephen's house, Oxford. Having served as assistant priest at St. Alphage, Southwork and St. Stephen, Lewisham. Reverend Coleman became vicar of St. Anthony, Nunhead, in 1948 and of Ellesmere Port, Cheshire in 1952. He was named to his post of general secretary of the Church Union in 1955. At present he is also proctor in convocation for the diocese of Southwark and member of the Church Assembly, Board for Social Responsibility. He serves on the Archbishops' Commission on Roman Catholic Relations and with the group engaged in discussions with Presbyterian churches. — Address: The Church Union, 199, Uxbridge Road, London W. 12, England.

mon councils would greatly tend to maintain particularly the unity of the faith, » and that they would bind the participants together in stronger bonds of peace and brotherly charity. It was clear from the outset that the Conference had no juridical or canonical powers, but it was no less evident that the Bishops of the Anglican Communion thus assembled together recognized their responsibility as pastors of their respective flocks and as a collective episcopate within their communion.

In spite of the misgivings held by the Archbishop of Canterbury and other Bishops in England, this first Conference issued a formal « address to the faithful, » and this document was given a particular character by being published not only in English but also in Latin and Greek. The addition of Hebrew was not, it seems, thought necessary or desirable ! More important, the Conference published a series of formal resolutions, which make it clear that the Bishops had both a clear conception of their place in the tradition of Catholic Christendom, and also a deep concern for Christian unity. « We desire, » the Bishops wrote, « to express the deep sorrow with which we view the divided condition of the flock of Christ throughout the world, ardently longing for the fulfilment of the prayer of our Lord « that all may be one as thou Father, art in me, and I in thee, that they also may be one in us, that the world may believe that thou hast sent me » ; and... we do here solemnly record our conviction that unity will be most effectually promoted by maintaining the faith in its purity and integrity — as taught in the Holy Scriptures held by the Primitive Church, summed up in the Creeds and affirmed by the undisputed General Councils — and by drawing each other closer to our common Lord, by giving ourselves to much prayer and intercession, by the cultivation of a spirit of charity, and a love of the Lord's appearing. » The Bishops who thus expressed their concern for the furtherance of Christian unity claimed to be « Bishops of Christ's Holy Catholic Church in visible communion with the United Church of England and Ireland, professing the Faith delivered to us in Holy Scripture, maintained by the Primitive Church and by the Fathers of the English Reformation. »

The proceedings and reports of the earlier Lambeth Conferences are little known today except to students of Church history. It is not surprising therefore that, in the popular mind, the interest of the Lambeth Conferences in Christian unity is thought to be something of recent origin. The reverse is true, and the theme of unity which appeared in the first of the Lambeth Conferences was to recur frequently as the Bishops of the Anglican Communion came together every ten years to discuss their common problems. They deserve a credit not often accorded to them for their pioneer work in bringing to the notice of the Church the evil of disunity among Christians, the importance of prayer and work for unity, and the basis upon which future unity must be built. They were, of course, men of their time. Anglicans, like other Christians, had many different and pressing problems which demanded immediate attention. It was one thing to talk about unity, but quite another to translate words into effective action. It must be borne in mind, too, that at this time, Christians outside the Roman Catholic Church were extremely indignant at the doctrinal developments which they saw taking place among their Roman Catholic brethren. So, while the Lambeth Conference of 1867 could in all sincerity adopt a positive resolution on the subject of Christian unity, the Bishops felt it necessary, at the same time, to warn the faithful against « the growing superstitions and additions with which in these latter days the truth of God hath been overlaid. » In particular, reference was made to the pretensions of the See of Rome and to the « practical exhortation of the Blessed Virgin Mary as Mediatrix in the place of her Divine Son. »

II. ECUMENICAL INITIATIVES
OF THE LAMBETH CONFERENCES
OF THE NINETEENTH CENTURY

The attack on Rome was renewed in 1878, when there was still vigorous reaction against the infallibility decrees of the first Vatican Council. On the other hand, the Bishops in 1878 again took the opportunity of asserting their desire to further the reunion of Christendom. Moreover, they anticipated the emphasis now being placed on the relationship between unity and mission. The official letter of the Conference commended among other things the following recommendation submitted by one of its committees : « Remembering the blessing promised to united intercession, and believing that such intercession ever tends to deepen and strengthen that unity of his Church for which our Lord earnestly pleaded in his great intercessory prayer, your Committee trust that the Conference will give the weight of its recommendation to the observance throughout the Churches of this communion of a season of prayer for the unity of Christendom. » « It seems to us, » the Committee added, « that intercessions for the enlargement of his kingdom may

well be joined with earnest prayer that all who profess in him may
be one flock with one shepherd. » Already, in 1878, the Lambeth
Conference was confronted with problems of Church relationships.
One of its committees was appointed to discuss the position of
Old Catholics, the Armenian and other Christian communities in
the East, and the Moravian churches which existed within the
territorial limits of dioceses of the Anglican Communion.

The report of the Lambeth Conference, 1878, contained also an
important statement of the basis on which the unity of the Anglican
Communion is built. Of the Churches within this communion, the
report asserted : « United under one divine head in the fellowship
of the one Catholic and Apostolic Church, holding the one faith
revealed in Holy Writ, defined in the Creeds and maintained by
the Primitive Church, receiving the same Canonical Scriptures of
the Old and the New Testaments as containing all things necessary
to salvation — these churches teach the same words of God, partake
of the same divinely ordered sacraments, through the ministry of
the same apostolic orders, and worship one God and Father through
the same Lord Jesus Christ by the same Holy and divine Spirit, who
is given to those that believe, to guide them into all truth. » Ten
years later, in 1888, these basic principles of Anglican unity were
related by the Lambeth Conference to the positive task of ecumenical discussion. In 1886, the General Convention of the (Anglican)
Protestant Episcopal Church, held at Chicago, adopted four articles
which were approved in a revised form by the Lambeth Conference
of 1882. Among the resolutions adopted by the Conference, we
find the following :

« That, in the opinion of this Conference, the following articles
supply a basis on which approach may be, by God's blessing, made
towards home reunion :

a) The Holy Scriptures of the Old and New Testaments, as
containing « all things necessary to salvation, » and as being the
rule and ultimate standard of faith.

b) The Apostles' Creed as the baptismal symbol ; and the Nicene
Creed as the sufficient statement of the Christian faith.

c) The two sacraments ordained by Christ himself — Baptism
and the Supper of the Lord — ministered with the unfailing use
of Christ's words of institution and of the elements ordained by him.

d) The Historic Episcopate locally adapted in the methods of
its administration to the varying needs of the nations and peoples
called of God into the unity of his Church. »

In popular language, these four points have become known as
the « Lambeth Quadrilateral. » They have undergone a further

modification, as for example in the reports of the Lambeth Conference of 1920, but their ultimate acceptance is implicit in all discussions and negotiations directed towards the establishment of relations of communion or of actual unity with other Churches. Having found an agreed basis for ecumenical discussion, the Bishops at Lambeth in 1898 were able to go further. It was agreed that the various constituent churches of the Anglican communion should « hold themselves in readiness to enter into brotherly conference... with the representatives of other Christian communions in the English speaking races, either towards corporate reunion, or towards such relations as may prepare the way for fuller organic unity hereafter. » It was noted that already such a conference had been proposed by the Church in the United States of America. In Europe the Bishops saw a hope of closer relations with the Church of Sweden and with the Old Catholic Churches.

They noted that in some countries, Spain and Portugal for instance, small groups had separated themselves from the Church of Rome, to adopt such sound forms of doctrine and discipline, and the hope was expressed that these groups might « be enabled such Catholic organization as will permit us to give them a fuller recognition. » Some of these hopes have been realized, some remain unfulfilled. Friendly, informal relations with the Church of Sweden have existed for some time. But so far as England is concerned, the formal relationship established by the Convocations in 1954 and 1955 simply allows qualified communicants of the Church of Sweden to receive Holy Communion in Anglican services, and, on suitable occasions, Swedish ecclesiastics to give addresses in churches of the Church of England. Full communion between the Church of England and the Old Catholics was established in 1932, and a similar relationship exists with other Churches of the Anglican Communion. In recent months, a relationship of full communion has been established with the Independent Church of the Philippines, with the Spanish Reformed Church, and with the Lusitanian Church.

All these Churches have been able to restore an Episcopal Ministry, through consecrations carried out by Bishops of the Anglican Communion. The Lambeth Conference of 1888 also expressed the hope that the barriers to fuller communion with the Patriarchs of Constantinople and other Eastern Patriarchs and Bishops might be removed in the course of time by further intercourse and extended enlightenment. The resolution on this subject is marked by a tone of condescension which is to be found elsewhere in the Lambeth Conferences of the last century. It « recommends that the counsels and efforts of our fellow Christians should be directed towards the encouragement of internal reformation in the Eastern Churches rather than to the drawing away from them of individual members of their communion. » The attitude has now changed to one of profound respect. Although relations with the Orthodox Churches are of an extremely friendly and cordial character, so far it has not proved possible to establish formal communion between any Anglican and Orthodox Churches. The present Archbishop of Canterbury is known to favour discussions with the representatives of the Orthodox Churches, and has personally done very much to encourage mutual understanding.

The principles on which relations of full communion should be based were already envisaged at the Lambeth Conference of 1888, but they did not find formal expression until the establishment of communion with the Old Catholic Churches in 1932. The concordat between the Church of England and the Old Catholic Churches is now accepted as the norm for any future relationships of this kind, and it is therefore worth quoting in full. In January 1932, the Convocations of Canterbury and York agreed :

« That this House approves of the following statements agreed on between the representatives of the Old Catholic Churches and the Churches of the Anglican Communion at a Conference held at Bonn on July 2nd, 1931 :

1. Each Communion recognizes the catholicity and independence of the other, and maintains its own.

2. Each Communion agrees to admit members of the other Communion to participate in the sacraments.

3. Intercommunion does not require from either Communions the acceptance of all doctrinal opinions, sacramental devotion, or liturgical practice characteristic of the other, but implies that each believes the other to hold all the essentials of the Christian faith.

And this House agrees to the establishment of intercommunion between the Church of England and the Old Catholics on these terms. »

Similar resolutions were adopted in 1963, when full communion was established with the three other Churches named above.

The Lambeth Quadrilateral, as has already been mentioned, was framed in connection with resolutions on the subject of Home Reunion in the Report of the Lambeth Conference 1888. So far as England is concerned, little was done at the time to initiate ecumenical discussions with other Christian bodies in the country, though the thought was not completely absent from the life of the Church of England. There were, however, other preoccupations. The Oxford Movement was gaining strength, and it was towards

the end of the last century that the most bitter strife was experienced. Moreover, developments in the educational field were
proving a point of deep division between the Church of England
and English nonconformity. Division within the Church of England
and animosity between Anglicans and Nonconformists were effective
obstacles to any considerable development of ecumenical thought
or activity.

III. ECUMENICAL ACTION
OF THE ANGLICAN COMMUNION
AT THE OPENING OF THE TWENTIETH CENTURY

The Anglican Communion, however, is wider than the Church
of England. At the first Lambeth Conference in 1867, 144 Bishops
were present. In 1897, the number had risen to some 200, and
of these more than 80 had been consecrated in or after 1890. The
earlier Lambeth Conferences provide evidence of initiatives taken
in the Provinces outside the British Isles, and by the end of the
century, the Churches overseas were growing rapidly. Many of them
were missionary churches, confronted with a situation wholly different from that of the Church of England and of the other Provinces within the British Isles. Already the folly of Christian disunity was becoming clear to workers in the Mission Field, and it
is therefore not in any way surprising that the early decades of
the 20th century are seen to be a period of ecumenical initiative.
The most celebrated of these is the movement which began in the
early years of the century with conversations in India between
Anglicans and Missionaries from a number of non-episcopal
Churches. At first it was a question of informal conversations
between people sharing common problems. Progress at first was
slow, and it was only after the war of 1914-18 that the conversations began to take a more positive turn, with a direction towards
unity itself. The Lambeth Conference of 1920 had provided a
new incentive. It called upon all Christians to « unite in a new
and great endeavour to recover and to manifest to the world the
unity of the Body of Christ for which he prayed. » Further, the
Conference recommended to the authorities of the Churches of
Anglican Communion « that they should, in such ways and in
the such times as they think best, formally invite the authorities of
other Churches within their areas to confer with them concerning

the possibility of taking definite steps to co-operate in a common endeavour in the lines set forth in the above appeal, to restore the unity of the Church of Christ ».

In South India, negotiations between a group of non-episcopal Churches had led to the formation of the South India Church, and in 1920 the episcopal Synod of the Anglican Church in India passed a resolution appointing a Committee to confer with representatives of this body. A little later the Wesleyan Methodist Church entered into the negotiations, and from then on, the work of discussion and negotiation was carried forward until the establishment of the Church of South India in 1947. As the negotiations proceeded, they gave rise to growing alarm in other parts of the Anglican communion, and particularly in England. It seemed to many that the basic principles laid down by the Lambeth Conferences of the last century were in some respects being seriously compromised. At one time, it looked as if the controversy would lead to a schism within the Church of England, if not within the Anglican communion as a whole. For the first time, the Anglican communion was confronted with a project for the reunion of a group of Anglican dioceses with Churches of Protestant tradition, and for the first time, the grave difficulties implicit in such a project were brought to light. Now that the history of those years can be viewed with more detachment, it seems inevitable that the South Indian scheme should have become a *cause célèbre*. The schemes now under consideration in other parts of the Anglican Communion today still arouse ardent opposition or fervent support, but Anglicans are becoming increasingly aware that the kind of problem which gave rise to acrimonious debate in connection with South India, must inevitably be considered, though dispassionately, wherever there is a move towards unity between episcopal and non-episcopal Churches. It should be noted that even today the relationship between most of the provinces of the Anglican Communion and the Church of South India is a transitional one. In England, for instance, the Convocations have agreed to a relationship of *limited* communion, and when this was accepted it was understood that a permanent relationship could not be established until certain outstanding difficulties in the Church of South India were resolved.

IV. NECESSITY OF THE EPISCOPATE
AND OF ORDINATION BY THE BISHOP :
PRINCIPLE AND APPROACHES

1. *Affirmation of the Principle.*

When two Churches enter into communion with each other, they recognize without any hesitation each other's ministries and sacraments. So, for example, an Anglican who goes to Holland, may communicate at an Old Catholic Mass, having no doubt as to the validity of the ministry or the sacrament. An Old Catholic visiting England, is in turn welcomed as a communicant, and he receives Holy Communion without any doubt regarding the sacrament or the priest who celebrates it. Other things being equal, it is comparatively easy to establish communion between two Episcopal Churches, where there seems to be no doubt as to the succession in orders on either side. By contrast, the attempt to bring into a unified ministry the ministries of Anglican and separated non-Episcopal Churches has proved to be one of the most difficult problems of the Ecumenical Movement. In the Church of England, as in the Anglican Communion at large, no one is allowed to minister as a priest unless he has first been ordained to the priesthood by a Bishop. The necessity of Episcopal Orders has always been asserted by the Church of England, and the principle has been affirmed again and again by the Lambeth Conferences. In 1958, the Lambeth Conference welcomed and endorsed a statement on Christian unity prepared by its Committee on Church Unity and the Church Universal. In doing so it accepted the following statement : « Loyalty to the age-long tradition of the Church, and to our own experience, compels us to believe that a ministry to be acknowledged by every part of the Church can only be attained through the historic episcopate, though not necessarily in the precise form prevailing in any part of the Anglican Communion. This ministry we believe to have been given to the Church by divine providence from primitive Christian times with its traditional functions of pastoral care and oversight, ordination, leadership in worship, and teaching. »

2. *Approach Used with the Churches*
of India and Ceylon.

In South India, as in other areas where schemes of union are under preparation, the Anglicans involved have always insisted that in any new united Church, the principle of episcopal ordination derived from the historic succession shall be accepted. So far as the future life of such a united Church is concerned, this has proved no obstacle to the non-Episcopal Churches taking part in negotiations for reunion. Difficulty arises, however, over the immediate integration of episcopal and non-episcopal ministries ; yet this integration is essential, if a new united Church is to be at once in communion with the Provinces and Churches of the Anglican Communion. While the majority of Anglicans consider episcopal ordination to be necessary, ministers of the other Churches concerned refuse to accept such ordination. They claim that they have already been ordained to Christ's ministry of the Word and Sacraments and that therefore they should be acceptable without any further ordination. Here we may note in passing a difference of approach. Anglicans, in common with other episcopal Churches, think of the ministry in terms of orders, Bishops, Priests, Deacons etc. Protestants, on the other hand, speak of « the ministry » without reference to any hierarchy of orders within it. Thus, for instance, a Methodist claims that he has been ordained to be a minister, not a priest, though some Methodists would claim that their ministry has a priestly character. The negotiators in South India effected a compromise. They agreed that all *future* ordinations within the united Church should be conducted by a Bishop with the assistance of Presbyters, but that all existing ministers at the time of union should be accepted as Presbyters of the Church of South India, without submitting to ordination or to any similar rite. Consequently, the Church of South India today has a ' mixed ' ministry. Since the inauguration of the union, all ordinations have been conducted by Bishops whose consecration derives from the Anglican succession.

The Anglican priests who went into the union have, of course, already been episcopally ordained. There remains, however, a considerable body of ministers who were serving in the other Churches and who have not, therefore, been episcopally ordained ; and to these must be added the number of ministers from non-episcopal bodies outside the Church of South India who, since the union, have been accepted for work in that Church without the requirement of episcopal ordination.

Other solutions to this problem have been sought in more recent schemes. For instance, in Ceylon and in the proposed plan for North India/Pakistan, the proposal is that the ministers should be integrated by undergoing a rite of unification. The unification rites put forward in Ceylon and North India are not identical partly owing to differences of local situation. In North India, the

situation is complicated by the existence of Methodist « Bishops. »
The approach, however, is largely the same. Unification is sought
by means of a rite in which *all* the ministers of the respective
Churches receive the laying on of hands with prayer. All are acknowledged as having already received from God, by virtue of their
ordination, grace for « the ministry. » On behalf of all, prayer is
offered to God that he will bestow on each, according to his need,
grace for the exercise of the ministry of a Presbyter in the Church
of God within the particular local Church (the treatment of
Bishops differs as between North India and Ceylon). These unification rites are based on the belief that any difference between
ministers not hitherto episcopally ordained and those already so
ordained will be transcended, and that the united Churches will
from the outset possess a ministry fully and without exception
accredited in the eyes of all their members and so far as may be
of the Church throughout the world. They have been submitted
to very searching criticism. To be satisfactory from an Anglican
point of view they must provide the essentials of ordination to the
priesthood, but some critics assert that they lack the necessary cer-
tainty of a sacramental rite by reason of the fact that the same
words and actions are used without difference in respect of episcopally ordained priests and ministers who have not previously been
so ordained. Here the underlying approach is itself questioned,
and it seems unlikely that the criticism will be met by improvements
in the form of service itself. On the other hand, there are some
who, while willing to accept the approach, are critical of the rites
themselves. Continued negotiations in Ceylon have led to marked
improvements, which may lead to acceptance of the rite by those
who believe that it is capable of conveying all that is given in
Catholic ordination to the priesthood. The proposed rite in North
India is much more complicated, and has been more severely
criticized. Allowance must be made for the fact that in North
India and Pakistan, non-Anglican influence has been strong during
the negotiations, whereas in Ceylon, the Anglican Church is in the
position of a strong majority.

3. *Approach Used with the Methodist Church.*

A new approach to this problem of integration has emerged from
the conversations between Anglicans and Methodists in England. In
the Report on these conversations, proposals are made for the
« reconciliation » of the two Churches and their ministries. The
attempt to « unify » the two ministerial traditions in one common
rite has been abandoned. Instead, a double rite has been devised.

In each district, it is proposed that the ministers of the Methodist Church shall be received by the local Bishop and four priests of the Church of England through the laying on of hands with prayer. By this means, the Anglicans seek to share with Methodist ministers the tradition of episcopal ordination, and the Methodist ministers come with a desire to enter into the spiritual heritage and continuity of commission treasured by Anglicans. The prayer before the laying on of hands includes the petition : « Renew thy blessings already given, and upon these thy servants do thou pour out thy Holy Spirit, to endue each according to his need with grace for the office of priest in the Church of God... » The laying on of hands follows in silence, and then the ministers are given a general authority to exercise the office of priest according as need may arise. In the second part of the rite the Anglican Bishop and priests of the district are received by representative Methodist ministers. The pattern of reception is similar, i.e. prayer for the grace of God is followed by the laying on of hands and a granting of authority to ministers according to necessity. The prayer offered by the presiding Methodist minister contains a petition for grace, but this is not linked with any particular order in the ministry — « pour out the Holy Spirit upon them for the work of a minister in thy Church. » Methodists do not, in fact, ordain Anglican priests who seek to minister within the Methodist church, and there is no reason to suppose that they would wish to regard this service of reconciliation as ordination. This latest proposal for the integration of ministries has met with criticism, though it is much more widely accepted than the rites drawn up in Ceylon and North India. Some Anglicans fear that the reception of Methodist ministers may not, in fact, convey the grace of priesthood, whereas, on the other hand, many Methodists (and some Evangelicals in the Church of England) take the view that the rite is so obviously intended to be an ordination as to be unacceptable to those who are prepared to recognize Methodist ministers as fully ordained, though not in the Episcopal tradition.

Given the fact that there are on both sides conscientious convictions which must be respected, it does seem to many in the Church of England that the form of reconciliation put forward in the Anglican/Methodist Report represents a definite step forward in the quest for a means of bringing together episcopal and non-episcopal ministries without causing offence to consciences on either side. In a short article, it is not possible to give this subject the extended treatment it demands. On the other hand, it is such an important problem for Anglicans that it deserves special considera-

tion, even within a survey of limited compass. Nor is it confined
to those conversations which take place between Anglicans and the
various traditions of Protestantism. In all ecumenical discussion,
sooner or later, some assessment must be made of the ministries of
Churches at present in separation. The Anglican may not believe
that the Methodist or Presbyterian minister is a priest in the broad
sense of Catholic tradition. He must, however, try to reach some
theological understanding of the ministry conferred in other
Churches, even though they lack the tradition of episcopal ordination. Similarly, it is not enough for a Roman Catholic simply to
condemn Anglican Orders. He too must ask what it is that Anglicans seek and are given in their ordination rites, and then seek
some form of reconciliation of these two traditions of ministry, in
the light of the conclusions he reaches.

4. *Attempts of Union in Africa and in Great Britain.*

So far as practical approaches to unity are concerned, Anglican
efforts have understandably been directed primarily to brethren in
the separated non-episcopal Churches. Schemes of union have
reached an advanced stage, not only in India and Ceylon, but also
more recently in Africa. Generally, the African schemes do not
reveal any special theological problems different from those which
have arisen in India, Pakistan and Ceylon. There are particular
problems related to the composition of the negotiating groups in
each area, but the general pattern is the same. Progress in Great
Britain has been much less rapid, but the conversations between
Anglicans and Methodists have revealed a degree of unity of which
many on both sides were previously unaware. Ignorance and prejudice, however, are more widespread in the Church at large than
they are among the experts who undertake the important of conversation and negotiation. This was painfully evident in the Scottish
reactions to the first report on conversations between Anglicans
and Presbyterians. Yet, in spite of the excitement aroused by this
report, the conversations have now been resumed, and are characterised by thorough theological discussion of disputed issues.

V. RAPPORTS WITH THE ORTHODOX CHURCHES AND THE ROMAN CATHOLIC CHURCH

The Anglican vision of unity is not, of course, limited to what
is immediately practicable. For many years, friendly relations have

existed between Anglican Churches and the Eastern Churches. In England, the work of fostering good relations has been undertaken by such bodies as the Anglican and the Eastern Churches Association, which has just celebrated its centenary, and the Fellowship of St Alban and St Sergius, which is noted for the quality of its theological conferences. There is now a prospect of renewed theological discussion between the Church of England as such and the Orthodox Churches. This is of particular importance when one considers the greatly increased weight of Orthodox reprensentation in the World Council of Churches. Until the most recent times, the promotion of understanding and good relationships between the Church of England and the Roman Catholic Church has largely been left to individual initiative. Generally, Anglicans have found it easier to enter into sympathetic discussion with Roman Catholics on the Continent than with those who are their immediate neighbours at home. This can be explained partly by the fact of highly developed theological traditions in such countries as France, Belgium and Germany ; partly by the fact that pastoral difficulties may arise where Anglicans and Roman Catholics, living side by side, both claim to be heirs of an authentic Catholic tradition. The natural tendency is for them to live over and against and in separation from each other, even though there is much which is common to their separated traditions. In England, the position is aggravated by historical and social considerations, which make it difficult to embark upon dispassionate theological conversations. This emotional atmosphere has, however, been greatly modified by the influence of Pope John XXIII and of the second Vatican Council. The Archbishop of Canterbury has now established a Commission which will be responsible for promoting good relations with the Roman Catholic Church in this country, and it is to be hoped that the Roman Catholic hierarchy in England will make similar provision in the near future. In the United States, there are signs of growing friendship, and it has long been recognized that the Mission Field provides many opportunities for friendly cooperation. One of the principal obstacles in the way of unity between the Church of Rome and the Churches of the Anglican communion is the bewildering variety of beliefs to be found within the Anglican tradition. Perhaps the greatest need for Anglican ecumenism today is that Anglicans should be more united among themselves.

The Sociological Situation in America

by Robert McAfee BROWN

Professor at the International Institute for Catechetical and Pastoral

A new religious pattern is emerging in the United States, and this pattern must be understood if the relationship between Catholics and Protestants is to be understood. It is very different from the former pattern, and one of the greatest difficulties in American ecumenical relationships comes from the fact that many Protestants and many Catholics are still trying to live in terms of the old pattern rather than the new one.

1. *America, a Protestant Nation.*

The former pattern could be described as follows : America grew to maturity as a predominantly « Protestant nation. » While it would be naive to pretend that in the past most Americans were staunchly Protestant, it would be incorrect to deny there was a Protestant « stamp » upon the culture, or that there was an « ethos » that could be described as Protestant. It was simply assumed that Protestant *mores* and Protestant ideals were normative in American life. All other *mores* and all other ideals were « different, » or « foreign » or « strange. » The politician who was not a white, Anglo-Saxon Protestant was, until fairly recent times, a rarity.

---

1. Robert McAfee BROWN, Professor of Religion at Stanford University formerly was Professor of Systematic Theology at Union Theological Seminary, and before that was Professor of Religion at Macalester College. He was an observer at the Second Vatican Council, representing the World Alliance of Reformed and Presbyterian Churches. He has written *The Bible Speaks to You, The Significance of the Church,P. T. Forsyth; Prophet for today. An American Dialogue* (with Father *Weigel*), and *The Spirit of Protestantism.* This spring his reflections on the Council were published under the title *Observer in Rome.* He has contributed to Scharper, ed., *American Catholics: A Protestant-Jewish View,* and has translated Suzanne de Dietrich, *Le Dessein de Dieu,* and Georges Casalis, *Portrait de Karl Barth.* He was recently co-editor with David Scott of *The Challenge to Reunion,* a study of the « Blake proposal. » — Address : Stanford University, Stanford, California, U.S.A. (Editor's note).

Public schools were a kind of secular extension of the Protestant Sunday Schools. In this situation, Roman Catholics were definitely a minority group, often persecuted, and usually « typed » in terms of national origins : one was either an « Italian Catholic » (in which case he deviated from the American norm), or he was an « Irish Catholic » (in which case he bore the legacy of generations of animosity engendered by English-Irish disputes in the old world). Catholics tended to congregate in the cities and to develop enclaves of their own, in which they suffered a double disadvantage : if they stayed among themselves they were accused of clannishness and a ghetto-like mentality ; whereas if they went out into the rest of the culture they were accused of trying to « take over. »

2. America, a Protestant, Catholic and Jewish Nation.

But the above is no longer an accurate description. America is no longer a « Protestant nation, » even though many Protestants act as if it were. And Catholics are no longer a beleagured minority, even though many Catholics act as if they were. Instead, America has become what can be called a « pluralistic culture » — in which to be « an American » is no longer to be a Protestant, but to be a Protestant, a Catholic, or a Jew. Protestantism is still the largest of these three groups, but it is a minority of the whole, and it seems unlikely that in the forseeable future any one of the three will become so overwhelmingly numerically predominant as to « take over. » The three groups, in other words, are faced with a situation in which no one of them can presume to run the show, and in which each of them must work out viable ways of getting along with the others.

3. Religious Pluralism and Secularist Conspiracy.

This situation is a hard enough one to adjust to. But it is further complicated by another factor. Thus far the description has been in terms of the « triple-melting-pot » theory that Will Herberg, among others, has helped to popularize. And while other analysts agree about the *fact* of religious pluralism, they do not all agree about the *extent* of the pluralism. Fr. John Courtney Murray, S.J., and Dr. Paul Lehmann, a Jesuit and a Presbyterian respectively, feel that there is a fourth group which can be labeled « secularist. »

Father Murray thus talks about « four conspiracies, » using the latter term not invidiously, but descriptively ; to « con-spire » is to « breathe together, » to share a common devotion to common ends. And the point is that the secularist « conspiracy, » like the Protestant, Catholic and Jewish « conspiracies, » embodies a deep commitment, for which the term « religion » is not inappropriate. It represents a deep faith, but in this case a faith in man, and what man on his own resources can accomplish. Thus the issue is not between those who « have faith, » and those who do not, but between adherents of differing kinds of faith, all of whom make genuine acts of commitment, albeit to different deities.

Dr. Martin Marty, a Lutheran theologian, describes this « fourth conspiracy, » secularism, as the fastest growing of the four, and claims that it is growing by reason of the inroads it is making into the other three. When confronted by this kind of evidence of a fourth faith, Herberg replies that secularism is indeed a major factor on the American religious scene, but that it is to be found largely *within* the other three groups. A great deal of what currently passes for Protestantism, for example, is no more than secularism with a thin religious veneer. The same thing, *mutatis mutandis*, turns out to be true in the Catholic and Jewish communities as well.

4. *Working out a « Modus Vivendi. »*

Nevertheless, whether one sees four competing « conspiracies » or three, each of which is liberally invaded by secularism, it is clear that the American religious scene is now one in which a number of groups claim the religious allegiance of a portion of the American people, but no one of which commands such an overwhelming proportion that it can expect to dominate the scene or behave in an imperialistic manner.

The latter point is important. One of the practical outcomes of the new situation is that each group must, for its own protection in the community, work out a *modus vivendi* with the others which makes plain that it does not have designs of engulfing them and destroying them. Terms must be found in which a tolerable civic life together can be achieved. Each group will naturally hope that the persuasive inner logic of its own position, coupled with the fruits of faith in the lives of its members, will persuade others to join it, but each group must also recognize that both coercion and annihilation lie beyond the limits of persuasion. If one group, for example, seeks civic legislation that will blatantly benefit it and work a hardship on the other groups, it will discover that it encounters stiff opposition in the body politic.

The problem, of course, is intensified by the fact that while the groups have differing *ultimate* commitments, they must find areas of agreement in the realm of their *immediate* actions. This involves a greater attempt at sympathetic understanding than has characterized any of these groups in the past. It means, for example, an attempt on the part of the Protestant to understand why the Catholic feels that the burden of « double taxation » is unjust when he sends his child to a parochial school. It means an attempt on the part of the Catholic to understand why non-Catholics occasionally feel perturbed about the use of « Catholic power » in the political realm. It means a willingness on the part of churchmen to appreciate the intensity with which other citizens dismiss organized religion as an outmoded irrelevance. It means a willingness on the part of the secularist to re-examine why Jews and Christians can hold an ultimate loyalty to God and involve themselves in civic reform because of rather than in spite of that loyalty.

A good symbol of the new openness that is beginning to develop is the election of President Kennedy in 1960. Even now it is hard to remember the degree of bitterness and venom that was engendered during the fall before the election over the issue of « a Catholic in the White House. » But the election of Kennedy, and his subsequent conduct while in office, has made clear that Catholicism does not have the sinister designs about « taking over » the country that its virulent opponents used to think it had. The assassination of the President in November 1963 gave a tragic confirmation to the fact that it is now possible not only for a Catholic to become president of the United States but also to give his life for his country in the carrying out of that high office.

What do all these facts mean for the carrying on of the Protestant-Catholic dialogue in the United States ?

5. *Welcoming the Pluralism.*

A new openness has been created by the very sociological situation just described. Whether the various groups particularly like the fact of pluralism or not, it is a fact they cannot disregard, and they must come to terms with it. Actually, it would be fair to say that the American Catholic experience with religious pluralism has been such that most Catholics would now voluntarily choose it in preference to a situation of close interdependence of church and state, wherein religious commitment and nationalistic commitment were inseparable.

6. *Ecumenical Openness.*

There is a happy concurrence between the recognition of the pluralistically open culture in the United States and the emergence of the new Catholic ecumenical spirit that was fostered by Pope John, even if not initiated by him. It is clear that Pope John's attitude released from silence many American Catholics who up until his pontificate had been afraid to express the kind of ecumenical openness that has since become not only possible but even normative on the American scene. For a long time, when a Protestant wanted to talk about American Catholic ecumenism, he would mention Father Gustave Weigel, S.J., and by the mention of Father Weigel's name he practically exhausted the list of ecumenically-minded American Catholics who were willing to stand up and be counted. Largely due to Father Weigel's pioneering spirit (coupled with the « official » endorsement given to such men by the whole spirit of Pope John's pontificate) there is now a much greater corps of dedicated Roman Catholics who, starting from the ecumenical premises enunciated by Pope John, can work more freely in the emerging ecumenical dialogue. The untimely death of Father Weigel in January 1964 — the man we could least afford to lose from the American ecumenical situation — only puts a greater burden on other similarly-minded Roman Catholics.

7. *Civic Cooperation between Catholics and Protestants.*

The combination of the new socio-cultural situation with the new Catholic ecumenical openness leads to a third fact ; the new situation makes possible a degree of civic cooperation between Catholics and Protestants that has not been possible in the past. Catholics and Protestants, for example, differ about the Dogma of the Assumption of the Virgin into Heaven ; they do not differ about the belief that all men are created in God's image and that the color of a man's skin is an irrelevant factor in determining where he is entitled to live. Thus, for example, Catholics and Protestants can work *together* for fair housing, for legislation to outlaw discrimination in public places, for the rights of all groups to register and to vote, even though they may still have many remaining areas of doctrinal disagreement. Catholic and Protestant legislators can work side by side, the Catholic no longer fearing that the Protestant is merely an « anti-Catholic bigot, » and the Protestant no longer fearing that the Catholic wants above all to deprive Protestants of the franchise until they kneel before the Queen of Heaven.

To be sure, there are still areas where it is hard to make common cause together. Whether one is a Protestant or a Catholic tends to be decisive in the attitude he takes toward Federal aid to public education, and the notion of federal funds for parochial schools is still one of the most hotly debated issues in public life — with the lines quite decisively drawn between Catholic support for the venture and Protestant opposition. There continue to be difficulties whenever the issue of birth control enters into requests for appropriation of funds available for public health projects. But beyond such issues as these, it is no longer possible to find Catholics and Protestants lining up politically simply in terms of being Catholics or Protestants. Neither major political party is predominantly a « Catholic » or a « Protestant » party : major bills before Congress always have Catholics and Protestants supporting them, along with Catholics and Protestants in opposition. The notion, then, that political involvement need separate Catholics and Protestants from one another is a notion that gets little support save when such matters as the two mentioned above are the subjects of the public debate.

8. *Catholic-Protestant Exchange on a Theological Level.*

A combination of the above three factors is making possible the beginnings of a Catholic-Protestant exchange on a deeper theological level than has ever occurred before. America is still far behind Europe in this matter, and if it can only be said that the theological discussion has begun, at least that much can be said. Various groups of Protestant and Catholic theologians are beginning to engage in on-going discussion ; seminary « exchanges » for a period of several days at a time are beginning to occur ; Catholic scholars are invited to speak to Protestant groups, and vice-versa ; publications under joing sponsorship are beginning to appear (the most notable being the recently inaugurated *Journal of Theological Studies*, published at Duquesne University, Pittsburgh, Pennsylvania, under the joint editorship of a Catholic and a Protestant church historian).

In the long run, of course, the latter type of interrelationship, on the theological level, must undergird the others, but it would be the thesis of the present writer that relations between Catholics and Protestants on the practical level make the interrelations on the theological level more possible, and vice-versa. At whatever points there is contact, the whole complex of factors at work is enriched.

Conclusion.

These words are written on the eve of the Week of Prayer for Christian Unity, and the Christian Unity Octave. During this week, Catholics and Protestants will be praying *for* one another. But, here and there, they will also be praying *with* one another. That the latter is now becoming possible is only because the former has always been possible. Surely, as we pray for one another, as we engage in common theological discussion, as we cooperate in civic matters, we will find possible new levels of common prayer together. As we come closer together, we may find paradoxically that at certain points we are farther apart than we thought. But whenever Christians are trying to make true the prayer of Christ that all his flock might be one, we can be sure that things are happening that make possible new penetration into human life by the Holy Spirit — and we know that no one of us is entitled to build boundaries around what may happen after that.

BRIEF BIBLIOGRAPHY

Will HERBERG, *Protestant-Catholic-Jew*, Doubleday Anchor book, revised edition, 1960 — the best overall survey.

John TRACY ELLIS, *American Catholicism* ; Nathan GLAZER, *American Judaism*, Winthrop HUDSON, *American Protestantism*, University of Chicago Press. — three historical interpretative studies, by adherents of the various faiths, each with additional bibliography.

R.M. BROWN and G. WEIGEL, *An American Dialogue*, Doubleday Anchor book, 1961 — an examination by a Protestant and a Catholic, of the faith of the other.

Wayne COWAN, ed., *Facing Protestant-Roman Catholic Tensions*, Association Press Reflection Book — a symposium by Catholics and Protestants illustrating some of the areas of difficulty and hope.

The Ecumenical Situation in Latin America

by Jorge María MEJIA

Expert at the Council, Director of « Criterio, » Buenos Aires [1]

1. *General Introduction.*

It is a great mistake to think that the ecumenical problem — understood as relations of all kinds but particularly religious ones between Christians of different faiths — does not exist in Latin America. It is quite true that out of 175 million Latin Americans, about 163 million are baptized Catholics, which means an overwhelming majority (estimated statistics but basically accurate); and yet the presence of non-Catholic Christians is not to be ignored. If the Orthodox form a very small percentage, chiefly settled in national groups (Greeks, Russians, etc.), Protestants have ceased long ago from being merely « a foreign group » (Anglicans have always remained something of that kind). The subsequent, but already time-honoured, arrival of communities with missionary intent (Methodists, Baptists, Presbyterians etc.), without mentioning various « evangelist » groups (of which the Pentecostists are perhaps the most characteristic) has given a new physiognomy to Latin American Protestantism. In Catholic eyes, it is generally thought of as a rather aggressive movement, of rather literal Biblism, with a keen sense of community, but not of « an institution. » This shows that the ecumenical problem definitely arises for us.

---

1. Born in Buenos Aires in 1923, Jorge María MEJIA studied philosophy and theology in the Seminary there. Ordained in 1945, he won his doctorate in theology at the Angelicum, Rome, and then his licentiate in Biblical Sciences (1950) at the Pontifical Biblical Institute. Since 1951 he has been professor of Holy Scripture and of Hebrew at the Faculty of Theology of the Argentine Catholic University. In 1955 he became director of the review « Criterio ». Theologian at the Council, he assisted as Observer from the Holy See at the World Council of Churches in Mexico in December 1963. Address : José Cubas, 3543, Buenos Aires, ARGENTINE (Editor's note).

It remains true that the problem has its own features, not identical with European categories, not even those in Spain. It must be promptly added that it is by no means certain that the problem is exactly the same all over Latin America. Whatever may be asserted, the Latin American continent is not a unity, neither in history nor in development, even religious. This affects the ecumenical situation and must be remembered in our analysis.

The reasons for our special ecumenical situation flow principally from our religious history. I am not going to retrace this history, which I presume known in outline, but I shall stress certain typical facts. Of these I select three :

1. In spite of Liberal revolutions, and interruption in spreading the Gospel (largely due to the suppression of the Jesuits towards the end of the XVII century), Catholicism has always been the traditional and official religion. It is not easy and it is always unusual — sociologically, I mean — for a Latin American, especially a political man, to profess any religion but Roman Catholicism. He may be a nominal Catholic but he could hardly be an Orthodox or a Protestant. In the Argentine, for example, the President of the Republic must be a Catholic, in accordance with our national Constitution ; he may not be a Protestant, although he may not have set foot in a Church since he was baptized. The consequences of this arrangement are probably apparent : the religious and sociological planes are always inclined to get mixed up and we slide unconsciously from one to the other. The Protestant or Orthodox fact is not only religious, it is also and even chiefly a sociological fact.

2. For the same reason, the non-Catholic Christian bodies have developed in a hostile atmosphere, especially where they have broken through this ostracism, and exercised apostolate among de-Christianized Catholics whom they have found in our country. That is the case for Protestantism ; it began as the religion of a few foreigners installed as a kind of colony, it has always remained « an outsider ; » it thus became extremely anti-Roman, if it was not so already. Latin American Catholicism in the eyes of Methodists and Presbyterians was positively anti-Christianism : religion *without* faith but with certain *works* apparently superstitious enough. This leads to our third fact :

3. The problem of Protestant missions. The situation appeared as an invitation to evangelical missionaries. They arrived long ago, especially from the United States. But the consequences of the war

1939-46, and the changes since then, especially in the Far East
(China is now Communist ; India and Indonesia practically exclude
missionaries from other lands) have brought us many new evangelical workers. Fairly well known statistics show the remarkable
increase of Protestant stations and personnel in the last ten or
fifteen years. The situation became more complicated — perhaps
embittered — by the character of the groups most active in evan-
gelizing. Unfortunately they were neither Methodists nor Presbyterians. They are the Seventh Day Adventists, Mormons, Jehovah
Witnesses, etc. for whom, as one of my Methodist friends said, the
larger Protestant Churches cannot be responsible. It will be easily
understood that the already existing conflict has become more
acute, sometimes even dramatic. It is not surprising that Catholic
bishops and pastors feel but little enthusiasm for any kind of
ecumenical tendencies.

Our first conclusion must be this : in Latin America ecumenical
activity has not appeared in a good light, and in some places has
not yet begun to do so.

*

*   *

2. *Factors of Change.*

The situation is beginning to alter. I think certain factors will
help to explain why and how.

A. *Intellectual Progress.* Under this intentionally general heading,
I allude to the great improvement to be noticed, at least in some
regions, in religious education, Catholic or Protestant. It is chiefly
seen among the Protestant clergy, but is not limited to them. A
deeper knowledge of their own faith has helped to give Catholics
a clearer sense of their dogmatic positions, and largely liberated
them from a troubled complex towards other Christians. Protestants also have learnt to distinguish between « Romanism » and
Catholicism, to use expressions which belong to them.

After the war, many of our young theologians did or finished
their studies in Europe, not in Rome only. Two aspects of the
training received were particularly helpful to them :
— presentation of a theology neither apologetic nor polemical ;
— a truly Biblical training.

I might add the importance given to positive studies, which
allowed our theologians to see Protestant thought at its source and

not in some kind of caricature. Our Protestant brethren did the same. Some have returned from Europe with a training chiefly Biblical far surpassing the polemical stage. Others went to the United States, where their studies turned on the scientific knowledge of Catholicism, since their mission was to be exercised in a Catholic setting. All this means that ecumenical activity is now setting in at Seminary and Theological Faculty level. Already there is an Evangelical Faculty and a Faculty of Catholic Theology in Buenos Aires. The importance of these as radiating centres on the general ecumenical situation is obvious.

B. *The Biblical and Liturgical Revival.* This factor is chiefly active among Catholics. It is connected with intellectual progress. Experience of the pastoral value of Holy Scripture has greatly helped Catholic priests to understand the efforts of our Protestant brethren to diffuse it and make it read. Fifteen years ago in Latin America, the Bible was almost an exclusively Protestant domain. One may speak of a re-discovery on the Catholic side. This affords a common ground, full of pastoral promise. The liturgical revival too, has shown Catholics, especially priests, the value of the community element, which has always been a characteristic among Protestants. A strange fact : the Protestants among us, most of whom have not a hierarchical type of Church, have a greater sense of belonging than the Catholics. The temptation to go over to Protestantism is in many cases connected with this desire *to belong* to something. By discovering their own Church through the liturgical revival, Catholics are better disposed to appreciate that of other Christians.

C. *The End or the Death Agony of Certain Politico-religious Notions.* This factor has some importance. It is connected with our history. After the Liberal revolution, militant Catholics all over Latin America tend to identify religion with politics and to dream of a State held together by both. The ideal of a Catholic State inspires various current names of similar meaning (Hispanism, Nationalism, etc.). In this kind of ideal there is no room for « heretics » or « infidels. » Typical of this notion is the booklet called « Las Sectas Disidentes » published under the direction of R.P. Alberto Garcia Vieyra, O.P. (Cuadernos A.M.A.D., Buenos Aires, 1958), in which the motivation of religious intolerance is explained. This kind of idea, fairly prevalent a few years ago, is being abandoned now. The following fact must be noted : our people know now that one can be a good, practising Catholic

without being intolerant — this was not easily accepted formerly.
What the laity now admit is accepted also and principally by
priests and bishops. The possibility of a pluralist society is beginning
to be understood. From the same fact the existence of civil and
religious « sects » is beginning to be acknowledged. I must declare
in all sincerity that a new peril is appearing on the horizon : a
politico-religious notion like the « Catholic City » has many chances
of success in a society such as ours. This success could lessen somewhat advances in the ecumenical perspective.

D. *The Positive Action of Some Individuals or Groups.* We can
now speak of ecumenical activity properly speaking. It is very
new and very limited. It is very discreet also, which makes it
difficult to evaluate the influence of these contacts in modifying
the general situation. The influence cannot be denied however. I
will give but one example. Contacts between Catholic and Protestant professors in the respective Theological Faculties in Buenos
Aires have led to relations between their students which have been
kept up after ordination, in their apostolic labours. It is probably
the first time that Catholic and Protestant pastors have been disposed
in some places to regard each other as friends. I give this local
example because I know it by experience and can judge by results,
at least in some measure. I am sure the same thing is happening
in other parts of our huge continent — in Mexico for example. In
the same strain we must mention the influence of some South
American or European publications, whose action is limited but
efficacious. These reviews offer contact between Catholics and Protestants, either by supplying ecumenical information, or because
Protestants sometimes contribute articles. There we have the
atmosphere of the Council.

E. *The Council.* In Latin America, as everywhere else, the proclamation and opening of the Council has had an enormous
ecumenical effect. I would even say that the Council has been
the major factor in the change that has come about. I will enu-
merate a few facts which have largely been the cause of this effect.

a) The creation by the Holy Father of the Secretariate for the
Unity of Christians, and the invitation to the different Churches
to send Observers to the Council, made an immense impression
on our people — heightened by the fact that one of the Observers
came from the Argentine. They understood then that the Protestant
phenomenon among them could not be ignored, and that trying

to suppress it was not enough. Positions were suddenly altered : « the enemy » had become the guest of the Pope.

b) The ecumenical attitude of Pope John XXIII and of many of the bishops during the Council, more or less known through information accorded, deeply impressed Catholics. This principally concerns the clergy and bishops. Some went to Rome with the anti-ecumenical focus I have described above : Protestants are heretics to be driven out of our countries. These bishops found themselves flung into a new situation. The situation had changed more than they had. They realized this by several indications, like the way in which the Pope and Cardinal Bea spoke of, and addressed, the Observers ; the speech by Monsignor Smedt at the Council, etc. Returning to their dioceses, they brought with them the awareness of this new situation and they imparted it — in varying degrees — to their clergy and institutions. I think the ecumenical bearing of this fact is decisive.

c) The public of Latin America could have been made aware of all this by information about the Council. This has not been what it could and should have been, if its pastoral character had been understood. It was a special, providential occasion to teach our people, through modern ways of transmission, the meaning of ecumenical activity, the Council's stress on this activity, the bearing of certain facts which escaped their comprehension, as for example, the presence of Observers at the Council. In spite of this neglect of opportunity, the slight efforts made have borne fruit. It can be asserted that after the Council, the Latin American peoples are more kindly disposed towards our separated brothers. They are better prepared to understand ecumenical action and to work for unity.

*

*   *

3. The Present Situation.

It is not easy to state accurately the present situation of Latin America in ecumenical matters. The Council is not over, and the few factors of change issuing from it and which we have just mentioned, have hardly had time to show everywhere and at all levels. Besides, the geographical extent of our continent, and the difficulty of intra-American communications prevent us from receiving both full and complete information. But thanks to some knowledge obtained through the truly Christian courtesy of M. Miguez Bonine, Argentine Observer at the Council, who has just travelled through several Latin American countries to visit the Methodist communities and whose ecumenical situation is one of his chief cares, and from our own local experience, we can outline the following facts.

A. *The Bishops.* The bishops are maintaining personal contact with certain Protestants, either for reasons of courtesy, or (in one case) for definitely ecumenical reasons. « Neighbourly » contacts have occurred almost everywhere, especially in the Argentine, others in Mexico, in the diocese of Cuernavaca. As far as I know, there has not yet been a pastoral letter on the subject — but I may be insufficiently informed here. [1] It is noticeable, however, that the bishops are taking occasion to speak favourably of our « separated brothers, » and even recognizing their existence publicly, by inviting them, for example, to special religious Services (the Requiem for John XXIII at Lima, where the situation is particularly rigid ; Cardinal Landázuri y Ricketts invited some Evangelicals to Masses celebrated during the week of Prayer for Unity).

B. *The Theologians.* It was at this level that fruitful contacts were expected. Meetings had started even before the Council ; to mention two cases : professors at the Catholic University at Santiago, (Chili) and a group of priests connected with the review « Mensaje » meet Presbyterian, Lutheran and Methodist ministers; professors at the Faculty of Theology of the Catholic University of Buenos Aires (Argentine) have occasional meetings with their colleagues of the Evangelical Faculty of theology and the Lutheran Faculty. In this second case it is important to note that the formal meetings began from informal friendly encounters and on Protestant initiative.

C. *The Clergy.* There is a definite change at this level. Not only priests and pastors are beginning to know one another, but they are considering the possibility of working together in certain matters. There have been two or three Biblical celebrations shared by Catholics and Protestants at Easter and Christmas in the diocese of San Isidoro, Argentine. There are groups of Catholic and Protestant families meeting together with their pastors (same diocese).

---

1. There has been, in fact, a pastoral letter on Protestantism by the Bishop of Temuco (Chili).

Catholic and Protestant chaplains of the American forces stationed
in the Canal Zone hold regular meetings (these are, of course,
Americans). The Maryknoll Fathers and Protestant missionaries
meet sometimes at Santa Cruz de la Sierra in Bolivia (these, again,
are Americans).

D. *The Laity*. Naturally, progress is slower. Where collaboration
can be fruitful is the social domain, of which I shall say more later.
A Catholic and a Protestant sociologist (the Catholic is a priest)
have brought out together the definitive study on the problem of
bandits in Colombia (the book is not for public circulation). A
whole series of tendencies are springing up among Catholics which
reveal a new ecumenical situation. People are beginning to admit
that the separated brethren are Christians too and not « worse than
infidels. » They believe in the obligation of working for unity. More
intellectual Catholic groups accept the idea of a pluralist society,
really free from the stand-point of religious liberty.

*
*　*

4. *The Future Task*.

The essential word of command for the future task of ecumenism
in Latin America is : do not go too fast. Century-old prejudice
cannot be removed in a few months. Besides, we have no right to
take over acquired positions. We must go forward prudently, taking
care to follow up the paths already open and of which we have
spoken.

As special undertakings I would suggest these :

A. *Instruction of Clergy and People*. As everyone knows, religious
ignorance is one of the scourges of Latin American Catholicism.
From the point of view under study, this instruction should insist on:
— unity as Christ's desire, and Christian responsibility ;
— the true nature of Protestantism and its difference from sects
(Adventists, etc.) ;
— the true conception of religious liberty.

B. *Intensify Collaboration in Certain Common Domains* :

— *diffusion of Holy Scripture* : the Protestant merits here are
well known. We Catholics have done, and seemingly do, nothing

like it (the Bishop of Cuernavaca, however, has just created a Biblical Society in his diocese). Some projects existing for this end, relying on vigorous approbation from the hierarchy, cannot be compared with Protestant projects (The Bible of the editorial Codex of Buenos Aires : mediocre paraphrase, illustrated in the worst « realistic » tradition, while the beautiful text of the Bible Society really invites thoughtful reading of the Word of God). It is eminently desirable that Catholics and Protestants should work together at a common translation of Holy Scripture and at its diffusion.

— *the social domain* : for us the time has come for big, decisive changes. Christians of every faith should take part and see that the changes made are compatible with man's dignity and his essential vocation. I quote from memory some aspects of the transformation already begun : primary education, the hunger campaign, agrarian promotion, over-population, migration to the towns, sanitary education. Collaboration with other Christians is not only desirable here, it is necessary. Certain projects of the World Council of Churches, already afoot in Africa and southern Asia, would be very welcome in South America. Bishops should encourage this collaboration.

C. *Examine the Mission Problem with our Protestant Brethren.* I think this is one of the most urgent and most difficult ecumenical tasks in Latin America, which is an extra reason for tackling it in all sincerity and confidence in God. What makes it difficult is the activity of sects for which the great Protestant Churches cannot and will not be responsible. On the Catholic side, there is distrust and a certain resentment over methods employed. On the other hand, it remains true that Latin America is a vast continent, wide expanses of which are waiting to receive the Good News. It is quite understandable that our Protestants are not indifferent to this need. In face of the problem, Catholics should not remain purely on the defensive. On the contrary, they should try and regard it as a decisive aspect of ecumenical activity, as a real *test* of Latin American ecumenism. Collaboration in other domains (like, for example, diffusion of the Bible) should bear fruit here.

*
*   *

That is what can be said of the ecumenical situation in Latin America at the moment of the Council. It may not seem much but it is a great deal if we compare the present situation with that of fifteen years ago. The Council is not finished. In the measure of the achievements and transformations it brings will ecumenical activity receive fresh impetus among us. With us, as everywhere else, the division of Christians is a cause for scandal, and animosity among them is worse. Especially as the very fact of recognizing each other as brothers cannot fail to win the confidence of all men in Latin America, and draw down God's blessing on us all.

3

Pastoral Activity in an Ecumenical Perspective

Ecumenical Prayer and Penance

by Xavier Seumois, P.B.

*Director of the African Catechetical Institute, Butare, Rwanda.
Professor of Religion at Stanford University, Standford, Cal., U.S.A.[1]
Formation, « Lumen Vitae, » Brussels[1]*

1. *Ecumenism, Coming of the Holy Spirit.*

« Blessed are the eyes that see what you see, the ears that hear what you hear » (Mt., XIII, 16-17). Yes, happy the men who saw the Coming, when Christ Himself was on earth. Happy also are the eyes that see the constant Coming in the heart of the very century in which they live, the Coming that is ever old and ever new, which is the passing of the Holy Spirit in His Church !

Ecumenism is the spiritual climate of our times. It is a coming of the Holy Spirit, making present in men's hearts, in an unexpected way, that intense prayer that rose from the heart of Christ the day before He was delivered up (John, XVII, 20-23). Action of the Holy Spirit within men's hearts ; it began by prayer, it is developed in prayer and through prayer. [2] If the problem of Christian Unity is arousing a particular and exceptional interest at the present time, and that in all sections of Christianity, it is on account of the Second Vatican Council. But when thinking of the Vatican Council we must never forget the immense capital of ecumenical

---

1. See the biographical notice in *Lumen Vitae*, XV (1960), no. 4, p. 670. — Address : 184, rue Washington, Brussels 5, Belgium (Editor's note).

2. Leo XIII was probably the first Pope in modern times to interest the body of the faithful in the question of Unity. In 1895, he instituted the novena of prayer between the Ascension and Pentecost, to hasten « the work of reconciliation of the separated Brethren. » The Octave for the Unity of the Church was inaugurated for January 18-25 in 1908 by two Anglicans, Revv. Spencer Jones and Lewis Thomas Wattson, and approved by St. Pius X, Benedict XV and Pius XI. The Abbé Couturier gave it a really ecumenical form, and it spread widely through his apostolate. He also set up what he called « the invisible monastery, » getting several communities, in different Christian communities, to take Unity as their principal intention.

prayer that it represents. [1] In the intense yearning for Unity, discernible among so many Christian confessions, we have a right to perceive the action of the Holy Spirit ; it is He in the hearts of Christians, Catholics or not, who is praying with unutterable longing (*Rom.*, VIII, 26), and developing this aspiration after Unity which Christ wished to be the dowry of His Church. [2]

One of the duties of religious education is to make « the signs of the times » (Mt., XVI, 4) understood, so that many may share the beatitude « Happy are those who see. » It must strive to open hearts to welcome the secret action of the Spirit, to listen to Him and join in His unutterable longing. Doing this, it contributes to the fulfilment of the wish expressed by Pope Paul VI to the Patriarch Athenagoras : « may the Lord open our hearts to the inspirations of His Spirit, and guide us towards the full accomplishment of His Will. » [3]

---

1. The idea came to John XXIII during Unity Week 1959. The many prayers ordered by the Hierarchy for the Council included its distant fruit, return to Unity. The Mass which opens each General Congregation is a peak-prayer for unity each time. The devout attendance of our brother Christians, the Orthodox, Anglican and Protestant observers, only a few steps away from the altar is a constant and sad reminder of the drama of our divisions, so that fervent prayer implores for all the chief fruit of this sacrament, the unity of the Mystical Body of Christ. This daily Mass at the Council, celebrated in the different Eastern and Western rites, leads to a truly spiritual experience, revealing the depth of the ecumenical dimension of the Eucharistic sacrifice. Its fruit is, through communion with Christ, communion between Christians. It is signified in the symbolism of bread and wine, welding the countless grains into unity; in the prayer of the Canon begging God to bestow peace and unity upon His Church; in the prayer after the Pater with its mention of Saint Andrew inserted by St. Gregory the Great to express communion with the patriarchal See of Constantinople, in the prayer before the Pax. With this view of Christian unity, signified and put into action by the celebration of the Eucharist, we appreciate Pope Paul VI's phrase in his letter to the ecumenical Patriarch Athenagoras I, on 29-9-63 : « May this celebration always increase « the feelings that are in Christ Jesus » in our souls, with the meaning and demands of His prayer to the Father : « that they may be one, I in them and Thou in Me, that they may be perfectly one » (Apostolos Andreas, 6 November, 1963, given in *Documentation Catholique*, 5 January 1964, col. 18).

2. The Instruction of the Holy Office « Ecclesia Catholica, » 20 September 1949 (AAS 42, 31 January 1950, p. 142 and seq.; *Documentation Catholique*, no. 1064, 12 March 1950, col. 330) attributes this desire for unity, manifest in nearly all Christian communities, to an efficacious inspiration of the Holy Spirit, which has stirred up fervent universal prayer for unity, and has already begun to grant it, by increasing and extending this desire. This action of the Holy Spirit can be seen not only in individuals but also in Christian communities not in full communion with Rome.

3. Letter to H.H. Athenagoras I quoted in a previous note to this article.

2. *Christian Prayer :*
Missionary and Ecumenical.

Joining in, through ecumenical prayer, with the spiritual Event special to our own time, brings us wonderfully into the essential of Christian prayer : prayer « in Christ, » made « in the name of Christ ; » prayer which Christ Himself continues by His Holy Spirit in the hearts of those whom Baptism has brought into His Mystery. Christian prayer renders present the eternal prayer of Christ : « Hallowed be Thy Name, Thy Kingdom come, Thy Will be done ! » This will is the achievement of the divine plan of salvation through the constitution of the People of the Alliance. Christian prayer also implores the Father to lead men to the Church which He wishes to be One. Thus it is *missionary*, prolonging the prayer of Christ as He gazed at the fields white for the harvest (John, IV, 35) or thought of the sheep which are His but are not yet gathered into His fold (John, X, 16), firmly convinced that God wishes all men to attain salvation and knowledge of the truth (*I Tim.*, II, 11). It is also *ecumenical*, sharing the aspiration of Christ the Redeemer, offering the sacrifice of His life that God's children who are dispersed may be brought to unity (John, XI, 52), unity which is an image of the unity between the Three Divine Persons (John, XVII, 21). When the religious training we give educates to missionary and ecumenical prayer, we are helping to attain the essential of the Christian attitude, the summit of charity; we are instilling « the thoughts that are in Christ Jesus. » [1]

Mission and ecumenism are closely connected. Today Christians realize that to be faithful to Christ, they must put themselves « in a state of mission. » At the same time they are aware that a return to unity is the indispensable condition for the world to believe that Jesus Christ is the One Sent by God (John, XVII, 23). The apostolic testimony hardly rings true on account of our divisions ; it must be given « in the Holy Spirit, » Who is the Spirit of love, peace and union. Mission and ecumenism cannot be separated either in prayer or in pastoral action and apostolic activity. [2]

---

1. *Phil.*, II, 5; see the ecumenical use made of this text by Pope Paul VI in a previous note to this article.

2. See *Missions et Unité*, by P. Le Guillou, Col. *Unam Sanctam*, Ed. du Cerf, 1960. In an interview accorded to the paper *La Croix*, Fr. Roger Schutz, prior of Taizé, said : « Mission is closely linked with ecumenism, one cannot go without the other. To reach the man of today we can no longer present ourselves as separate, since we profess this position of faith, that the unity of mankind will pass through the Unity of the Church or will never happen »

3. The Training Value of Ecumenical Prayer.

Real prayer is the expression of the soul's fundamental attitudes before God ; in consequence it helps to make them more precise and to drive them home more deeply. On the psychological plane alone, its educative value is immense, the more so because, wishing to be authentic, it tends to become prolonged in life, inspiring a behaviour which is in conformity with its object. [1]

Training in ecumenical prayer takes on significant importance from the fact that its authenticity requires the attitudes of soul expressed by Christ in His most solemn prayer, attitudes which meet the dominants in the plan of salvation. This fact, above all makes ecumenical prayer accord with God's will not our self-will, human desires or fantasies.

There is yet more in ecumenical prayer. The Master within, the only one who can really teach prayer, is the Holy Spirit. At the moment, His inspirations are prompting an intense prayer for unity in the Christian world. The instrument of the Holy Spirit, the religious education must strive to prepare hearts to be more ready and open to receive this unction (*I John*, II, 27) penetrating the deepest fibres of the soul, provided barriers and obstacles are removed. Religious education too, anxious to let itself be guided by the Holy Spirit, will help to live God's present action, to perceive the Event, which is always a call. It will supply occasion to give faith's answer in prayer.

Ecumenical prayer has a more positive role still over Christian unity. It is the indispensable spiritual preparation for the re-union of Christians. To prepare it means to remove obstacles which prevent or delay it, and to develop the factors which will facilitate it. The obstacles are principally of two sorts : on one hand, divergences of faith which mean there is not entire communion in one faith, therefore unity is imperfect until dogmatic essentials are made

---

(*La Croix*, 30 Nov. 1963). M. Jean Guitton in his discourse in St. Peter's Basilica, 3 December 1963, said : « Most of the problems which grip us by the throat (like war, and poverty) would be settled as well if Christians were united » (*Doc. Cath.*, 5 January 1964, col. 81).

1. We are not reducing the value of prayer to that of a psychological operation, by referring to interior attitudes. It is and it remains the immanent activity of the theological virtues; but the supernatural organism grafted on to natural faculties cannot normally exercise the theological virtues without the active co-operation of these faculties. This thought brings out the importance of the psychological substratum, and notably of the interior attitudes, not only in the act of prayer itself, but also for education in prayer.

absolutely clear ; on the other hand, a mass of psychological dispositions, made up of prejudices against people and institutions, which
have resulted in the establishment of a second wall of separation,
not a dogmatic one this time but moral, preventing « fraternal
communion. » Christian unity, signified and made real in Eucharistic communion [1] is impossible unless there is communion in faith
and fraternal communion. Obstacles to the latter mostly come from
the fact that we are prisoners within a collective mentality, imposing
prejudices and behaviours from without. This mentality is in fault
since it runs counter to the Gospel attitude. Through religious
education, truth must replace prejudices, justice replace hasty con-
demnations, charity replace coldness and antipathy. Ecumenical
prayer is among the privileged means at the disposal of religious
training to instil these moral and psychological dispositions which
directly prepare the spiritual climate needed for re-union.

4. Qualities of Ecumenical Prayer.

Prayer is necessary to obtain from God the grace of the restoration
of unity in the one Church of Christ. [2] But we are not alluding
chiefly to petition when we speak of the educative value of ecumenical prayer. We mean prayer plunging straight into the ecumenical
climate, passing the confines of the Catholic Church to join in the
prayer rising from all Christian communities, from Christianity in
travail of unity. It shares the spiritual desires and motions prompted
by the Spirit towards reconciliation. Ecumenical prayer is entirely
dependent on the movement of the Holy Spirit. This gives it special
traits which are religious attitudes which education should cultivate.

a) Prayer in the Full Perspective of the Mystery of the Church.

Aware that it forms part of the tremendous supplication for unity
stirred by the Holy Spirit in the different Christian communities,

---

1. See the fine Communion antiphon in the Mass for Unity. With some
Churches, division is the more tragic because we already share so many benefits
ever since the beginning: « We belong to Him (Christ) through the gift of the
Gospel of Salvation, by the same baptism, the same priesthood, with the same
Eucharist, the one sacrifice of the one and only Lord of the Church » (Paul VI
to the Patriarch Athenagoras, letter quoted already). And in spite of this communion in so many gifts from the Spirit of God, the summit of Eucharistic
communion is not possible!

2. We need to implore the gift of unity; humanly insurmountable obstacles
oppose its restoration. The devil, source of divisions, can only be overcome by
prayer and fasting (Mark, IX, 28). Unity is that peace which is a supernatural gift from God (John, XIV, 27), to be obtained from Him by prayer.

ecumenical prayer strengthens the conviction that baptism has made us all brothers in Jesus Christ. If the visible unity, desired by God, does not exist, invisible bonds already unite us. Our separated brothers are also disciples of Christ, they already belong fundamentally to the Church through baptism.

In the very act of praying for unity, each one consciously proves his incorporation with Christ, since Christ is then prolonging in them His prayer at the Last Supper. Christ present in His members, to whatever confession they belong, causes a mystical union between them which, at the very moment of prayer aspires and turns towards perfect union, which will make us *One*, as the Father and Son are *One* (John, XVII, 21). The invisible mystery of the Church, the very life of the Holy Trinity communicated to men in Christ through faith and love (John, XVII, 3), is lived as a reality in ecumenical prayer ; this invisible reality leaves the sphere of intellectual thinking to become part of life.

To train this interior attitude of ecumenical prayer, centred on the entire Christ, aspiring towards an ever fuller participation in the life of the Trinity, means that education must stress what unites Christians beyond their dividedness, [1] and unfold before its pupils the spiritual riches possessed by the Churches which are not in full communion with Rome. [2]

b) *Prayer which is Aware of our Insertion in the History of Salvation.*

Through revelation God has made it known to us that His plan of salvation implied the Church, both One and Visible. Our present divisions are openly not in accordance with God's will. Ecumenical

---

1. Speaking to the Observers on the 17 October 1963 (*Doc. Cath.*, 3 November 1963, col. 1421) Paul VI called them « dear brothers in Jesus Christ » « to whom we are all united in faith and baptism, » « who are fed by the same Gospel, and hear in the depth of their hearts the same joyous call of St. Paul to the Ephesians · « One Lord, one faith, one baptism, one God and Father of all, who is above all, through all and in us all. » See the passage from the letter to the Patriarch Athenagoras, previously quoted in these notes).

2. Paul VI, opening address at the Council's Second Session : « We hold in high esteem the religious patrimony, original and common, which among our separated brethren has been preserved and even in some part, felicitously developed. We are delighted to see the studious endeavours of those who seek in all sincerity to bring out and extol the authentic riches of truth and spiritual life which these separated brethren possess, and that with the intention of improving our relations with them » (*Doc. Cath.*, 20 Oct. 1963, col. 1356). To the Observers on the 17 October he expressed « his respect for you all individually and for the Christian institutions and values which you represent. »

prayer fits in perfect accordance into the divine plan of salvation, since it begs « that this Will may be done » when God wishes and by the means He chooses. By these traits it brings forward attitudes of readiness and trust. It is for religious training to develop these interior attitudes.

The attitude of readiness towards the development of the plan of salvation, rouses a constant effort of continued renewal in the Alliance. The more Christians live according to the Gospel the more they increase the bonds of invisible unity, and to the same extent they draw nearer visible unity. The aspiration after unity, inherent to ecumenical prayer, stirs up the determination to grow in faith, in charity, in a more evangelical way of life. The Church reminds us of this in the Epistle of the Mass for Unity : « I entreat you to live in a manner worthy of the vocation to which God calls you... »

The way towards unity is an ascent, which Christians make together, even if separated, through their striving to grow in the life of faith and love. To imagine we have got there, that there is no more progress to be made in the lived understanding of truth is to stand still on the road to unity ; a true Christian never remains stationary ! [1] This progress forward in faith and charity is made by interior conversions many times repeated. The attitude of readiness, proper to ecumenical prayer, untiringly brings with it the *metanoia* which accompanies the earthly phase of the kingdom of God.

Confidence, which ecumenical prayer directs towards the divine plan of Salvation is nothing else but the unshakeable hope of the Bible. God will carry out his plan, in spite of contrary appearances of difficulties which seem insuperable to human eyes. The People of God is travelling forward, strong in the victory of Christ and the gift of the Spirit, which is the Spirit of Unity. God is Emmanuel, « God with us, » the more we live the realities of the Alliance. These convictions of Moses, Isaias, and all the Prophets, especially of Christ who « is with us all days, even unto the consummation

---

1. Words of Paul VI to the Observers, 17 October 1963 : « Divine truth should be ceaselessly studied more deeply in order to pessess it and live it more intensely. « Seek in order to find, and find in order to seek still further. » Saint Augustine's phrase, which We have heard you quote, Sir, with keen delight, applies to all of us — a true Christian never remains stationary. » Shortly before, Paul VI quoted the passage from the Epistle to the Philippians III, 13-14 : « Forgetting the things that are behind, I press forward with all my strength, and I run towards the goal, for the prize which God calls us to receive in Christ Jesus. » And in his letter to the Patriarch Athenagoras : « Forgetting all that is behind, I press forward to what lies ahead seeking to capture Him as I have been captured by Him. »

of the world » (Mt., XXVIII, 20), give a halo of absolute confidence to ecumenical prayer : Yahweh reigns, Christ is master of
the world's history, His plan of Salvation will be fulfilled in and
through the unity of Christians, thanks to His interventions in
history — when He wills it, by the means He selects. [1] Our trust
is absolute because our ecumenical prayer is truly the prayer of
Christ in us, the prayer of suppliant Omnipotence. [2]

c) *Prayer which Invites Conversion.*

Division is the result of our collective sin. Concerning it we could
quote plenty of passages from the Prophets which call us to penance :

« The hand of the Lord is not shortened that it cannot save,
        neither is his ear heavy that it cannot hear.
            But your iniquities have divided
                between you and your God ;
        and your sins have hid his face from you
                that he should not hear. »

(Isaias, LIX, 1-2).

Ecumenical prayer brings awareness of this sin and urges towards
a conversion which prepares the way for re-union. This conversion
is a change of mentality and heart, sorrow for faults against union,
an ascetism and penance in expiation.

A change of mentality and heart. Every Coming of the Holy
Spirit poses a question. The aspiration after unity which He rouses
forces us to re-consider our judgments and behaviours concerning
our non-Catholic Christian brethren. The thought of their relation
to Christ makes indifference and prejudice give place to good-will.
We pray for our brothers in Christ, loved by Our common Lord,
who long as we do, to grow more and more in Him, and who are

---

1. The Church puts these sentiments into our hearts by the Introit and the
Gradual psalm of the Mass for Unity.

2. Paul VI expressed this trust at the opening of the Second Session of the
Council : « Aware of the enormous difficulties which stand in the way of the
desired unification at present, we humbly put our trust in God. We will go on
praying. We will try to give better testimony of our endeavours at authentic
Christian life and fraternal charity. And when historical reality threatens to
disappoint our hope, we will remember Our Lord's encouraging words : « What
is impossible for men, is possible with God » (Luke, XVIII, 27). — In his speech
in Saint Peter's Basilica on the 3rd. December 1963, Jean Guitton said : « Before
the throne of God our ecumenical prayer dies away in an act of surrender,
which is the highest peak of love. »

convinced as we are, that only in the path of re-union can we receive together the riches of Christ in all their plenitude. We thank God for the supernatural gifts which they have preserved and developed. The more sincere this prayer, the more eager we shall be to achieve union in sectors where it is possible notwithstanding dogmatic divergences : human relations, [1] some meetings for prayer, co-operation in social activities, ecumenical collections and assistance, [2] collaboration on the pastoral plane at diocesan and parish levels.

Sorrow for faults against union. Ecumenical prayer, plunged in the intensity of Christ's sacerdotal prayer which each Eucharistic celebration makes present among us, can find no other explanation for its remaining unanswered than the mass of sins, collective and individual, against unity. Begging Almighty God to bestow the gift of unity upon His Church once more, our supplication is full of contrition. We humbly admit the faults of our own Church, the acts of our ecclesiastical leaders which contributed positively to cause division ; we ask pardon from God — and from our brother Christians — for what we have not done in the past to avoid division and restore unity, and for what we have done which has proved a scandal and an obstacle to our brethren. [3]

An ascetism and penance in expiation. Penance is necessary, for there is no doubt that the enemy, the father of lies and dissensions,

---

1. On the 17 October 1963, Paul VI said to the Observers : « Approach one another, meet, greet, know and talk to one another; what could be more simple, natural and human ? Certainly. But here there is more than that : listen to one another, pray for each other, and after many years of separation, after such sad disputes, begin to love one another once more. This is what make our present meeting memorable and full of promise. »

2. Doctor O. Cullmann, starting from the biblical meaning of communion (koinônia), suggested as a first step towards perfect unity (koinônia in the sense of Eucharistic communion), unfortunately not yet possible, actions of mutual help between separated Christian communities, in the shape of a collection made in one Church for the benefit of the poor of another Church. That is koinônia, in the sense of mutual help, a communion that can be effected here and now.

3. Paul VI, in his opening address at the Council's Second Session : « If fault can be imputed to us in the causes of this separation, we humbly ask pardon from God, and forgiveness from our brothers whom we have offended. And we are ready, as far as in us lies, to forgive any injuries against the Catholic Church, and to forget the sorrows She has endured throughout the long series of dissensions and separations. May our Heavenly Father deign to accept this our public declaration, and lead us all to the peace of true brotherhood. »

has sown cockle in the Heavenly Father's field. This kind of devil can only be cast out by prayer and fasting (Mt., XVII, 20).

This ascetism lies in interior renunciation. Steeped in the ecumenical climate, prayer helps us to see better the essential of our dogmatic positions, without confusing them with accessory elements, to which we may cling inordinately. It lies in making our own life and the outer aspect of the Church more evangelical. The renewed youth, the interior freshening of the Church, which John XXIII and Paul VI hope will be the chief result of the Council, will contribute positively to the ecumenical effort because it is in line with the basis of the Unity movement : the meeting of all Christians in an effort of greater and more integral fidelity to the essential, God's plan for His people. The Unity hoped for is not to be seen as a return pure and simple to the Roman Church, but more as a convergence, or for the Orthodox, a reconciliation. The Catholic Church too must grow in Christ, increase in the spirit of the Gospel, for re-union to become possible. [1]

Inter-confessional prayer. In the evening of January 5, Pope Paul VI and Patriarch Athenagoras I, surrounded by prelates of their suite, at the Apostolic Delegation of Jerusalem, recited the Our Father together, each in their own tongue. The next morning at the Greek Orthodox Patriarchate, they prayed together, reading St. John XVII verse by verse, the Pope in Latin, the Patriarch in Greek. The Pope gave the Patriarch a chalice, symbol of the perfect communion which both desire.

All inter-confessional prayer stresses what unites : baptism, the Gospel, faith largely common, the same hope and the life of Christ in each one. At the same time, the tragedy of division is acute ; the present was a chalice ...destined for the same Eucharistic sacrifice ; but con-celebration was not yet possible. [2]

---

1. M. Jean Guitton said so eloquently in St. Peter's before the Pope and the Council : « Woe is me if, before our brethren eager for fresh agreement, I clumsily confuse dogma with some formula, method with some usage, life with some manner of living, thus making narrower this path to the union for which Christ died... Let us imagine that all our brothers wish to enter the Catholic basilica. It would lengthen its nave, raise its cupola. It would remove its useless or antiquated decoration so that all could move freely in its sublime simplicity. It would keep the same form, the same structure. Nothing essential would be modified in dogma, in worship, in power. But this same unalterable form, enriched by such great affluence and so much suffering, would then have its full development, perfect plenitude, anticipated glory. And what testimony that would be before the world ! »

2. Some Observers remarked that assistance at the Council Mass together drew closer the consciousness of Christian unity ; but at the same time, since

On certain occasions, inter-confessional prayer could be arranged in order to train the ecumenical spirit. It makes us aware of the invisible dimensions of Christ's Mystical Body, of the state of the adoptive children of God which our separated brethren possess by their faith and their baptism, of the unseen presence of Christ who has promised to be in the midst of two or three disciples gathered together in His name. Such an atmosphere of faith intensifies desire for unity, fervour in prayer, resolution for conversion to the entire Gospel. It unites hearts in authentic charity.

Such prayer is inconceivable without respect for the religious convictions of all concerned. The formulas used must avoid what might offend the beliefs of others. If Catholics, Protestants or Orthodox do not express the full content of their faith, notably over their conception of the Church, it is neither hypocrisy nor dissimulation. Each one prays according to the lights of his faith, without abandoning any of it ; but since prayer is not a profession of faith, it need not express the full content at all times. [1]

Inter-confessional prayer prepares hearts for the longed-for moment of re-union, opening out towards that pluralism in Catholicity, outside which future Christian unity is hardly possible. [2]

---

divergences in faith prevented Eucharistic communion, it also stressed more painfully the drama of separation. Jean Guitton in St. Peters : « If non-Catholic ecumenism was exactly the same thing as Catholic ecumenism, there would be no longer a problem but a kiss. »

1. At the 74th. General Congregation of Vatican Council II, Cardinal Bea gave this answer to criticisms of these prayers in common. « The Instruction of the Holy Office in 1949 recommended these prayers in certain cases. We all pray together for the unity Christ desired for His Church, and the how and the when we leave to God. Such prayer is necessary. Popes have asked for it, and bishops must encourage it. Thus understood, ecumenism will do good to Catholics themselves, and will hasten the greatly desired Unum sint (Report from *La Croix*, 27 Nov.). In his exhortation for Unity Week 1964, Paul VI resolutely envisaged the perspective of inter-confessional prayers (*Osservatore Romano*, 18-1-64).

2. In his discourse in St. Peter's, on December 3, Monsieur Jean Guitton said : « To be Catholic is also to proclaim that unity will only be perfectly achieved when the legitimate forms of Christian and human diversity can find their place and rightful liberty in the bosom of the Church. »

Education in the Ecumenical Spirit

by Paul MAILLEUX, S.J.

*John XXIII Centre for the Study of the Christian East,
Fordham University, New York*[1]

The Church Defending Herself.

In the days when armies took citadels by storm, it was not usual
for the besieged to be on friendly terms with the soldiers encamped

---

1. Born at Ouffet (Liège) in 1905, Father MAILLEUX had the good fortune,
while attending the College Saint Jean Berchmans, to meet the Ukranian Metropolitan André Scheptitzky in 1921. The prelate, who had just left Russia where
he had been interned during the war, interested him in the spiritual needs of
Russia. Two years later, Father Mailleux entered the Society of Jesus, where
he managed to become fluent in Russian, and after his priestly studies, he was
appointed to direct the Boarding School Saint George, founded in Constantinople in 1921, for the sons of Russian emigrants. At that time the Boarding
School was at Namur, Belgium; during the war Father Mailleux transferred
it to Meudon, not far from Paris, since most of the boarders came from there.
About 90 % of the scholars in this school were Orthodox, while the establishment was run chiefly by Catholic priests. Many of the boys came from families
deeply attached to Russian religious traditions. Collaboration was quickly organized in a truly ecumenical spirit. The aim and object of those who directed
the school could be summed up in the words of the author of this article:
« to develop as fully as possible all the elements of authentic Christian life,
which the Christian not in complete union with ourselves have preserved, perhaps even cultivated better than we have. » Need it be said that the boys
learned to write and speak their ancestral Russian with ease, more than that,
the school's liturgical life was organized in the traditional Russian style,
according to the Julian calendar always followed by the Russians. The fathers
of the Latin rite adopted the Byzantine rite for their own Offices.
Before long, the Orthodox priests, relatively numerous in the vicinity of
Paris, discovered that they were very welcome visitors whenever they called
to see their young friends or parishioners in the school. Collaboration between
the Orthodox clergy and the school board thus became closer and closer with
real profit on both sides. When occasion arose, the school did its best to
encourage any of the older boys who were thinking of consecrating their lives
to the service of souls in the Orthodox clergy.
In June 1954 (notice the date), Father MAILLEUX made a speech at the Old
Boys' Dinner, from which we quote the following passage as characteristic of
the spirit of the College St. George:
« St. George's is very dear to us because it allows us to carry out an attempt

below the ramparts. Caution and distrust were a necessity. For a very long time this has been the attitude of the Church when indicating the safest attitude for the faithful towards Christians separated from Her.

For centuries after the Reformation and in many countries, Catholics found themselves in a position very similar to that of a city in the state of siege. In the British Empire, in Holland, Germany, Switzerland, the Scandinavian countries and in North America, Christians in union with Rome were only a minority, often a mere fraction, and sometimes poor and ill-instructed. In Imperial Russia where Orthodoxy was the State religion, Polish, Lithuanian and German Catholics were in a like position. In all these countries, politics, finance, commerce, industry, higher education were nearly always directed by non-Catholics. The best way to a successful career did not lie in proclaiming attachment to the Roman Catholic Church. Less than forty years ago, it was quite

---

unique of its kind. Belonging to the same Christ, wishing for only one Church, Christians of East and West have been divided none the less for several centuries. This division is diametrically opposed to the rule of charity which Christ left us; it humiliates and weakens us terribly in the eyes of the non-Christian world. I know quite well, that if division persists, it is because neither of the groups will so much as listen to a word of bargaining or compromise in their search for Truth. But must this devotion to the integrity of faith necessarily entail reciprocal ignorance and even antagonism, in which the two fractions of Christianity too often live ? By its very existence, the College Saint George refutes this. Suffering in silence what divides us, we labour in complete cordiality to save the spiritual values which are common and dear to us both. We have got past the stage of degrading hostility, we can say so with pride. We are in the advance-guard of working in sheer depth for Unity.

« Visitors to our college have often remarked that a spirit reigns here which is seldom found in similar establishments. Most of the teachers are of different nationality and even different religion from the majority of the boys, and yet we have a family spirit, a mutual cordiality which many envy. Explain this spirit as you wish, but may I suggest that it is a reward and constant blessing from God for the example, possibly unique, which our college gives of authentic and intelligent charity among Christians. »

The school still flourishes at Meudon, and remains one of the most accessible meeting-places for Christians of various confessions. The parents of the boys have formed an association of their own accord to which they have given the Russian name « PLAMIA » (the flame), where they meet together, Catholics and Orthodox, to study the religious questions raised by their daily life in the setting of Paris.

Since January 1957, Père MAILLEUX has been living in New York. He is superior of the John XXIII Centre atached to Fordham University for studies and publications on the Christian East. — Address: Soloviev Hall, Fordham University, New York 58, N.Y., U.S.A. (Editor's note).

normal to see advertisements in the Boston or New York papers which ran : « Wanted a cook... a trustworthy servant. Good *Catholic not wanted.* » Such wording could not tend to foster very cordial relations between Catholics and non-Catholics. Do we realize how strong the temptation to get in among influential Protestants must have been for a young man, say from Ireland, arriving in the United States, poor and friendless, but with plenty of ambition ? At that time, Catholic teachers had no choice ; they would have had no sense of realities then, if they had not tried to keep together the young Catholics they could reach, and warned them very seriously of the danger of becoming unfaithful to the Church. In some countries, of course, such as Spain or Belgium, Catholics were in a better position, but the directives of the Church were formulated in view of the most exposed regions.

In order to protect the faithful and to invite non-Catholics to reflect, the Church issued strict rules about relations with separated brethren in religious matters. She forbade the reading of their books, frequenting their public prayer, and any share in their worship which might look like approval. These rules became more and more severe. In the XVIII century, Franciscans and Jesuits could preach and hear confessions in Greek Orthodox churches ; in the XIX century, this was no longer permitted. When ecclesiastical authorities allowed a mixed marriage, it might not be celebrated in the church ; the couple made their promises in the sacristy with no signs of exterior pomp. Many considered this an unnecessary and vexatious order and resented it ; the Church's real aim was to impress on Catholics, how much she discouraged such marriages.

Need it be said that the Church was as eager for the salvation of the separated brethren as of the Catholics, but the pressure under which the faithful lived in many places forced Her to be chiefly concerned with their protection. The apostolate among non-Catholic Christians was thought of in almost the same way as the apostolate among non-Christians. Individual souls that could be reached were invited into the Church. Towards the non-Catholic communities. the position was not unlike a state of war. Very few dreamed of a collective reconciliation.

2. *In the Spirit of the Good Shepherd.*

In the course of this century, as regards human relations, opposition between Christians of different confessions has weakened. Reasons for this are several, the fact alone matters here. Without ceasing to protect Her faithful with great care, the Church of today can afford to widen Her horizons and look more serenely upon the groups of Christians separated from Her. She can study their exact position with more attention, appreciate their deep aspirations, look for possibilities of a collective reconciliation, at least with certain groups.

This evolution proves progress in the evangelical spirit and the Catholic educator cannot ignore it, still less regret it. Besides, whether he likes it or not, young Catholics can less and less be trained in a kind of camp enclosure. Formerly, the different Christian confessions were fairly well separated geographically. Now, voyages and migrations bring Christians of different confessions into constant relations. The young must therefore be given as adequate an intellectual and moral preparation as possible to meet these encounters.

No Catholic today can simply accept the divisions among Christians which have grown up in the past. Many grave reasons oblige him to desire the unity of the Christian world. The teacher with psychological sense will know how to choose the reasons most likely to arouse the interest and zeal of his pupils. The fundamental reason is Christ's desire, and His prayer that all may be one and recognized by their love for one another. Then there is the scandal which division among Christians causes in the non-Christian world. Finally, there is the enormous waste of energy entailed in the lack of co-operation in missionary work. It would be well to point out to minds sufficiently mature how the modern nations aspire towards surpassing their own particular ideas, and tend towards a « supra-national » unity. The United Nations Organization is an attempt at a vast human society on a world scale. Christians cannot possibly infuse the spirit of Christ into this society if they present the sad spectacle of disunion.

It is all-important for the young to see the work for union from a really supernatural point of view. It is the only way to avoid their becoming quickly wearied and discouraged before the immensity of the task. During centuries of schism, the positions of the Christian groups have hardened ; ignorance of each other has done nothing but increase, disconcerting prejudices have accumulated. It seems illusory to hope for a swift reconciliation ; with many groups, it seems even humanly impossible, divergences are enormous. For-tunately, what counts in God's sight is not the immediate result, but our good will and efforts to put an end to division. The schisms had happened long before we were born, they have hardened with the passage of time ; we are not responsible for all that, but only in so far as we make no attempt to put an end to them. Not to care would be blameworthy before God. On the contrary, our efforts to re-establish Christian unity, closely unite our wills to that of Our Lord, and glorify His Father.

Is not teaching the young to pray for Unity, initiating them to an altruistic, truly apostolic prayer, eminently elevating, a prayer which will attune theirs to the prayer of Christ ?

3. *To Form a Sound Judgment.*

During the centuries when the Church had to stand largely on the defensive, Catholic teachers strove to train the young in a resolute opposition to schism and heresy. In our time, this chiefly negative attitude should give place to a positive one : one of un-failing attachment to Truth. Why ? First, because life is given us not to fight against something, but to build up something positive. Then, to be better heard by our separated brothers. Opposition arouses opposition ; it provokes hostility. But who can resist an invitation to seek fuller and higher truth together ?

From kindheartedness, the young will easily suggest reconciliation between divided Christians by making a few concessions even in doctrine, or not alluding to points of disagreement. They must be made to understand as soon as possible that such concessions are out of the question. There is an objective truth to which the Church must remain faithful. She must remain what Christ wished Her to be, and teach what Christ has wished Her to teach. Error is always dangerous and to be detested. If God has in some way taken the trouble to reveal Himself to men through the Word Incarnate, if He has wished to unite them to Himself through the Church, we on our side must do all we can to welcome His gifts in their entire plenitude. Besides God's precepts are not arbitrary ; they have their profound reason in the nature of things. They could not be modi-fied or suppressed without injury to the progress and happiness of man.

To inculcate sound judgment on so basic a matter, it should be explained to the young by examples they can grasp. They can be shown, for example, how a « supra-national » pastoral authority in the Catholic Church has largely contributed to its maintenance of unity and its independence from the temporal power. To sup-press the pope's authority would not only go against Christ's wish, but would do serious harm to the Church. Divorce is another easy example for the young to understand. The Catholic Church never grants divorce strictly speaking. Protestants and Orthodox allow it in certain cases. [1] In itself, it is always an evil ; Christ condemned it explicitly, and St. Paul used the image of conjugal union to describe the union of Christ with his Church. How can She who must be the light of the world make concessions in such matters, without failing gravely in Her mission ?

The century of Ecumenism must not ask the Church to alter her doctrine ; She cannot. But She can be asked to formulate it more fully or more accurately to make it easier to understand. It is not enough to declare the truth ; it must be made comprehensible and easy of acceptance for those who are to receive it. In her desire for reconciliation with those in separation from Her, the Church of today thinks much less of anathemas than of enlightenment. Her theologians study the writings of their theologians in order to understand their position better, to find what implicit requests lie beneath their attitude of refusal, to see how Truth may be put to them in order to be better understood. The young can be invited to help in this, each according to their capacity. They will gain much by doing so, since nothing will help them to penetrate further into the understanding of Catholic dogma themselves, than the effort to make others understand it.

4. See Good Wherever it is to Be Found.

Love of the whole Truth obliges us too to recognize among our separated brethren all the elements of authentic Christian life which they have preserved, perhaps even cultivated better than we have. In a famous address on 10 January 1927, Pope Pius XI said : « If there are mutual prejudices, these prejudices must go. Do we know how much that is good, precious, and Christian, lies in these fragments of the old Catholic faith ? Separated blocks from a gold-bearing rock are gold-bearing also... »

The Holy Father was referring to the Eastern separated Christians, but his words can equally apply to the Reformation groups. Most Protestants have an intense trust in Our Lord Jesus Christ. In that we have but to imitate them. Our faith in the intercession of Our Lady and the saints does not interfere with our belief that Christ is the one Mediator between God and ourselves ; all grace is

---

1. They rely on a text of St. Matthew XIX, 9, which can be interpreted in several ways: « Whosoever repudiates his wife, except for infidelity, and marries another, commits adultery » (trans. Segond). « Whosoever repudiates his wife — I am not speaking of fornication — and marries another, commits adultery. » (see note, Bible of Jerusalem) (Editor's note).

obtained for us by His merits. Protestants also read God's word in Holy Scripture with tender veneration. Here again we can but praise and imitate them, while never losing sight of the fact that Christ left us His Church to keep His Word alive and give us its authentic meaning.

The Eastern Churches can give us much more precious help and example. It has been pointed out several times that the majority of the reforms approved by the Fathers of the Second Vatican Council have always existed in the customs of the Eastern Church : use of a language understood by the people, concelebration, communion under two kinds, active participation of the faithful. These Churches have always retained a permanent diaconate. Deeper penetration into their life reveals that collective devotion in the liturgical life has retained a greater place than among us. The Paschal mystery has remained more central not only in theology but in the life of the people. The language of symbols is understood better among them than among us, the sense of, and reverence for, the sacred has been better preserved (with the Russians, for example, the laity, especially women, never go into the sanctuary ; only a priest may touch the altar, walk in front of it, etc.).

Our sincere readiness to recognize among Christians not in complete union with us the spiritual values which life under different conditions has permitted them to develop, is bound to make them willing for friendly and fruitful exchanges of view with ourselves. Better understood by us, they will be better disposed to understand us.

5. *Possible Pitfalls.*

Honestly admitting the spiritual values preserved and developed by other Christian communities does not mean losing sight of those possessed by the Catholic Church. That is quite obvious, and yet it must be foreseen that some young people will fall into this danger. Having merely heard a Baptist preacher on television speaking with moving eloquence of the tenderness of Christ, they will find that no Catholic preacher suits them ; after attending one religious service in an Oriental Church, or simply listening to a few records of Russian religious music, they will discover they have an Eastern temperament and will declare that the Western religious world has no longer any appeal for them. The wise teacher will seize this opportunity to form the pupils' judgment, teaching them to distinguish between what is of divine origin and therefore essential and unchangeable in our religious life, and what is human assistance, variable from circumstances of time and place. This provides an occasion to replace the religious life of these young people on its solid, rational basis.

Others, taking part in ecumenical action and burning with zeal for the « aggiornamento » of the Church, will chafe against the slowness of elderly pastors in introducing reforms which the young consider indispensable. Here is the opportunity to develop their spirit of faith, showing them that the Church of God is not the one built by their dreams but the one willed by Christ when He chose Peter and the other apostles to be its foundation-stones. In making His choice Christ foresaw the imperfections of the apostles and of those who would come after them, and accepted them in advance. We must all therefore give the reverence and help they deserve to members of the hierarchy as authentic delegates of Christ.

6. *Training in Tact.*

If it was once advisable to recommend to the young a reserved attitude towards non-Catholic Christians, the objective to aim at now is more the creation of an atmosphere of understanding and approach. The popes are giving a most noticeable example in this, and Cardinal Bea has expressed the fundamental reason several times. Once a person is validly baptized, even outside the Catholic Church, he is organically united to Christ, he is a member of Christ's mystical Body, and although imperfectly, a member of the Church. Every baptized soul is a child of God and has a right to our fraternal affection.

The first mark of this affection will be to give them the attention they deserve. This means that our young people should learn to know the Christian communities not united to Rome in their present concrete reality, that is, their multiplicity and variety. Every Catholic with a little culture should acquire as clear a knowledge as possible of the dogmatic positions of the chief of these communities, especially if he lives among them, so as to be able to speak of them with justice and objectivity. Nothing will wound our separated brethren so much than precipitate behaviour towards them, without troubling to grasp their real thought.

One way of rousing youthful interest in ecumenical questions would be to teach them the history of past initiatives for the reconciliation of Christians. They could read an account of the Oxford Movement, the Malines Conversations, the World Council of Churches ; they could be interested in the activity of the monastery

at Chèvetogne, the community at Taizé ; a biography of Newman
or Soloviev will open new horizons to them.

In order to make them appreciate that the unity sought for
must not entail a uniformity which would impoverish us, they
could be allowed to assist occasionally at the Eucharistic sacrifice
celebrated in a rite with which they are less familiar. Nowadays
long journeys are not essential to meet Catholic priests belonging
to one of the Eastern rites. Besides Catholic priests of the Byzantine
rite are now authorized to celebrate their Offices in a modern language understood by those assisting at it. It is thus quite easy to
join in their prayer. Active participation in a ceremony of this
kind does more than theoretical teaching to make young people
realize which are the essential parts of the Mass, divine in institution,
and which are the elements introduced by man.

After so many centuries of polemics, rivalry, and even religious
wars, we must strive to clear the atmosphere for the future by
instilling the following convictions into the young :

1. Christians separated from us wish their dignities as men to
be scrupulously respected. They must be able to feel that the love
of Truth is our unique guide in our overtures towards them in
matters of religion. The love of Truth and of Good is the only
motive acceptable to God. We must banish from our hearts anything like confessional Chauvinism ; it is not a question of winning
others over to our own ideas, or to a human society to which we
belong, but solely of uniting together more closely to God. To
train an ecumenist, each one must first grow in perfect rectitude
of heart and in respect for our neighbour.

2. We never have any right to doubt the good faith of those
who are separated from us in beliefs. Whatever may have been
the attitude and responsibilities of the leaders in past centuries of
schism, people alive today who profess to be Orthodox, Lutheran,
Anglican, Presbyterian... do so through fidelity to a national and
a family spiritual heritage. For them their religious tenets are a
precious patrimony which was the basis of their religious and moral
life. Their attachment to their religion, therefore, deserves our
respect in all it contains that is lofty and positive. The task of the
Catholic ecumenist then is to make these Christians perceive that
what they are asked in order to make union possible, is not to
renounce positive values of this religious patrimony but to surpass
them. We would not be responding to the call of the Holy Spirit
in our time, if we kept up a bitter contest with non-Catholics, by
seeking to reduce them to silence by hurling quotations from Scripture or the Fathers at them. On the contrary, the young should

be taught to follow the line of conduct which Père Lacordaire once mapped out for himself : « I never strive to convince my adversaries of their error, I seek to join them at a higher level of truth. »

Christian unity can never be achieved without perfect unity in faith. When circumstances have become favourable, it will be for the theologians, under the direction of the hierarchy, to engage in dialogue with theologians of other confessions, in order to try and dispel oppositions which are still very serious. That is a task for specialists requiring profound knowledge of theology and of the history of the Church. Nevertheless, Union cannot be achieved as a fact, still less can it be permanent — the Council of Florence was the tragic proof of this — unless it is desired and understood by the Christian people. The education of rising generations must therefore aim at augmenting this desire.

Experience has proved that public discussions on controversial subjects usually bear no fruit, and it is very difficult to maintain a peaceful note throughout, especially with the young. On the other hand, in social activities encounters can be both revealing and fruitful. While striving together to bring a little more happiness into the world, young Christians of different faiths can learn to know and love one another.

It would be good to teach the rising generation to make positive efforts to render more cordial inter-confessional relations which have remained strained, or at least cold and uneasy, for too long. In Europe, Professor Oscar Cullmann has initiated organized collections among Protestants for Catholics in need, and vice versa. These kindly gestures have touched and brought nearer together many hearts. Initiatives of this sort could be multiplied to great profit. When we are preparing a fête in parish or school, why should we not invite the Greek or Russian Orthodox priest in the neighbourhood to come with a delegation of his own ? He is in charge of émigrés, he often feels very much alone. Are we truly Christian if we take no notice of his solitude ? Each one's zeal will prompt personal initiatives of this kind. All such acts must be done with natural ease and tact ; we will come together by greater and greater practice of this charity which Saint Paul describes so fully in his letter to the Corinthians.

Charity does not mean lack of prudence or desirable reserve. Clumsy advances which could spoil everything must be avoided. We need hardly say surely that it would be unwise from an ecumenical point of view to specially arrange meetings between young men and young girls belonging to different Christian faiths.

Mixed marriages are never to be encouraged, but on the contrary, to be discouraged. Except in very exceptional cases, when both partners have rare spiritual vitality, mixed marriage remains one of the greatest obstacles in the details of daily life to the coming together of Christians belonging to other confessions. Orthodox and Protestants do not want them any more than we do.

In case any over-cautious adviser considers these efforts at education in an ecumenical spirit to be too complicated and dangerous, if he ruefully regrets the days when the Church recommended reserve and isolation for the young, let him not be unduly dismayed. The haunting desire for unity perceptible in the élite of today is undoubtedly the most exhilarating phenomenon of our time, not only in its final objective, but also in its invitation to get beyond our own littleness. When we urge the young to love Truth for its own sake with all their hearts, when we encourage them to extend as far as possible their efforts to understand their neighbour, with a delicate charity in all that concerns him, are we not leading them with still more ardour towards the end of all true education, to become more deeply Christian ?

Suggested Instruction
in Ecumenical Education
at the Different Ages

by Jacques Desseaux

Contact Agent for the Diocesan Secretariate for Unity, Versailles [1]

These « suggestions » are the result of team research. [2]

The research was carried out for the diocese of Versailles, and was accompanied by *Principes généraux* for Ecumenical education. We have not repeated these here since we considered that other writers in this Review would set them down better than we could.

This work is only useful as what it set out to be, a very small attempt inviting readers' opinions, whose only ambition is to be of service, according to Our Saviour's will, to the cause of Christian Unity in the souls of the young who will make the Christians of tomorrow.

I. FOR CHILDREN UNDER NINE

Which are the favourable moments for a general and implicit instruction on ecumenism ?

---

1. Monsieur l'Abbé Jacques Desseaux was born in Paris in 1923 and ordained at Versailles for the Service of the Diocese in 1949. After the Major Seminary, he continued Theological studies at the Institut Catholique, Paris. He was professor of Church History at the Major Seminary, 1951-1963, and since 1957 he has been vice-director of Denominational Education. He was appointed contact agent for the diocesan Secretariate for Unity in 1963.

2. The compiler wishes to express his most sincere thanks to Mgr. Renard, Bishop of Versailles, and Mgr. Rousset, Bishop auxiliary, Director of Religious Instruction in the diocese, who have encouraged this research. He would like to say also that it could not have been completed without the help of Monsieur l'Abbé Descouleurs, vice-director of Religious Instruction, Sœur Marie-Geneviève, Mademoiselle Brien, Mademoiselle Sauthier, Mademoiselle de Jandin, and Père Caffin of the Oratory who kindly composed the file for the 14-16 years of age.

1. About the Creation.

Of all the things He has created, what God considers finest and what He loves most are human beings, ourselves. He knows and loves each one, as anyone loves their own child.

God wants everyone to call Him « *Father*, » even those who do not yet know Him or who are not united with us, because they are our « brothers. »

2. About Our Lord.

Our Lord came to draw all men together in the Father's love. He comes to us (Christmas...) to show us more clearly what the Father wishes, and how to please Him (syllabus 2nd. term). When He prayed to His Father, He uttered His great longing : « *Father, that they may be One.* » « May they love one another as we do ! » May no one stay apart from us.

3. About the Church.

Christ wants all to be within His family, in His Church. He began in Palestine... Through His Church the Risen Jesus calls, unites men, women, in His family.

He is called the « Good Shepherd. »

Every day He calls, unites more men, women, children... He will not have finished His work until everyone in the world is grouped round Him, till there is « *one fold and one Shepherd*, » when He has brought all men to the Father.

During Unity Week, prayer should not make distinctions among our separated brothers.

1. It should be more *a thanksgiving* that we can say « OUR FATHER, » and can say it with all men.

2. It should be an occasion to *appreciate better phrases which express Christ's desire :* « that they may be one, » « thy kingdom come » — « thy will be done » etc.

The Holy Spirit makes this desire grow in our hearts.

The children should be told that plenty of people are praying that all who believe in Christ may be truly united.

II. FOR CHILDREN FROM 9-12 YEARS

For the first time, children will hear a priest or teacher talking about Protestants, Orthodox, Anglicans, etc. At least at first they will not grasp the difference of their religious positions, but from the way in which we speak they will grasp our attitude within the Catholic Church towards these separated brothers : we want and are waiting for their complete belonging to the Catholic Church, we are sorry that they are separated.

In the perspective of teaching respect for others as such, and as separated brothers, chapters of History syllabuses relating to Protestants can be read again (see COLOMB, *Au Souffle de l'Esprit*, II, chap. VIII and IX).

1. In Teaching.

In preparation for Unity Week, it may be possible to take a chapter on the Church : « *The Unity of the Church* » in connection with the Epiphany. But all instruction must strive to make children grasp a clear idea on the division of Christendom, and *Christ's desire.*

Set out from Christ's desire to group all men round Him to lead them to the Father : « Father, that they may be one. » Parable of the Good Shepherd : « I have other sheep... » « There shall be but one fold and one Shepherd... »

Our Lord wants all who believe in Him to be very united, to believe all He has said, to be grouped round the Bishops united with the Pope, as the apostles were round Saint Peter.

It is not only Catholics who are followers of Christ. There are the *Protestants* ; they are children of God. They wish to live with Christ as children of the Father. They believe that Christ gave His Holy Spirit to help them to live as children of God. They listen to the Word of God as we do. So they are *our brothers.*

They are our *separated brothers.* They are not fully part of God's great family, the Church of Christ. They do not believe all that the first Christians believed, everything Christ said — for example : some find it hard to believe that at Mass the bread and wine become the Body and Blood of Christ through the words and actions of the priest.

There are the *Orthodox* ; they believe all the Church teaches in Christ's name, but they do not accept that the Pope holds among bishops the place of St. Peter as head of the apostles.

They too are our *separated brothers.*

All men are going forward, more or less near to the Church of Christ. See Schema : COLOMB, III. *Avec le Christ Jésus*, p. 117 taken up by F. DERKENNE in *Vie et Joie*, III, p. 64 (Pupil's book).

This schema shows clearly that Christ's Church longs to gather all men together ; and the place of Protestants, quite near.

It is not entirely their fault that they are separated from us. We love them as Our Lord does... We want to be all united together in the Church of Christ.

To make men believe in Christ, all Christians should be united. « That they may be one that the world may believe. »

There is no need to put forward the actual figures of Catholics, Protestants. The average child will gather little from numbers ; figures mean little when they are too high.

If desired, however, the numbers can be transposed to the pupil's class level. Supposing we are a class of 30 ; 5 would be Catholics, etc. This method often tells very vividly ; we discover by it that in Sweden there would be only one or two Catholics among several hundreds of children...

2. *In Prayer.*

We pray with our separated brothers that we may become united. If we love Our Lord we want our separated brothers to become our brothers completely, just as they want it. Together we ask the Father that His kingdom may come. Point out that each Our Father we say is said with our Protestant and Orthodox brothers.

It would be good to take the *Mass for Unity* with the children during the week. Use texts from the Mass for the prayers in class...

With a view to the Mass for Unity, study particularly :

— *The Collect..*

— *The Epistle* : « you await but one thing : the Kingdom of God ; you all have but one Lord... There is but one God who is the Father of all and who dwells in all... »

Be gentle and patient, bearing with one another...

Think over our attitude towards our Protestant brothers.

— *The Gospel* : « I pray not only for them, but for all those who at their word will believe in me, that they may be one as thou Father in me and I in Thee... » and the remainder of the text.

— *The Prayer over the Offerings* : we offer Christ's sacrifice for all those who bear the name of *Christian*, which means Protestants and Orthodox.

— *Prayers before the Communion* : the first : « Lord Jesus, who hast said.... »

*

*   *

Use the hymns for Unity : O Seigneur, rassemblez dans votre Église... D. 13.

Seigneur, tu cherches tes enfants... D. 34. See bibliography.

Show the children that we do not pray alone, our separated brothers pray with us during this week.

Explain that there are Protestant brothers who devote their lives to praying for the unity of Christians.

Some Protestant formulas of prayer might be used ; see the Office for Christian Unity by the Brothers of Taizé (this Office is meant for adults... choose from the simple prayers); see the collects particularly.

Part of the record « Dimanche à Taizé » Studio SM might be used (See bibliography).

3. *In Actual Life.*

Show the children that every time they make an effort to understand others, to avoid disputes, they are working with Christ for the unity of His Church...

Each time anyone could say at our behaviour : « See how they love one another, » they are working for Christ's great wish.

Help them to see the effort God asks from each one by starting from the practical deeds of everyday life.

Educate their eyes of Faith concerning their Protestant companions :
— do I know any ?
— what is my first thought on meeting them ?
— what does Christ think of them ?
— do I really love them as Christ did ?
or is my first thought : they do not believe all the Church teaches ?

III. FOR CHILDREN FROM 12-14 YEARS

1. *General Directives.*

In general, follow the *Orientations pédagogiques pour une catéchèse de pré-adolescents,* as put forward by Père Babin and Abbé Bagot, in the « Sel de la Terre » series, Mame editions.

At this age questions can be treated historically, taking care to fulfil certain conditions.

a) The history of separations, or efforts in the Church for unity, must not be taught as a series of stories or even as merely secular history ; all must be presented as from within the Church, within God's plan for the world, and His will for unity, bringing out the sad and painful side of the separations (texts no. 5, chap. 17, p. 134 COLOMB, *Au Souffle de l'Esprit,* Tome II. — Text p. 152, COLOMB, *Aux sources,* no. 3).

b) This presentation from History will appeal more to adolescents if some heroes or saints are introduced, great attention must be paid to the evolution of hero-worship at the different stages of adolescence (cf. *Orientations pédagogiques* quoted above).

For example, the class could take :
— St. Francis of Assisi and his relations with the Jews and Mussulmans ; Strasbourg File no. 141.
— St. Thomas More and the Church in England : Strasbourg file no. 141, and *Au Souffle de l'Esprit,* no. 2, ch. XI.
— Père de Foucauld (cf. *Témoins de Dieu,* Centurion editions).

c) According to the geography syllabus of the class, religious ideas could be made concrete by asking what religions prevail in different regions between one great city and another. Example : Between Paris and Jerusalem what religions would you find among the inhabitants you would visit ?

When speaking of Unity itself, the following points could be taken :
— Throughout her history, the Church lives the mystery of Christ's death and resurrection in each of the sacraments, especially in the Holy Eucharist. In instituting this sacrament, Christ wished it to be the symbol

of Union between all His brethren. The Eucharist is the new Alliance, the life of union with God and our brothers in Christ.

— Explain or give a new awareness that not all Christians are grouped within the One Church of Christ. Many Christians are not in communion with us with the same Eucharist. And yet they, like us, long for Unity (speak of our separated brethren's efforts for Unity : Brothers of Taizé, encounters with Protestants, Unity Week, World Council of Churches...)

2. *How Shall we Reach Union ?*

It is not by human industry alone (point out the difficulty of union between nations, the members of a family, a class).

God's grace is necessary to achieve this union « when and how He wishes » (John XXIII).

In the meanwhile :
— pray,
— keep our own faith vivid and deep,
— purify our own souls individually,
in order to achieve the Union desired by Our Lord « that they may be one that the world may believe. »

We must make :

a) *An effort of charity* : « Love one another as I have loved you. » Our desire for union must be concrete, practical. Think how we can establish solid union in our own little communities :

— at home with our parents, brothers, sisters ;

— with companions in our district, leisure-hours (stadium, recreation), go to meet others, come out of ourselves ;

— at school (no jealousies, antagonism, but friendliness, mutual help, team spirit). « In our time, a Catholic should always think, act and behave as if being watched by an unbeliever or a separated brother who, while silently watching and pondering over what he sees, will say to himself : « See how they love one another. »

— if we have any contact with companions of other beliefs (Protestants...) we should think of them as brothers.... Is this always our attitude ? Do we know how to create links ? (we are all Christians, let us find points in common and see what unites us). Do we esteem them ? do we admit their value (they have something to give us). Do we respect their beliefs ? (take a concrete fact, study it, judge it in comparison with the Gospel, see how to act or react towards it).

b) *An effort of prayer* : more personal, more frequent prayer for Unity. Make the class find in the Ordinary of the Mass passages where we pray for unity and the universal Church. Texts from the Mass for Unity. If a class Mass can be arranged, bring out these texts.

A map of the religious world could be made use of :

cf. « Propagation de la Foi » 5, rue Monsieur, Paris VII.

cf. COLOMB, *Au souffle de l'Esprit*, II, chap. XX. The Church in the World.

cf. *Informations catholiques internationales,* no. 100, The Church in the World.

cf. Missi, 1958, no. 2 ; 1960, no. 1.

cf. COLOMB, *Au souffle de l'Esprit,* II, « The History of the Church, » chap. VIII, « Separated Brothers », Chap. XI « False and True Reform. »

IV. FOR ADOLESCENTS (14-16 YEARS)

1. *Psychological Support.*

Once a youngster begins to understand his own responsibility concerning his character, future, relations with others, his free time, he wants his budding personality to be recognized and considered before anything else.

In his religious evolution, he will be tempted to reject whatever does not satisfy his intellectual and emotional needs : to make his own God.

This applies especially to pupils of 3rd. and 2nd. Grades in secondary studies. With these classes put forward the ecumenical problem in relation to the study of liberty arranged in religious instruction.

2. *Presenting the Problem.*

1. It is first of all necessary to make these youngsters feel that *disunion among Christians is a scandal.*

The great idea at this age : « all religions are good » favours toleration, regardless of diversity in the Churches. The Reformation attitude, as a revival, an excuse for private judgment, flatters their own personal phase.

In one way, Luther is a hero for adolescents ; he knew how to break with unworthy authority.

It may be well to start from Luther's drama of conscience, showing up its good qualities to the full. Follow up Luther, after his decision to break away, in the search for an authority, to avoid the split into rival churches (Anabaptist crisis).

With the help of the chart of Christian sects (*Fêtes et Saisons,* no. on Sects) show how this wish for a Church of the pure, by breaking away and beginning again, has crumbled the Reformation Churches into fragments.

Point out the constant of such reactions in their own stand within a J.E.C. group, a Scout patrol, a set of pals. Analyse with them how disunion can creep in among friends through want of understanding and forgiveness, by forgetting self-sacrifice and patience.

From there, lead their thoughts to Pope Paul VI at the Holy Sepulchre, thinking of all the sins committed by Christians in the past and at the present time, of our own sins. Arouse deep regret and uneasiness at the division of Christ's family (read the Pope's prayer at Jerusalem).

2. Admitting this tragedy, *call upon them to take part in the hopes of the ecumenical movement.*

The Unity of Christians must start from Christ and His Holy Spirit.

Real reform within the Church is individual conversion to Christ which draws others into a movement towards Him.

Analyse the behaviour of the young fellow who, in order to react against the stream of insincerity or the tyranny of « the roughs, » forces himself to live a life beyond reproach, and draws the better-minded after him. For one who wishes to improve the tone of his class or team, there will no longer be question of condemning or despising the undesirable, but of creating another movement working against the too human incline, with a few others, in order to save the rest, the least tractable included.

There is food for thought in the meditation on the leaven in the mass of dough, for any adolescent.

Efforts at conversion and fidelity to Christ from all Christians of any Church is the indispensable basis for drawing God's children together.

The more Christians form the leaven of Christ the sooner will they find ways to understanding and unanimity.

3. *In Conclusion.*

Adolescence seems to us the time to see ecumenism as the holiness of the Church through the conversion of Christians, therefore of each one to Christ.

Reducing the ecumenical problem to that of « true and false reform in the Church » may seem to be curtailing the question. And yet is it not a necessary step with the young during the phase when they are thinking principally of themselves, of the quality of their own lives, and judging — with considerable harshness — the failings of their elders.

After this personal invitation to follow Christ with all His brothers even of the separated confessions, we may teach them more easily through dialogue, the historical aspects and universal dimensions of the ecumenical movement.

V. FOR THE SENIORS

Instruction on ecumenism supplies the occasion to instil a real idea, as accurately as possible, of the true catholicity of the Church. Young people of today have some difficulty in finding their balance in face of the Mystery of the Church. From the influence of audio-visual techniques and information (press, radio, television), and from facilities of contact (holidays abroad, relations, exchanges, etc.), they are either tempted by relativism, because they fear ghetto and sectarianism, or else they harden into a kind of integrism, from a kind of subconscious bewilderment before the complexity of problems, and because they fear to question, to think things out.

In other words they are threatened by two forms of non-engagement. That is why :

a) The teacher must have a resolutely missionary attitude, that is he must have a *mentality of dialogue* He must seek to find out with the pupils what is lacking to separated Christians since they have not had the Church ; then what separated Christians will bring to the Church (which has lost nothing essential) when they return to positive realities. He must show that the Church respects and continues the authentic religious values of separated Christianism.

This means that he needs *a positive and a mystical mentality.*

He will point out that the yearning for unity is an urge of faith, a proof of spiritual vitality, a testimony of missionary Christianism.

It is on this condition that his teaching on unity will be really heard by his pupils.

b) The educator must strive to rouse an adult type of loyalty. Care over this will lead him to unmask mechanisms of false authenticity : sincerity is not truth, engagement is not partiality ; he will stress the definition or true idea of religious tolerance.

He will strive to unmask the process of passive annexation
— either rationalist : for the problem is on the sin-redemption plane ;
— or pharisaic : negation of facts from principles.

He will bring out the irreductibility and transcendence of the Catholic event (see Hasseveldt, *Mystère de l'Église* — Holstein, *Jésus-Christ, maître de pensée*).

He will make the different planes clear: theological, polemical, historical, spiritual. He will remake the History of History by showing the position taken in the History of the Separations to consider the separated Brothers on these planes. Historically, the movement is : polemical, theological, historic, spiritual.

He must show the relativism of the historic forms of the Church, placing the principle of constant reform in the Church, as the Council is actually doing. The reality of the Incarnation will be situated in its double aspect of engagement and transcendence.

c) The teacher must help his pupils to situate their own lives in the Church, assisting them in this towards a personal discovery of the Church.

Why am I a Catholic ?

The fact of being born in a certain place has given me the chance (grace), an extra one (vocation) of accepting this situation by a personal choice (adult faith); this choice gives me a place in this small fraction of humanity which bears and can spread Salvation in Christ (the Catholic Church).

My attitude to this problem corresponds to my adult engagement in the Church.

I cannot reach this depth if I have no behaviour or experience of engagement (Catholic Action, spiritual Movement, etc.), if I have a formalist, individualist conception of my faith.

d) A few suggestions for the upper classes in colleges and institutes :

Why not take advantage of a lesson on Montaigne or Descartes to see whether the idea of the Church's catholicity of these « Christians » had not become strangely impoverished, in favour of another catholicity or universality, that of reason.

What should be thought of phrases like these : « We are Christians in the same way as we are Périgorians or Germans » (Montaigne).

« I have the religion my king and my nurse have » (Descartes).

Occasions of national or international campaigns could be for working with students of other confessions (Hunger Campaign, UNESCO). It would be good here to work with « Pax Christi » (Route de la Paix). The young should be prepared for their ecumenical contacts during the holidays, contacts becoming more and more frequent.

We consider that organized interconfessional relations only seem desirable for older children and students, and that these should be in connection with Youth Movements (J.E.C., J.O.C., J.I.C., M.R.J.C., Scouts, etc.).

VI. LITURGICAL ACTIVITIES

1. *Celebrations.*

a) *Typical schema* :
— an opening hymn
— reading passage from God's Word (commented or meditated)
— a prayer
— a concluding hymn.

b) *Advice* :
There could be several readings from Scripture (3 or 4), separated by hymns, meditations or short readings, commentaries.

In any case, it is better to keep to one theme, and not choose too long or too difficult passages, for young people are not capable of long-sustained attention.

If there is question of small prayer groups (classes, small groups of boarders), the texts can be chosen by the children themselves. If they read them also, practices will be needed.

During a celebration, it would be well for the priest presiding to make a very short homily, to guide the few minutes of silent meditation.

With large and mixed groups, this homily would be better placed even before the opening hymn, especially if the children are not accustomed to celebrations.

In the ordinary way, the whole meeting should not last more than half-an-hour.

c) *Material* :
1. *Catéchistes* : no. 13, pp. 45-49 (Themes : readings, spoken choruses).
2. *Brochures de la Semaine de l'Unité* (prepared celebrations). Centre Unité Chrétienne, 5, Place Fourvière, Lyon.
3. *Un dans le Christ* : Brochure of the C.P.L., 78 p., 8 complete celebrations on Unity. Notes on catechesis, preaching, prayer by the assembly and by the celebrant.

4. *Unis dans la prière* : Brochure by M. GILLOT at Veules-les-Roses (S.M.) published under the auspices of the Association de l'Unité.

5. *Union* : November 1957, p. 32. Indications for the Mass for Unity, p. 34. Indications for a Prayer Watch.

6. *L'Angoisse de l'Unité* by Père TAVARD. Bonne Presse. Collection of texts about Unity.

— « Soli Deo Gloria, » studio S.M.

— Office de Noël à Taizé, studio S.M.

— Dimanche à Taizé.

— Eastern Liturgy.

— Russian Choirs.

— CEFAG Photo on Unity (Rue de Grenelle, Paris VII).

2. Prayers in Class.

— Use the special intentions suggested for each day, but also and above all, pray with Scripture texts relating to Unity (Old and New Testaments).

— Have no hesitation in making them an activity under direction.

— Consult the annual booklet of the Centre Unité Chrétienne and the Brochure mentioned below by Roger AUBERT (No. 7. Knowledge of the different Churches.

VIII. GENERAL BIBLIOGRAPHY — RECORDS

1. From Ecumenism to Unity.

1. *Encyclicals* : « Ad Petri Cathedram » of Pope John XXIII.
             « Aeterna Dei Sapientia. »
2. *Missi* : 1957, no. 1 : The Ecumenical Movement, its history, the Catholic participation.
          1963 December : Ecumenism « Towards Unity. »
3. *Actualités religieuses dans le monde* :
          no. 33-34 (August 1954)
          no. 43   (1 January 1955)
          no. 44   (15 January 1955).
Religious situation in the world towards the Unity of Christians.
4. *Informations Catholiques Internationales* :
          no. 64, the Ecumenical Movement.
          no. 100, the Ecumenical Movement.
5. *Fiches « Vérité et Vie »* of Strasbourg (1, rue de la Comédie).
          Pédagogie de l'œcuménisme. Fiche no. 386.
          Le Dialogue entre chrétiens, P. Congar. Fiche no. 375.
6. *Cahiers d'Action religieuse et sociale* :
          no. 160, the Ecumenical Movement.
          no. 161, the Catholic and the Ecumenical Movement.
          no. 226

no. 317, the Secretariate for the Unity of Christians.
no. 323, Protestant conception of Unity.
7. *Echanges.*
L'Unité des chrétiens (Review edited by the Helpers of the Holy Souls).
8. *Brochures du Centre de l'Unité Chrétienne* de Lyon (5, place Fourvière).
Abbé Paul COUTURIER and Christian Unity.
How does Ecumenism stand at present ?
Spiritual Ecumenism.
Prayer and Christian Unity.
9. *Documents catéchétiques.*
December 1959 : The Unity of Christians.
10. *Pages Documentaires IV,* elements of bibliography on Ecumenism :
apply to Père MICHALON, Place Abbé Larue, Lyon 5.
11. *Fêtes et Saisons,* no. 181, January 1964, « L'unité des chrétiens. »
12. *Fiches « Ensemble »,* 32, Rue de Noyon, Amiens,
     nos. 15-16-17-18-19-20-21.

2. *Knowledge of the Different Churches.*

1. *Informations Catholiques Internationales* :
     no. 9   « Les Églises orientales ».
     no. 136 « Un mois chez les Orthodoxes Grecs ».
     no. 160 « Église Latine et Églises d'Orient ».
2. *Fiches « Vérité et Vie »,* of Strasbourg (1, rue de la Comédie) :
     Fiche 392. The Orthodox Church.
     Fiche 410. The eve of the Reformation.
     Fiche 436. The drama of Martin Luther.
3. *Cahiers d'Action religieuse et sociale* :
     no. 305. Separated Christians of the West.
     no. 313. Separated Christians of the East.
4. *Brochures du Centre de l'Unité Chrétienne,* Lyon, 5, place Fourvière.
     Notes on the Anglican Church.
5. *Ecclesia* :
January 1962 « Numéro spécial sur l'Unité » : « Ces chrétiens qui sont
nos frères ».
6. *Missi* 1963. — One thousand million Christians.
7. *La semaine de prière pour l'Unité chrétienne* (Roger AUBERT).
Édition Pro Apostolis, Brussels, 8, Chaussée de Haecht.
Excellent booklet which gives information on the different confessions,
with prayers and suggested hymns for each day of the week. Useful once
pupils have grasped the respective positions of our separated Brothers.
The author stresses positive values.

3. *School Books.*

1. *Le Mystère de l'Église* (Roger Hasseveldt). Éditions de l'École, ch.
35, especially the paragraphs « Œcuménique », « Hors de l'Église pas de
salut ».

2. *L'Église* (by Père BUYS and Père DELCUVE). Éditions Casterman, ch. 18, contains some good pages on Unity.

3. *Au souffle de l'Esprit* (Ch. COLOMB). Éditions Desclée, Tome II (History of the Church):

    Chap. 8. Separated Brothers.

    Chap. 11. False and true Reform.

    Chap. 20. The Church in the World.

4. *Jésus-Christ vivant dans l'Église.*

    Chap. 10. Reform of the Church. — The Council of Trent.

5. *L'Église familière et mystérieuse* (Album « Fêtes et Saisons »).

6. *L'Église* : Matter for catechesis with adolescents.

Éditions Mame by Père BABIN and Abbé BAGOT.

Part II : the Church on earth journeying Heavenwards.

First mark of the Church : Unity : Fiches 15-21, 22-24.

This set of files is by far the best to use in catechesis on Unity for boys in Poetry. Great profit will ensue from studying the doctrinal and psycho-educational notes in file 16.

4. *Scripture Passages.*

John, X, 11-16 : The Good Shepherd.

John, XVII, 21-23 : Prayer for Unity.

Matt., VI, 7-13 : The real prayer : the Pater.

or Luke, XI, 1-13.

I Cor., XII, 12-20 : Comparison of the Body.

Eph., I, 22.

Eph., IV, 1-6. One Lord.

Eph., V, 8-14 : The New Life in Christ.

Phil., II, 5-11 : Preserve Unity in humility.

Rom., VIII, 30 ; XII, 21.

Isaias, XLII, 1-7 : First hymn of the Servant of Yahweh.

Isaias, I, 10-18 : Denunciation against religious hypocrisy.

5. *Hymns.*

Ta Parole, Seigneur est vérité	Fiche	Z 18
Pitié, Seigneur	»	Z 50
Nous te rendons grâces	»	C 7
Seigneur, en ton Église	»	D 36
Un seul Seigneur	»	I 46
Fille de Sion	»	Y 3
O Seigneur, envoie ton Esprit	»	K 17
Seigneur, tu cherches tes enfants	»	D 34
O Seigneur, rassemblez dans votre Église	»	D 13
Marche de l'Église	»	K 4
Seigneur, seul Maître du monde	»	B 24
Aimons-nous les uns les autres	»	D 1
Vers Toi, terre Promise	»	E 18

Booklets : Éditions du Chalet. Les 2 Tables, no. 9 « Jérusalem nouvelle »; no. 8 « Chants d'Unité ».

6. *Records.*

« *Aujourd'hui Noël à Bethléem* » — speed 45, Jericho 601 (Testimony of a Little Sister of the Community under Père Gauthier).

« *Jérusalem Nouvelle* » (9 hymns for the period of the Council) Pastorale et Musique PM - 250 - 48 S.

« *Prière pour l'Unité* » — speed 45 SM (Prayer sung by the Brothers of Taizé).

7. *Teacher's Personal Culture.*

For his own personal culture, the teacher would draw profit from the following works :

Charles MOELLER : *Mentalité moderne et Évangélisation,* 2nd. edition, revised and enlarged, Brussels, Lumen Vitae, 1962, Paris, Office Général du Livre.

— Jesus Christ for non-Catholic Christians ;

— Our Lady and non-Catholic Christians ;

— The Church and Separated Christians.

L. BOUYER : « Paroles, Église et Sacrements » in *Le Protestantisme et le Catholicisme.* Desclée De Brouwer.

SCHLIER, VOLK, DE VRIES : *Unité de l'Église et tâche œcuménique.* Ed. l'Orante.

To receive information regularly, a subscription can be paid to the review *Vers l'unité chrétienne,* from the Centre Istina, 25, boulevard d'Auteuil, Boulogne-sur-Seine.

N.B. These bibliographical suggestions are far from exhaustive. Any further information can be obtained from M. l'Abbé DESSEAUX, 22, rue Maréchal Joffre, Versailles.

The latter will most gratefully receive any suggestions, criticisms or accounts of experiences connected with Christian Unity.

Reflections
on the necessity for Pastoral Guidance
Concerning Mixed Marriages

by Élisabeth DECOUDUN

*Licenciate in Religious Instruction at the Institut Catholique de Paris,
Contact agent of the Ecumenical Circle in the Banlieue Sud de Paris*[1]

Introduction.

A detailed study of catechesis and œcumenism cannot ignore the delicate problem of marriages between partners of different faiths, to be found in each Christian confession.

1) How are these Christian cells formed ?

2) How do they live their life of faith ?

3) How can they attain a spiritual unity, so necessary for conjugal harmony for any one wishing to give God the place He should hold in every home ?

4) What help can the ecclesial authorities give to these men and women seeking to develop their faith ?

A group of these homes with different faiths in the Paris districts discreetly sent round questionnaires within their social setting (middle-class), so that knowing the answers to the two first questions, they might try and suggest an answer to the two further ones. Examination of the replies to the questionnaires, which gave solid proof of frankness and seriousness, permitted a few constants common to most of the homes to appear. Here is a rapid survey to serve as the subject of our article :

The « average » mixed marriage (pardon the use of this statistical term) is the result of a chance meeting, on a holiday for example, of two young people whom their divergences of confession have taken unawares, although both are more or less serious adherents of their Church.

---

1. Born on 14 February 1920, Madame Elisabeth DECOUDUN married a Calvinist on 11 August 1942. She has five Catholic children (aged from 13 to 20). — Address: 26, rue Victor Hugo, Montrouge, Seine, FRANCE (Editor's note).

The consent of the families was given in spite of these diver-gences, religious disapproval having quickly faded away before social considerations.

Advice was asked from religious advisers ; it did not seem to have provided the spiritual help needed, since the couple were left to themselves after the wedding.

When the wedding took place in the Catholic church, the Pro-testant partner was displeased over the written promises he or she had been obliged to sign as if they were mistrusted. Then came the ceremony itself, celebrated in two parts : consents in the sacristy, Mass elsewhere (the enquiry revealed great variety in these cele-brations, in parishes of the same diocese and during the same period).

Family planning caused no problem.

Over baptism of the children, there was no difficulty in the choice of god-parents, since the family was unaware that the Roman Church does not allow non-Catholic sponsors. Usually, the priest has said nothing about this rule in order not to hurt feelings.

It is no longer possible to follow up the evolution of the « average » mixed marriage beyond the first months, during which the desire to consolidate conjugal unity often leads the couple to go to church together on Sundays. From the moment that this unity is firmly settled emotionally and intellectually, it is the per-sonal reactions of the individuals and the intensity of their faith which conditions the religious life of the home. If the journey thus far has not led simply to the conversion of one to the religion of the other (which is relatively rare), it can plunge both into a great spiritual isolation due to the disconnection between two different religious practices in the same home. In this case, one, or sometimes both, of the partners abandon practice. Sometimes anxiety over the children's education or uneasiness over the rivalry of two doctrines, make their appearance. There lies the danger of syncretism, indifferentism, or hardening with no religion.

On the other hand, amongst homes which continue to practice, a real desire to look further towards a deeper spirituality can be observed at least in one of the partners (usually the wife). This often leads them to movements of Christian action, or a real per-sonal effort towards religious culture.

Briefly, those are the elements, which formed the basis for the effort of pastoral research which we now set down.

1. *Necessity for a*
« *Catechesis about Mixed Marriages.* »

Examination of these constant characteristics strengthen the earnest wish to remedy certain painful situations, to supply grave lacunae, or to bring up dispositions which could be altered for the better. This leads us to think there could be an appropriate pastoral. The whole of this pastoral would make up what could be called a « Catechesis *about* mixed marriages. »

Such catechesis would not go in one direction only, for we are not thinking merely of the religious education of parents and their children who are in this complex situation, but of « *an education outside the home,* » reaching the whole Church ; pastors, clergy and laity are not sufficiently informed of the problems as they really occur.

The mixed marriage is the sad fruit of separations, and as such is an anomaly in the Church of Christ. This actual situation has so much disturbed the « Churches » that they have considered it as an unapproachable taboo down to the present day. « Do everything possible to avoid mixed marriages ! » This recent phrase uttered by Pastor Sweeting has become a slogan repeated more or less openly everywhere.

The problem is much deeper, and that is why the question of mixed marriages calls the « Churches » to reflection, meditation and examination of conscience. We think that this sincere search can lead *very far*, and is part of the Lord's educational paths.

2. *Marriage : Warnings-Celebrations.*

If we have placed these two very different points together in the same section, it is because they are intimately connected in public opinion through the shock unanimously sustained by the fiancés, their families, pastors and many priests, over marriages celebrated in a Catholic church.

« The affront » of the written promise, of the formulas employed, like that of the consents given in the sacristy (the most usual custom in France) is keenly resented. The new atmosphere of ecumenical dialogue is disturbed by the continuance of these out-dated regulations — although various experiments have sought to attenuate them.

Warnings. The stumbling-block to this dialogue remains in the problem of the choice of promises — which the Reformed Churches do not usually impose as an obligation. Here lies the tender spot of a mixed marriage and the crucial knot of the situation. Unsolved, and apparently far from solution, it is subjacent in the exigence of warnings. We cannot go into the subject here, which deserves full development by itself. At least we can hope, in the not too distant future, for the suppression of certain formalities which give offence, the remains of an epoch of more or less mutual distrust.

Celebration. Let us suppose that the engaged couple are thinking of a wedding either in a Temple or a Catholic church. The question arises of the celebration.

They want the giving of consents, an essential act of the marriage, and for us Catholics, the « Sacrament » itself, to take place in the most authentically true ecclesial and liturgical setting. The principle of two successive celebrations not being theologically accepted by the « Churches, » we only mention it, because several cases of this kind were reviewed in the enquiry, (it used to be the custom in some countries).

Outside the fundamental question of disobedience to the law of the Roman Church, a marriage in a Temple presents no difficulty in its liturgy for the Catholic partner. But a marriage in a Catholic church presents difficulties of a pastoral order to both parties, Catholic and Protestant. Our marriage liturgy is but slightly elaborated and is often followed by what is called a nuptial Mass, containing two prayers taken from the Scriptures said after the Epistle and Gospel. One of them seems particularly well chosen in its typological references to the wife.

And yet the question is whether the principle of this Mass is to be continued or abandoned, in the case of a mixed marriage. Why ?

The Mass is rightly thought of as « Sacrament of Unity, » for the Eucharistic liturgy is both memorial of the Institution, and the rendering present of the Redeeming Sacrifice.

Marriage also is « Sacrament of Unity » in the visible manifestation of God's plan for each couple, and the consecration of human Love, image of Divine Love (cf. St. Thomas, III, q. 65, art. 3).

There is an hiatus in the juxtaposition of these two celebrations at a mixed marriage. Can we, without loss, straight after celebrating one (consents and witness of the couple's Unity) stress their spiritual separation, immediately afterwards, by offering Eucharistic communion to only one of them ? It is not a question of scrambling over or minimizing this separation. It exists, and finds the culminating point of its suffering at this moment of Worship. Is it the right moment to render it more vivid, just after the couple have joy-fully been united for ever ? It does not seem so to us. In a case like this, should a mixed marriage be condemned to a hasty cele-bration stripped of the solemnity required for so definite a step in Christian life ?

Remembering that liturgical history records that in certain ex-ceptional cases, there existed an ancient custom of a liturgy without the Eucharist (cf. *Les signes de la Nouvelle Alliance.* A.G. MAR-TIMORT, p. 199), could not a mixed marriage be counted as an exceptional case ?

We would also suggest a marriage liturgy inserted into a liturgy of the Word, where the basic aspirations of worship for the two ecclesial families would be happily found. This suggestion does not fall into the snare of a dangerous syncretism, because the basis of these aspirations have one and the same source. « Sacrament » or « Mystery, » marriage could be an occasion to bring out the common source of worship rendered to the Blessed Trinity for every Grace, especially that of Love shared.

3. Family Planning.

The small amount of questions asked on this subject attracted our attention. If it seems that most Christian couples of one faith (apart from a few militants) pay little attention to this problem, the fact remains that the Christian masses must be educated, as we know, at the young people's level.

We would have thought that comparison of two different trainings on conjugal morality in a home of mixed faiths would have had the same effect as the comparison of two different spiri-tual trainings when it arouses a re-action of awareness, search and deepening in a vital longing for union on both sides. This effect was not produced, or if so, it was eliminated in most cases. Why ?

To remain objective, one might think that this point was treated with reticence in the questionnaire from a sense of modesty and reserve, which would justify the answers. After careful reflection over the analysis of several other experiences of life in a mixed mar-riage (which some families were kind enough to impart to us), it would rather seem as if each one had looked for and found a modus vivendi which satisfied the conscience of both parties, in a relative ignorance of the recommendations of the Catholic Church (especially concerning certain limits of the use of the conjugal act).

We have no intention of undertaking here either criticism or approval of these limits, but we can say that explanation by this modus vivendi, which of course varies according to circumstances, does not satisfy our wish for clear and enlightened conjugal ethics.

Our hopes turn towards very young couples, whose serious outlook on various planes is usually deeper than that of older couples, (homes of less than five years compared with homes of more than ten years married life). It must be admitted, the older ones tend to give this delicate matter a second place, chiefly striving to reach a conjugal unity difficult to attain, when the progress of ecumenism did not yet allow partners to pursue it on a religious terrain. Publicity accorded nowadays to birth control prompts young couples to think over this question more readily. These young couples will soon be asking for a serious study of this question to be undertaken not only by theologians, doctors, sociologists, but also with them, that they may submit the facts of their daily experience. As regards human and religious training, this demand should be welcomed with pleasure and respect. We know that research of this kind has begun already in some places, but we think they would be more fruitful if studied interconfessionally.

4. God-parents at the Baptism of the Children.

Another surprise sprung from the enquiry concerning the baptism of the children ; it is the choice of god-parents.

The fact that a difference of religion causes so little anxiety is probably due to the « Churches » giving but vague instructions on this point. It sometimes happens that it is only the rough but frank attitude of the Catholic priest, when the registers have to be signed, that the partners of a mixed marriage discover the truth : the Roman Church does not allow non-Catholic god-parents. But little prepared, and led by convention, these families misunderstand, and are hurt by this stipulation. Besides, in the Reformed Churches sponsorship has a different meaning. God-parents represent the family not the Church. For the Catholic Church, the god-father is a « representative of the Church, » ... a « guarantee » for authentic adult dispositions, responsible with the parents for the religious education of the child (cf. MARTIMORT, op. cit., p. 166).

Experience proves that a Protestant is at least as loyal to the discharge of the responsibilities he believes that he has towards a Catholic child, as a Catholic would be. But can he in conscience consider himself to be « a representative of the Roman Church » ? Of course he cannot. Nor can the Catholic Church impose that upon him, which is the logical reason for the restriction. Some consider the position as a manifestation of a sincere reverence for their Faith, and the dedication of their own baptism.

None the less, objections to this regulation are many, which proves that there is a lack of comprehension among Catholics as well as Protestants. Whatever his beliefs, cannot a baptized soul validly represent the Church of Jesus Christ ?

To avoid confusion, we would say that unity in diversity presupposes complete communion in faith at least. This is not the case with Protestants and Catholics. It is difficult to see how some one can make a sacramental act as guarantee for another who will not share the same communion of faith. The minds of Catholics must be clearly enlightened about this in parishes and in catechism classes. The values of engagement would find their right place and useless disappointments avoided. Too much insistence cannot be laid on the gulf made between some unfervent souls and the Catholic Church, and the resentment of our separated brethren, each time one of these « irregular » sponsorships is discovered. We must also denounce a deplorable practice, which is happily already on the decline : secret baptisms or « re-baptisms. » Among the families of mixed faiths, several cases appeared in the enquiry. It had caused serious spiritual conflicts. A grandmother, a female relative brings a Protestant child already baptized or on the verge of being so, and has it baptized or « re-baptized, » sometimes with the consent of one parent, sometimes without the knowledge of either. What lack of appreciation of the value of the Sacrament ! This helps us to realize the degree of sclerosis in the Catholic mentality some thirty years ago. We must have the humility and the courage to admit it.

5. *Education of the Children
in a Mixed Marriage.*

Education of the children, issue of a mixed marriage, is directly influenced by the parents' degree of religious equilibrium. Therefore it can vary a great deal according to circumstances. In spite of that, one constant stands out: these children escape religious indifference more than others, contrary to what one might expect. Generalization would give a false impression, but for a good majority, the enquiry corroborated this.

The phrase « Our children are ecumenical » appeared several times in the replies. What did it mean ? The children of a « mixed union » (if we may use such an expression), no matter what their place of baptism and education, carry in their veins the heritage of two patrimonies once diametrically opposed.

In other words, whether we like it or not, aversion for Papists from Protestant ancestry, and the haughty contempt of ancient Catholic stock for heretics fuses in their heredity. We know that this is not nearly so vital for the psychology of the being as was once thought, and we do not give it more importance than it deserves. The facts are there, the presence of two aversions gives an extra-ordinary openness of heart and a spirit of religious tolerance which is nearer to true charity than to indifference. It is also true that they possess the wealth inherited from both patrimonies.

Obviously, there are experiments that fail, and opposite results, but they are rare. Religious instruction for children of mixed marriages falls upon special ground, where a search for the simple truth, a kind of natural elimination of the superfluous, bringing out the essential seems to come spontaneously.

It will be said... confusion, syncretism, beware ! Where the parents practise little or not at all, there is admittedly danger. In these cases, the influence of pastors, priests or chaplains, has a very great importance. The children of parents separated from any religious contact, always risk becoming « separated » themselves, which does not apply only to mixed marriages. But at least they dislike hearing religion attacked, whether their own or another. They remain fairly sensitive to the religious fact.

It is evident that children in general feel safer when their parents practise, and are each faithful to their ecclesial community. When only one parent practises, the problem of the other parent is harder for the child than in a home of a single faith. A great difficulty arises when the mother holds a different faith. A Protestant father is usually aware of his responsibilities and attenuates the problem for his wife and children. For the latter, religious instruction is received at Sunday School, the mother standing aside. It can happen that the husband is anxious for her to develop her Catholic faith. In cases of « sanatio in radice, » a much ignored possibility, the parents find their spiritual balance with the mother's religious practice and the children profit by this. In frequent cases, where the mother is a Protestant, the children Catholic, and the father not practising, the situation becomes acute ; too heavy a burden weighs on the mother, who cannot bear it through lack of competence. The counter-testimony of the father is an added sorrow for her, and drifting away threatens those families most.

To conclude, plenty of young Protestant and Catholic wives who do not share their children's faith, wish to know something of the catechetical instruction these will receive, in order to help with their education. Certain conditions are needed here. Ecumenical sincerity allows no proselytism. Therefore, together with the presentation of catechistic instruction a serious revision of their own religious beliefs must be available for these wives in order to maintain the equilibrium of their own faith.

This would be a new pastoral orientation, delicate indeed, but greatly desired by those concerned. We think this suggestion deserves to be examined, so great is the moral and spiritual need of help for these young wives.

6. *Pastoral guidance for Homes of Mixed Faiths.*

It has been found that this can hardly be arranged by the opening initiative of pastors and priests, especially with families who have drifted away from the Church and no longer seek for contact. These homes especially cause missionary anxiety. But there certainly are families of mixed faith, desirous for religious growth, many more than is usually believed, in which the faith of both partners, far from slackening, is strengthened, purified, increased by comparison of two different creeds. They think they should bear witness to the Grace thus received, offering their moral and spiritual help to all those who suffer from this situation. The very fact of facing the same problems, meeting the same difficulties, gives them easier access to similar homes. The need of grouping by affinity, so often noticed in other movements, notably in Catholic Action, also declares itself here.

In these kinds of groups, identity of situation unleashes long pent-up feelings. The opportunity of telling one's own personal history and being sure of sympathy, confident that they will meet neither contempt nor polite indifference, leads to a liberation of the conscience, a development of the individual and of the wedded couple. As one of them put it, there is an « unloading process » which affects both partners, and allows them to express sentiments which neither of them no longer ventured to utter to the other. By degrees, it becomes easy to think, not of the past, but of the future, and plan the outlines of a catechesis. From such points of contact, which may vary but always begin from the couple's problems, they turn naturally towards a deeper examination of religious problems — even as far as theological reflection and spiritual renovation.

A wish to come in contact with their parish, with priests and pastors, is soon felt and carried into effect. There is also a desire in each partner to preserve the other's faith. The wish to convert is rare, most reject vigorously this idea. On the contrary, fresh interest in the Church of each, and desire to give testimony helps them to go forward and undertake responsibilities in civic or in parish life. It need hardly be said that these enterprises must be known to pastors and priests who help the homes in both difficulties and development. The enterprise in the Paris region, still small in numbers, seems satisfactory enough to be continued.

Those married very recently, who profit by a clearer ecumenical atmosphere, have chances of being less ignored in their parishes. And yet, the desire to consolidate quickly their new union in an enlightened spirituality, and to give their future children a balanced education from the start, makes some eager to join in the experience of these groups from their earliest days of marriage.

Besides that, many engaged couples — whose choice is fixed in one or the other perspective — express the wish that those experienced in mixed marriages should give them the testimony of their Christian life. Although useful, we think this testimony would not be enough. Rather than leave them in ignorance of so many problems and difficulties, in order to avoid a kind of spiritual anguish settling down beside their human enthusiasm, why not prepare them for this arid path, arming them against discouragement, disaffection or spiritual neglect ? An inter-confessional commission of priests, pastors and families of mixed faiths could study the possibility of sessions in preparation for a mixed marriage, attendance being strictly reserved for engaged couples only, who have already consulted priests or pastors.

Conclusion.

We have purposely left it to the conclusion of this article to stress the question of the ecumenical education of the young, for it could bring about a perceptible alteration in mentality, which would lead, in all probability, to a decrease in the number of mixed marriages.

A Christian catechesis, as it is thought of now, catechesis of authenticity and simplicity, anxious to bring out fully the true values of Faith, must not consider ecumenism as a new chapter on the syllabus. It must be seen as a new spirit to animate and transform. Our younger generations must be trained in this spirit. They must be taught sufficiently clearly, besides the truths of Faith based on Scripture and on Tradition which explains it, the

---

1. The Community at Taizé in Burgundy organized at Cormabin, since last year, a « catechesis-retreat » for mixed marriages, with the aid of a Benedictine monk of Ligugé ; two sessions in 1963. (Editor's note).

historical development of the Church of Christ, and the origins of the human quarrels and separations. The whole picture should be put before them with sincerity and without compromise. From their early years, they should gradually be made aware of the other Christian communities, and of their vitality and spirituality, instead of discovering they exist during adolescence or even when grown up.

In this perspective, catechists giving religious instruction, will not fail to arouse and foster in the children a Love for the Other and respect for his Faith. The first advantage : freedom from the painful surprise of two young people falling in love only to discover they are sharply divided by religious imperatives.

Will not the first reaction of young people be to reject the thought of a mixed marriage, knowing what difficulties arise and the inevitable spiritual mutilation imposed on one of them ? From different experiences of regular ecumenical encounters organized in youth groups, university or other, the phenomenon of increased mixed marriage does not seem prevalent... Is not that a sign in itself ? We do not mean to defy the spontaneity of human love that selects for itself with no apparent constraining force. Yet it cannot be denied that education counts for much in the behaviour of the individual and the construction of their social and religious personality.

It is for the Church of Jesus Christ, in its different « families » to be particularly exacting over the training of children and of youth. All this with a view to obtaining for the Christian, of whatever faith, a full human and religious development, so that he may be free with the holy liberty of the children of God, to answer « Yes » to the Divine call.

Will this eliminate the problem of mixed marriages ? Probably not, because there will always be those who refuse to be enlightened. At least the « Churches » will have provided the maximum light.

But since it is not certain that the will of God is only to call Christians to « marriages among the same confessions, » and because the Divine Will may be that the inter-confessional dialogue of the « Churches » should sometimes pass through the narrow path of mixed marriages, it may be that the Divine Will shows itself at times by calling two people separated in Faith to join together and form a providential home of unity, an early and humble seed of the Unity we are all seeking.

We are conscious that such an allusion irritates many Christians. And yet, the experience of life in a home of mixed faiths, augmented by that of many such homesteads, verified and asserted by the

anonymous confidences revealed through the enquiry, makes it a
duty for us to maintain this thesis :

Those who being « one flesh » under Love's influence, and
by a long, difficult, slow, steep path become « one spirit, » praying
in Christ Jesus, meditating and suffering the sorrows of separations
with Him, but also experiencing sometimes the unspeakable joy
of catching a glimpse of what rediscovered Unity could be, have no
right to refrain from declaring these first fruits to those who doubt
their existence.

An Ecumenical Experiment in a Parish

by Pierre GRESSOT

Parish Priest of Bourguignon (Doubs).
Secretary of the Pastoral Commission for Unity in the Pays de Montbéliard[1]

Mutual Goodwill.

On the 30th September 1963 the Second Session of the Vatican Council was solemnly opened in Rome. Almost at the same time, in a little village of the *Pays de Montbéliard*[2] the local Catholics inaugurated a new chapel dedicated to St. Bernard. At the door of the sacred edifice, the pastor approached the priest with a Bible in his hand. « We have brought you » he declared, with the elders of the Church at his side, « a copy of the Holy Scriptures. We take this step after 422 years of separation, as 52nd pastor of this village. There are certainly some who will fear what may come of

---

1. The Abbé GRESSOT comes from an Alsatian family, related to Protestant and Catholic families as also to those of mixed religion. In 1949, a year after his ordination, he was appointed curate and began his apostolate in that region of Montbéliard, characterised by working-class and industrial problems and by its mixed population of Protestants and Catholics. In 1955 the Abbé GRESSOT became Parish Priest of Glay in the heart of the Protestant population, at the very moment when the Lutheran Centre of the district was beginning to evolve in an ecumenical direction. It was thus that an ecumenical vocation began to burgeon in the author's mind. Since 1957 he has been taking part regularly in the meetings for the furtherance of ecumenism held at Chatelard and organized by the Centre for Christian Unity at Lyons; he is also in re-lationship with Père le Guillou and the Istina Centre. Contacts with the Protestant world are increasing as a result of the activities of the Protestant Centre of Glay. Since 1963, when he became Parish Priest of Bourguignon, the Abbé GRESSOT has had charge of ecumenical questions throughout the Montbéliard region. He has contributed to several reviews : *Expériences œcuméniques* in « Pages Documentaires », IX, of the *Centre Unité Chrétienne* of Lyons, in « Vers l'Unité chrétienne » of the *Centre Istina,* and in « Correspondances » edited by *l'action Protestante,* etc. — Address : Curé de Bourguignon (Doubs), FRANCE (Editor's note).

2. Clairegoutte, near Héricourt (Haute-Saône).

this initiative. But, I say emphatically, there is no need to fear when our gift is the Holy Bible. »

Replying to the Pastor, the Vicar General explained that in dedicating this chapel to St. Bernard, account had been taken of the unspoken desires of all the local Christians, St. Bernard having been a saint of the days before the separation.

« Certainly things have changed » said people to each other on their way home. It would indeed have been unthinkable, only a few years ago, that such a spectacular manifestation of mutual goodwill should have taken place in the *Pays de Montbéliard*. How could it have happened ?

The Seed Cast in the Earth.

At the outset, indeed, prospects had been none too bright. In early days the *Pays de Montbéliard* had been swept into the current of the Reformation. The Lutherans of the district, who were in a majority of 90 per cent up to the middle of the last century, were in control. It was only as a result of the extraordinary growth of the Peugeot industrial works that the whole sociological situation was transformed. In the course of the last century a land of Protestant traditions was the somewhat nostalgic witness of far-reaching changes in the make-up of the spiritual communities there present. For quite a long period the policy of the two sides was, at best, one of mutual unawareness. Only a few pioneers made any attempt at that time to bring about a rapprochement. We may mention amongst these, Canon Flory, Archpriest of Montbéliard, who, during the dark period of the occupation, provided the Lutherans with altar-breads for the Communion Service, and resolutely took his part in the first ecumenical contacts of the Abbé Paul Couturier.

What a sombre picture of the relations of separated Christians — one side « putting up » with the other ! Then a simple little seed is sown in the earth. Nothing yet to indicate future events at Clairegoutte !

The Leaven in the Lump.

About 1953 the outlook improved. On the Protestant side the Glay Institute [1] became a centre for lay formation, and since then has been visited more and more assiduously by the Lutherans of

---

1. Near Hérimoncourt, in the Pays de Montbéliard.

the region. This Centre works on the lines of the great ecumenical assemblies (Evanston — New Delhi) like a ferment for the internal renewal of local Protestantism. The *Montbéliardais* began to rid themselves of their special brand of umbrageous anti-Catholicism. They began to see for themselves in its true proportions the mission of Christians in the modern world.

Similarly the Catholic parishes were preparing for the C.P.M.I. Mission. They were seriously reflecting upon the obligations laid upon them by their missionary presence in an industrialised region so much under the influence of various currents of the prevalent materialism, whether of a Marxist or capitalist character.

Each in its own way, the Christian communities began striving to gain a deeper understanding of their faith, to put it more fully into practice in daily life. There were no spectacular manifestations, but the possibilities of fruitful dialogue were already there in embryo.

That dialogue would begin rather hesitatingly, like a seed which sends forth shoots in its first gropings towards a still unfamiliar world. Some priests, some pastors, some layfolk, entered into friendly relations with one another in the course of the ordinary events of daily life. The welcome given to the refugees from the Hungarian revolution of 1956, collaboration in the planning of educational trips for foreigners visiting the district, were some of the stages in this evolution.

Then, little by little, the two sides learned to know each other better, like each other more and more. A desire for deeper spiritual relations made itself felt, and the first series of inter-confessional meetings took place.

Spiritual Rapprochement.

Every two months, in fact, a small team of Catholics and a small team of Protestants began to tread the path of spiritual rapprochement. The meetings opened with a Bible reading and a prayer in common. An exponent then made clear the theme of the coming discussion. Questions came up for discussion as varied as the Encyclical « Pacem in Terris, » the evolution of the respective liturgies, the distinctions between Catholic Action and Protestant Action, the position of the workers. Then the discussions began, inspired by the desire, not to convince, but to know, each other, without in any way neglecting points of difference.

Little by little, the two parties got so far as to organize a « Week of Unity. » (This event is now heralded by a simultaneous chiming of the bells of both Protestant and Catholic places of worship.)

Pastors and priests, delegated for the purpose, were entrusted with the formation of two permanent Committees. On the eve of the Week of Unity preparatory circulars and suggestions for preaching are handed to the combined gathering of priests and pastors, to enable them the better to co-ordinate their efforts. On the occasion of deplorable events like the Peugeot social conflict, the religious authorities of the *Pays de Montbéliard*, Catholics and Protestants, took up a common line, as the faith of both alike dictated. Permanent bases were laid down for dialogue which promised greater achievements. (We may note, in passing, the valuable spiritual aid given by religious communities who had been kept informed of the progress made as a result of these contacts.)

On the Protestant side, the « Ecumenical Committee of the Lutheran Inspectorate of Montbéliard » took under its wing an *interim* group which had spontaneously sprung into being in the midst of the pastoral conference.

On the Catholic side a « Pastoral Committee for Unity » came into existence, the efforts of which are now upheld by a Diocesan Secretariat of Unity which extends its activities all over the Diocese.

When the New Delhi congress took place, and when the General Assembly of the French Protestant Federation met at Montbéliard, the opportunity was taken by all the Catholic Communities to pray for these gatherings, in order that the Light of the Holy Spirit and the Blessing of God might be brought down upon them. In response, the Synod of the Lutheran Church approved, almost unanimously, an address inviting Protestants to pray for the Council. Unobtrusively emerging from the earth, the little ecumenical seed had become a plant and had begun to put forth branches.

Rediscovery of Fasting.

And, lo, as its branches spread out more widely, the plant had become a tree !

In quite a humble fashion, in the course of an interconfessional meeting, the idea of an ecumenical fast arose as follows :

In 1962, during a campaign against hunger, the Catholics found themselves rediscovering the deep inner meaning of Lent in the form of three traditional practices, deeply rooted in three practices essential to the Christian life, viz :

Prayer — (glorification and service of the Almighty Father).

Fasting — (renunciation of excessive attachment to created goods).

Almsgiving — (giving practical expression to brotherly love).

On the Protestant side, repentance has also been expressed through fasting [1] (in the Reformed Churches of French Switzerland a Sunday in September is traditionally set aside as a fast-day). Practical expression was as a matter of course given to this act of penance by contributing to some work of charity through a collection. A deeper appreciation of the spiritual treasures to be gained during the time of preparation for Holy Week and for Easter made itself felt in close coincidence with the fast.

All this gained in significance when it was noted that, starting in the XVI century, the fast of the Montbéliard Lutherans had been undertaken with a view to the reconciliation of the divided Protestants (Lutheran and Reformed). As the Council was now placing before Catholics a renewed Ecumenical goal, the paths being pursued by both sides in search of unity thus came together. Ties seemed even closer when we reflected on our responsibilities as Christians living for the most part in rich countries, at grips with the Algerian problem, which laid on us a particular responsibility in God's sight. We were thus led to think out together a gesture of reconciliation and reparation.

« *Pacem in Terris.* »

On the 6th April 1962, the Protestant and Catholic church-bells summoned Christians to gather in their churches at 7 o'clock instead of at table. Assembled in their respective places of worship, the faithful brought their offerings (savings that were the result of giving up their meal).

The offerings were placed in a « marmite de la faim » (pot for the hungry) in the course of services based on the respective religious traditions of the confessions concerned, whilst the prayer of both assemblies was offered for Peace through fair redistribution of wealth. The money collected was handed over to a re-settlement centre in strife-torn Algeria (this centre had already been taken over by a local Protestant Committee).

Since then this fast has become a regular event. In 1963 a joint « micro-enterprise » of the CIMADE and of the *Secours Catholique* set before itself the objective of « making the desert flower » by the boring of two wells which would render possible the agricultural development of an uncultivated region (LAGHOUAT). On the 22nd March, Protestants and Catholics of the entire district went to

---

1. Similar customs exist in Drôme and Ardèche (Editor's note).

their churches once more to place there a humble token of Ecumenicism and a modest testimony to the brotherhood of man.

The size and the fervour of the congregations was a surprise to priests and pastors and the results greatly exceeded the hopes of the organizers. In addition to the successful sinking of the two wells, and of the restoration of livestock to a whole region of Africa, 21,600 francs were sent in addition to help finance the operation « ESPERANCE » started by the Taize community in Latin America. « It is clearly not possible as yet to form an estimate of the spiritual effects of all this on us and on those who have benefited by the sums raised » declared the final joint communiqué of the two Committees, « but we are already conscious enough of these to render thanks to the Lord. »

« Blessed are the Peacemakers for they shall be called sons of God. »

On the Road to Ecumenism.

And now how far have we advanced ?

The fraternal dialogue has started and has been placed on a permanent basis — a prudent dialogue, the participants in which are themselves surprised to see how far its repercussions make themselves felt, throughout the Universal Church and indeed on a world scale. The road of spiritual emulation stretches out before us with prospects undreamt of at the start. We feel that we ourselves have been spiritually enriched and our souls widened.

« Ecumenism obliges Christians to live what they believe and to believe what they live in ever closer proximity to Christ » averred Professor Lovsky in a phrase of deep meaning. [1]

No doubt the Christian communities have much to do still each in the direction of its own renewal, but our prayers of spiritual emulation are already opening a way to Unity.

We are now conscious of living in a great epoch of Church history. May we be enabled, without quenching the light of the Spirit or trying to precipitate His action, to permit Him to bring about those miracles that the world awaits. « When the mustard seed grows up, it is greater than any garden herb » (Matt., XIII, 32).

---

1. Extract from *Correspondance,* bulletin of the Protestant Action of the Pays de Montbéliard.

Towards an Ecumenism of Charity

The Meaning
of the International Eucharistic Congress at Bombay
November 1964

by René DEBAUCHE, S.J.

Chaplain at the Maison Saint-Vincent, Jumet [1]

For a long time the Ecumenical movement has found and still finds an urgent and heart-searching backing in the demands of the « mission » : *Caritas Christi urget nos.* How shall the world recognize the authentic features of Christ in the Church, if She does not manifest in her own body the unity and charity of Christ ? This work of unity among Christian brothers must be achieved in various directions. If there is one way in which Christians, alive to the Gospel's demands, can already work together, it is in the « service of the poor and of mankind. » Professor Skydsgaard stressed this in his address in the name of the observers at the Council, to Pope Paul VI, 17 October 1963 : « It has been said that Pope John XXIII wished that this Council should lead the Church from being the Church « in itself » into being the Church « for all men. » Is there a better way for us to meet one another than to come out of ourselves, trusting in the forgiveness of our sins, without considering our preferences and our merits, in order to live in the world. Thus we shall be truly the disciples of Christ,

---

1. Father René DEBAUCHE was born in 1897. He studied at the college Notre Dame de la Paix, Namur. After his first two years in philosophy and Letters, he volunteered for active service in World War I, 4 August 1914. He entered the Society of Jesus in 1919. After his higher studies at Louvain, he became master of Poetry and Rhetoric. Later he obtained the Chair of Philosophy in the Institut Gramme, Liège, then at the Faculty of Namur University. For thirty years he was chaplain in popular scout-groups. He has founded homes for orphan boys with Mr. R. Bracq, deputy for the Attorney General. He works efficiently for morally neglected children. — Address : 184, rue Washington, Brussels 5, BELGIUM (Editor's note).

Who did not wish to live for Himself alone, but solely for the world. »

We, Christians of all creeds, can assuredly always go forward in this direction of a « Church for the world » for the glory of God. The Council itself must go further in this way, and appeals from well authorized sources are inviting it to do so.

Here, for example, is a summary of the suggestion made by Cardinal Gracias of Bombay at the 75th. general Congregation, 26 November 1963 : « The Cardinal regretted that the schema does not insist on the struggle against want. He spoke of co-operation among Christians and of their acting together in the service of the poor. Like Paul VI, he pointed out that « the poor person is the image of Christ, the living sacrament of Jesus. » He quoted figures from a book by P. de Lestapis revealing the unfair division of possessions, and the extent of the hunger problem in the world.

We should send a petition to the Pope asking that the next session begin with the examination of schema 17 : the Church and World Problems. This would be a fine preparation for the International Eucharistic Congress at Bombay, which will consider this very subject. It must be « neither a triumph, [1] nor propaganda, but a manifestation of love for the poor, following Christ's example, who said : « I came not to be served but to serve. » It will bear witness to the charity of Christ, which has its source in the Eucharist » (La Croix et le Monde, 28-11-63).

The co-operation of Christians, a common activity in denouncing unjust division of goods and in the struggle against want, is the spiritual step which the Cardinal wishes the Church to take.

And the Eucharistic Congress at Bombay will give tangible proof of the real meaning of the Eucharist, if it can be, on the part of all, a manifestation of effective love for the poor.

The Cardinal's proposal echoes the *Message to the World* sent out by the Council Fathers, 20 December, 1962.

Here are some extracts from it : « Far from turning us away from our earthly duties, our adherence to Christ in faith, hope and charity, binds us entirely to the service of our brethren, like our adorable Master, Who came not to be served but to serve. For that reason the Church was not founded to rule but to minister.

---

1. The directives given by Mr. Visser 't Hooft to the delegates from the World Council of Churches on their arrival at New Delhi will be remembered. He recommended avoiding any show of « triumphalism. »

From all parts of the world, we have brought with us the material and spiritual distress, the sufferings and the aspirations of the peoples entrusted to us. We are aware of the problems which harass them. Our solicitude goes out to the lowest, the poorest, the weakest. Like Our Blessed Lord, we are moved with compassion for the crowds who suffer from want, hunger and ignorance. We feel at one with all those who have not yet reached a really human development, for want of sufficient mutual help.

That is why we humbly and earnestly appeal to our brothers whom we serve as pastors, and also to all our brothers who believe in Christ, and to all men of good-will, to unite in building up a city that is more just, and with a better sense of brotherhood. For God's plan assuredly is that through charity, the kingdom of God should in some way, shine out upon earth, as a distant glimmer of His eternal kingdom. »

This same message was repeated by the Pope at Christmas '63, since the gentle glow of that night calls us to link a chain of love with all the children on earth, beginning with the poorest and most forlorn.

« Our wishes, » said the Holy Father, « must reach... men's serious needs. Our love cannot be ignorant of the great suffering, deep longing, pitiful privations, which affect wide layers of society, or whole peoples... What does the modern world need most, what wishes can correspond to these necessities with wisdom and foresight ?

The needs of the world ! The problem makes one dizzy, so wide, so many and so boundless are these needs. Some, however, are so obvious and so urgent that we all know something about them.

In the first place, there is Hunger. We had an idea it existed. Now, it is a positive discovery. Yes, it is a scientific discovery ; half the people on earth have not enough to eat...

If we lack the miraculous power of Christ, to multiply loaves in order to feed the hungry, we can at least hear in our heart the pleading from the crowds weakened and crushed by want, and echo the compassionate cry from the Divine and yet so human Heart of Christ : « I have pity on the multitude... who have nothing to eat » (Matt., VIII, 2)... We would hope that our sympathy for the poor will manage to stir up this *new love*, that by prudent use of a new economic system will multiply loaves to feed the world. »

The Holy Father asks that self-interested and humiliating benevolence should be replaced by scientific and technical assistance,
not in a patronizing spirit, but in one of solidarity and brotherhood.

We are much inclined to think that the texts quoted above
formulate the deep and synthetic meaning of the Council. Why
else episcopal collegiality ? Why the liturgical revival ? Why the
return to the Bible ? If not in view of the love of Christ and of
our neighbour from whom He is inseparable.

If everything is not inspired by, and working towards, charity,

Christ's Teaching.

During the week preceding the Passion, while Our Lord was in
Jerusalem, we see His enemies fiercely hostile to Him, laying snare
after snare for Him (Matt., XXI-XXII). And yet, encircled by
hate, Christ launches the commandment of love and suggests its
basis.

« When the Pharisees heard that Jesus had reduced the Sad-
ducees to silence, they laid plans together, and one of them, a
doctor of the law, sought to catch him, saying : ' Master, which
is the greatest commandment of the Law ? ' Jesus said to him :
' *Thou shalt love the Lord thy God with thy whole heart, with
thy whole soul, with thy whole strength.* That is the greatest and
the first commandment. The second is like to it : *Thou shalt love
thy neighbour as thyself.* On these depend the Law and the
Prophets. ' »

The Law and the Prophets, that is, all the Old Testament, to
which Christ gives us the key : love of God and our neighbour
(Matt., XXII, 34-40).

After His reply to the doctor of the Law, Our Lord added :
« This do and thou shalt live. » [1] So true is this, that St. John
echoes it, saying, « he who is without love, abides in death. » [2]
Then Christ explains by the parable of the Good Samaritan what
we should understand as real love for our neighbour. The story
is well known.

A man was going from Jerusalem to Jericho. He was attacked
by thieves, who wounded him and left him half-dead. A priest
came down the same road, saw the man and passed on. Then came
a levite. « He drew near, » glanced at him, got no further than
curiosity, and went on his way also.

---

1. Luke, X, 28.
2. *I John*, III, 15.

« But a Samaritan who was on a journey, came near him, and was filled with pity. He dismounted, approached and bound up his wounds pouring in wine and oil. He laid him on his own beast, took him to an inn and looked after him. The next day, he paid the inn-keeper to look after him until he came back. » [1]

Who was neighbour to the man who had fallen among thieves ?

In Our Lord's eyes, to be really a neighbour to others requires an active and efficacious *pity*.

In St. Matthew's text, when He had answered the doctor of the Law, Our Lord took up the attack ; He asks the Pharisees :

— « What think you of Christ ? Whose son is he ?

— David's.

— But if he is the son of David, how is it that David calls him Lord ? »

In the words of Christ there is an invitation to see in the Messias a higher value than that of a man, or even of one sent by God. He is the Only Son, as St. John says in his Gospel, the One truly begotten.

But if Christ took human flesh, if He pitched his tent among the caravans of men travelling through the desert towards the promised land, if He became our brother in our human kind, born of a woman, as St. Paul says, a woman of our own race, it is because He wishes to make us His brothers in divinity.

O marvellous exchange ! cries out St. Thomas in the Office for Christmas. Christ all alone has no meaning. But He becomes fraught with meaning in associating to Himself all men who will accept this gift. And when Christ unites us to Himself, we become like Him, we are in Him as regards the Father who is in heaven. He is the one mediator between us and the Father since He is the Only Son. And it is when we are united to Him that we can truly say the Our Father.

Christ is the vine, we are the branches ; He is the Head and we are the members, He is the Shepherd, we are His flock. This divine and human reality cannot be separated. Since the Incarnation, to love Christ, yet not to love other men has no sense.

Our Lord solemnly proclaimed : « I was hungry and you gave me not to eat ; I was thirsty and you gave me not to drink... »

What you did not do to the least of my little ones, you did it not to me. [2]

---

1. Luke, X, 33.
2. Matt., XXV, 42-45.

When we neglect to feed those who are hungry, or to clothe those who are in need of it, we withhold food and clothing from Christ ; we refuse Him. The second commandment is like the first, in a strong, not a weak, sense ; a likeness tending to identification.

The Church for the World.

In India, alas, as in many other parts of the world, there are children who are hungry, who are dying of hunger ; children without clothes, without shelter, sick children without care.

A Eucharistic Congress must not look like a devout and well fed pleasure-trip.

Yet we must admit humbly and sadly that we Western Christians are quite capable of being satisfied with a comfortable and emotionally fervent congress. What a contradiction it will be if we refuse food, care and clothing to Our Lord Himself !

Cardinal Gracias well understands the essence of the Eucharist in asking that the Bombay Congress may be a token of the whole Church's love for the poor. We would like each pilgrim to Bombay to come as a delegate from his Church. Could a collection be made in every diocese, so that the sums realized could be used to build houses for the homeless, a technical school for the young unemployed, or a maternity clinic for poor mothers ? Might one suggest that pilgrims fast in order to share only a little, but really, in the world's hunger ; and could they bring material, rice and medicines, to provide clothing, food and medical aid for those in need of these things.

This should be the beginning of a universal campaign of Christian peoples against all kinds of want.

For this, tremendous, gigantic, unified efforts are needed. In face of such a boundless, superhuman task, says the Pope, one man unaided is like some one trying to empty the sea with a thimble. So we must pray for an increased, concrete, universal and efficacious charity. This love for the poor, overflowing from the *Pope's* heart must spread from one to another. Thus the Church and all Christians will create a spirit of brotherhood among nations, which will oblige political and social leaders to work together to repel hunger, sickness, ignorance...

If only through active charity, we could force the leaders of the different countries to abandon the dire folly of armaments, so as to equip the world to feed its growing population ! To feed the hungry, present and to come, is problem ONE. Christ's words should ring in our ears : « I was hungry and you gave me not to eat ;

I was thirsty, and you gave me not to drink ; I was naked and you clothed me not ! »

The essence of our faith is the universal brotherhood of men, rooted in adherence to the One King. The Kingship of Christ is first of all in the poor.

To wish to break spiritual bread among the Churches, without being at the world's service, and breaking « material » bread *for all men*, is mere literature.

In a booklet called « Is Mao right ? » Scheyven shows us the head of China haunted with the desire to feed and clothe hundreds of millions of men, so that each can have his daily bowl of rice and his annual blue suit.

Mao does not believe in Christ.

But his effort, at least that one, to feed and clothe his people, will surely call down God's blessing.

If Mao should die, I think Christ would say to him face to face : « Thank you. I was hungry and you fed me... »

We have faith in Christ and we love Him.

But do we love the « Christus totus, » the whole Christ, Head and members ? Perhaps we are like Mao, living a contradiction.

Pray God our contradiction may not be worse than his.

Let us pray and get to work so that the Eucharistic Congress at Bombay may not only be a manifestation of love in words, but in deeds and in truth.

Pastoral Guidance on Ecumenism : Prayer, Encounters, Co-operation

With the kind consent of its Author, we here reproduce long extracts from the dossier drawn up by the Very Rev. Fr. Dumont, O.P., Delegate of His Eminence the Cardinal Archbishop of Paris for ecumenical questions, and director of the Study Centre « Istina. » This document was printed in « Les dossiers de la Semaine religieuse de Paris. » [1]

I. PRAYER THE ONLY AUTHENTIC AND SURE WAY OF APPROACH TO ECUMENISM

The only authentic and sure way of approaching the problem of Ecumenism is to do so by means of prayer. This is true without doubt about all manner of things, but here requires to be given particular emphasis. The problem of unity, which is the problem of the Church, is at once recognizable as being on that plane which the theologians call *theologal*. It cannot therefore be genuinely approached except in a *climate of faith*, inspired by *hope* and in a spirit of *charity*. Of the sheepfold He has founded Christ is *the Door*. No-one can enter it but through Him. It is then by praying with Christ, by praying His own prayer : « Father, that they may be one, » by praying that prayer in Him and through Him, that we must enter upon any apostolate with a view to unity.

It is by this means, moreover, that the break-through effected by the Ecumenical Movement has taken place in the Catholic world. One could not therefore be regarded as qualified to enter the world of ecumenical gatherings unless one had made oneself familiar, at least to some extent, with the history of the movement of prayer for unity which has led to the inauguration and then to the development of the *Week of Prayer* in January in the form in which that is almost universally observed today. There is no question here of entering upon the historical field for history's sake,

---

1. *La Semaine religieuse de Paris,* 9 rue de Fleurus, Paris VI. In this brochure will also be found concrete cases of interference of ecumenical preoccupations at ordinary pastoral work.

but of *making one's own the spirit in which we ought to pray and induce the faithful to pray.* [1]

II. FROM PRAYER TO ECUMENICAL GATHERINGS

Introduction.
General Recommendations.

The apostolate for unity can assume very different forms. In every case, however, we shall let ourselves be guided by the three following principles :

a) *We should organize nothing except in complete agreement with the local religious authority.* This agreement can naturally be taken for granted when the matter is one of initiatives concerning Catholics only. It must be explicitly obtained whenever the *active* participation of members of other confessions is involved.

b) We should be on our guard, both in speech and in writing, not only, as is obvious, against all error, but also *against all slipshod doctrinal assertions* which could give rise to confusion in the minds of Catholics and could foster in non-Catholics the illusory idea that reunion is easy.

c) We should *avoid*, in our references to our separated brethren, *all tactless and wounding expressions and everything inspired by a polemical spirit.* As regards this latter point, we must eschew well-worn manners of speech to the wounding implications of which, as concerning our separated brethren, custom may have blinded us.

1. *Meetings Specifically Intended*
for the Catholic Faithful.

A. *At religious ceremonies.* — The principal of these is clearly the *Holy Mass.* It is then to Mass that precedence will be given. This will be a particularly favourable occasion on which to explain to the faithful the bond that links the Church with the Eucharist, the Sacrament of Unity. This is an essential point in ecumenical pastoral teaching.

This will often require a serious effort on the part of the clergy, for this important point in catechesis is generally left in the shade because

---

1. The essentials of this subject will be found in the work by the Rev. Fr. Maurice VILLAIN, S.M.: *L'Abbé Paul Couturier,* Paris-Tournai, Casterman. l⁰ ed., 1957, 376 p.

of some confusion in the notion of a Sacrament and a tendency to reduce it to the confines of a « cause of individual grace. » The liturgical movement has already done much to restore the full and true notion of what a Sacrament is — a notion that has remained so real to our Eastern Orthodox brothers — but it still remains for this « rediscovery » to be made use of in the teaching given to the faithful.

In cases where the celebration of Mass seems inopportune, or if it is desired to make use of a longer period for the purpose of a doctrinal or documentary *exposé*, a *sermon-lecture* will meet the case, followed by *Benediction of the Blessed Sacrament* or the singing of *Compline*.

The prayer for Unity provides an opportunity for talking in concrete fashion about the mystery of the Church under its various aspects. Matter is provided thus for numerous sermon-lectures, whereby the conscience and the faith of the Faithful can be opened to the reality of the Mystical Body of Christ, whereby they are enabled, as it were, to lay a finger on the sinister effects of the division of Christians on the coming of Christ's Kingdom here below, whereby too means are provided of recalling or suggesting what duties we have of justice or charity towards our separated brethren, etc.

Akin to the sermon-lecture, with readings, is the devotion of the *Holy Hour*, which lends itself to active participation on a large scale of clergy and Faithful, with hymns, prayers in litany form, etc.

B. *Manifestations without religious ceremony or worship.* — It is obvious that liturgical celebrations do not normally attract the attention of any but practising Christians. It is, however, to the advantage of all that a wider public should be given an interest in the problem of unity — it is often a way of bringing people to take a new interest in the religious problem and in the Christian life.

This object is best obtained by *lectures* given in places of entertainment. It will be easy to discern, in this place or that, whether or not it will there be found helpful to make use of a room without religious character. In several places cinema halls have been employed with success.

This type of meeting can take the form of lectures on a *subject of Church history*, touching the divisions of Christians or their efforts to reunite : or on *certain special characteristics of Christianity* as practised in this or that locality (the Christian East provides, in this connection, abundant and most interesting subject-matter of a kind which is well calculated to increase the knowledge already possessed by our Catholics of the mystery of the Faith and Christian life). Lectures could also be given on certain *subjects of current interest concerning the Ecumenical Movement* (origin and development of the Ecumenical Movement in the non-Catholic churches, the great assemblies, their growing relations with the Catholic Church, etc.).

It is obvious that only lecturers who are well-informed and have sufficiently specialized knowledge about these various themes, can fruitfully be asked to tackle these subjects.

Another form of meeting is that of the *scenic play*, setting forth in a living and concrete manner the drama of Christian division. Such plays are based either on the Bible or the liturgy, or indeed on both.

Again, a *sacred concert* can be given in which suitable pieces will be performed, deriving either from traditional sources of piety, from the liturgy, or from the religious folk-lore of other countries or other Christian traditions.

One can also welcome the idea of showing an appropriate film (this is done at the big ecumenical assemblies) or of lantern-lectures illustrating the liturgical and iconographical traditions, as well as the life, of different Christian communities.

2. *Mixed Meetings with Active Participation of Non-Catholics.*

General Principles. — Until now we have only been considering manifestations organized by Catholics and intended principally for a Catholic public.

The increase of interest in the cause of Unity is, however, so great today that we shall soon be led to take a further step forward, indeed to organize some manifestation in the course of which our separated brethren will have an *active part* to play. Experience proves that no such step should be taken without previous careful thought.

It will always be good — and therefore desirable — that Catholics should take serious steps to familiarise themselves with the problem of Unity, whether in the domain of prayer or in that either of information or of formation. A parish priest or chaplain of Catholic Action who is anxious to make this step forward must *have well in hand the group of Catholic layfolk* whose help will be essential. This group will itself need to be sufficiently trained to participate in the ecumenical action to which it will find itself being invited (most often, moreover, at its own suggestion).

Another principle is that nothing must be done without the knowledge and the co-operation of the non-Catholic clergy, or of the responsible ecclesiastics of the religious body with which it is desired to enter into contact. This will allow, among other things, for a minimum of preparation on the part of all the participants, for meetings which must take place in the right spirit, one not of compromise but of clarity and loyalty.

These principles having been once established, how can we bring about the participation of our separated brethren in the various kinds of meeting which we have envisaged above?

A. *Meetings Intended for a Large Number of People — Sacred Concerts, Scenic Plays, Lectures*. — Orthodox and Protestant choirs are generally glad to participate in *sacred concerts* organized in common. There is no objection to the sung texts being presented and explained by some member of the non-Catholic community concerned. Naturally a manifestation of this sort does not take on its full significance unless Catholic choirs are also taking part. The choirs of neighbouring parishes will be able to unite on such an occasion. While there should be no question of giving an exhibition of artistic virtuosity, pains should however be taken to ensure that all be well and devotionally carried out. A final chorus could be sung by all the choirs united. The object and the meaning of the manifestation could be set out in a brief introduction by the priest responsible for the concert, and the closing address could be entrusted to the responsible non-Catholic minister, or *vice versa*. The gathering would not break up without reciting the *Our Father* in common.

A similar order could be observed in regard to the *scenic plays* in which members of the different religious bodies will play an active part. The introduction and closure would be made on the lines above indicated.

Greater discretion will have to be observed about inviting a *non-Catholic lecturer* to address an audience predominantly Catholic. Before a large gathering it is important not to choose as themes of such lectures disputed questions of doctrine. Lectures of this kind before large audiences do not provide suitable occasions for the fruitful exchange of views. It is impossible, in practice, for Catholic doctrine to be adequately set out in the form of replies to a non-Catholic thesis, and to allow this involves a risk, by no means illusory, of disturbing or even undermining the faith of Catholics.

With this important exception, it is a fact that a large number of subjects, historical, spiritual or of topical ecumenical interest, can be dealt with in lectures that our separated brethren are requested to give. We have here a means of obtaining information of a most valuable kind that is capable of contributing efficaciously to closer understanding and better feeling. As a result of such talks, indeed, we usually obtain a clearer idea of what we have in common with our separated Christian brothers, and of what is an essential element in the Christian Revelation : *faith in Our Lord Jesus Christ, God and Saviour*, as also *our personal allegiance to Him* through this same faith, the gift of God and Source of our salvation.

It is self-evident that, as in the preceding manifestations, the priest who is responsible or who was chosen to preside, will introduce the subject and present the speaker, making clear at the same time the object and scope of the invitation that has been extended to him. At the conclusion of the lecture, the presiding cleric will sum up briefly, if need be making, with due tact, any clarifications which seem called for. Here again, the Our Father will be recited in common to round off the meeting.

B. *Meetings Intended for Small Audiences.* — a) *Meetings intended specifically for the purpose of prayer.* — The first object of the *Week of Universal Prayer for Unity* was to synchronise, to render *simultaneous*, these prayers of the different Christian communities in order that, at the same time, they might present themselves before God, upheld by the eternal prayer of His Son, « *semper vivens ad interpellandum pro nobis.* » But the more fervent groups, though praying separately in this manner, could not but feel also a profound need to unite themselves with their separated brethren in prayer. From *simultaneous prayer* an ever-increasing urge was felt to pass on to *prayer in common*.

Such a desire seems to us to be perfectly legitimate. We would even be tempted to say that, in this matter of the restoration of unity, nothing decisive will be achieved until such time as prayer in common has become the normal thing in accordance with this exhortation of Our Saviour : « Amen I say to you, if two of you agree over any request that you make on earth, it will be granted them by my Father who is in Heaven » (Matt., XVIII, 19).

None the less we are here treading upon delicate ground. The division of Christians is essentially a rupture of ecclesiastical *communion* between those within the Church and others in the triple domain of doctrine, of hierarchical allegiance and of worship. Only the restoration of unanimity in the *profession of faith* (rejection of grave error or heresy) and inclusion in the *one and only hierarchical structure of the Church* (renunciation of schism) could lead to the re-establishment of *full communion in the public worship* of the Church, and above all to the *reception in common of the Eucharist,* Sacrament of Unity.

This is the reason why Canon Law forbids Catholics to enter into « *communicatio in sacris* » with members of separated churches, and *vice versa* (not without some exceptions in certain clearly defined cases which will be mentioned below). In the eyes of the Catholic Church, there cannot be *intercommunion* in the strict sense of the word, i.e., the holding of public worship (principally sacramental) in common, between members of different Communions, that are separated from each other by grave divergencies in regard to revealed doctrine or depending on hierarchical organizations which are unrecognized by each other. The Church is one unique « Communion » and not a juxtaposition of disparate communions. And this communion inevitably implies unanimity in faith, membership of a common hierarchical structure, and participation in the same sacramental worship.

We have said that the prohibition pronounced by Canon Law *principally* applies to sacramental worship and, primarily, to Eucharistic worship. This does not mean that all non-sacramental worship carried out in common with the active participation of our separated brethren is authorized. Were that so, it would be permissible for us to take an active part in all Protestant services, since no sacramental character is attributed to them. It is obvious that, whilst being essentially adoration and praise offered to God, public worship is a proclamation of the faith of the community that holds it and an affirmation of its existence as a specific community. This constitutes an obstacle to the common participation in such worship by members of different religious communions.

We must however, it would seem, make an exception in favour precisely of prayer in common, even public in character, of which the professed and specific object is to obtain from God that He will give us the grace to surmount our divisions and to put an end to them. In such circumstances, indeed, Divine worship is no longer a manifestation of the special character of this or that community, but quite to the contrary — without denying the existence of such a separate character — it is rather a manifestation on the part of the body concerned of its profound desire to find itself one day united with all the other divided communions.

Since such a manifestation of public prayer held in common can only be an exceptional event, all the circumstances, including those affecting persons and places, must be taken carefully into account, and in the way in which it is conducted the function must never exceed the limits outside which the application of canonical sanctions might be justified.

Given the actual state of things and state of minds that surround us, mixed meetings for prayer will be held exclusively for the benefit of comparatively small gatherings. They will not be organized in buildings officially and habitually dedicated to some form of religious worship, but will take place in business or entertainment halls of seemly and dignified appearance. The specific object of such meetings will always be as we have already stated, to obtain from God for all Christians the grace of unity and the right means of attaining to it ; knowledge of the Truth in humility, charity, the spirit of witness to God and service to one's neighbour. The text of the prayers must never contain anything contrary to the Catholic Faith.

It is generally very easy to find agreement with the responsible authorities of other communions on this subject, all the more because recourse is usually had by preference to Biblical texts and those from the Liturgy which are so impregnated by Holy Scripture. The same will be true of chants and hymns, some of which can be borrowed from the familiar *repertoire* of our separated brethren. It will be all to the good if, in the course of such meetings, room can be found for the reading of texts of Scripture (principally from the New Testament). These, without being prayers in the strict sense of the word, are yet peculiarly fitted to awake in us those attitudes of mind and inward feelings of the heart which bring about that mutual sympathy that is the first step towards reunion and unity. Certain passages in St. John (there exists a tuneful recitative of the sacerdotal prayer, John, XVI, that could be sung by a good soloist) and in St. Paul (the whole of the Epistle to the Ephesians, but above all IV, 1-16 ; *Phil.*, II, 1-11 ; *I Cor.*, XII, 4 to XIII, 13) ought to become familiar to all the faithful. Indeed such readings (if well done and with a minimum of introduction, recalling the situation of the primitive Church and sketching out briefly the application of this to our own times) should induce in the hearers a taste for Holy Scripture, together with a deep sense of the mystery of the Church.

Such meetings must not only be held in the January Week (even though on that occasion it is easier to bring out their true object). In places where local Catholics show keenness about the meetings, it is permissible and beneficial to renew them in the course of the year. It will then be possible, in favourable circumstances, to arrange for different religious groups to take part in turn.

b) *Mixed meetings for information purposes.* — We have already spoken of the *active* participation of members of non-Catholic religious bodies at meetings intended to give information to large audiences by means of lectures and documentary *exposés*. In the case of smaller gatherings consisting of persons sufficiently instructed in the apposite fields, one could *make more people participate* and *touch upon problems in greater detail*. In small groups of fixed composition one could more easily and more efficaciously proceed to exchanges of views, to a genuine « ecumenical dialogue. » The same care as has been indicated above as needful should be exercised in the choice of speakers and lecturers.

It should not, however, be thought that meetings of this kind should always be for the purpose of hearing what are, strictly speaking, lectures. The meeting may take the form — and this will not be the least fruitful — of *simple conversations* on a given subject, chosen by general agreement, which will enable both sides to obtain an exact knowledge of the doctrine and practice of their separated brethren in this part of their Christian life. This will usually lead to the conclusion that, when we take life as it actually is, and the actuality of thought in so far as it moulds our lives, our differences are often much less pronounced than they would appear to be if we judge from the way in which they are formulated in the abstract by either side. This would seem to apply to such doctrines as grace, justification and the sanctification resulting therefrom, also to the question of merit, etc.

c) *Mixed meetings to organize work.* — This kind of meeting should be reserved for *very small* groups, otherwise they risk being useless or even giving ground for grave objection. What are here in question, strictly speaking, are study circles which, in practice, can take two principal forms : *circles for Bible study* and *circles for the study of theology.*

N.B. One of the effects — we venture to say beneficial effects — of ecumenical gatherings is to make us realize vividly (save in cases which are happy, but rare, exceptions) our inferiority vis-à-vis our separated brethren, particularly Protestants, in the matter of practical and familiar knowledge of Holy Scripture — this in spite of the progress made by the Biblical Movement among modern Catholics. Far from deterring us from entering upon this field, this humiliating reflection should on the contrary spur us on to buckle to the task ; it can only be of benefit to our normal pastoral ministrations, over and above our specifically ecumenical commitments. The means at our disposal for such work are today more than abundant ; it is for us to make use of them, unafraid, to give up, if need be, for the time being, other activities which might seem to promise more fruitful results on the pastoral plane.

C. *Individual Action.* — « Ecumenical meetings » are not necessarily group meetings. In the domain of the apostolate for Unity there is room for action as individuals which must not be neglected.

a) *Members of the Clergy.* — Such individual action is called for in the first place from the clergy. We have already, in passing, indicated one of the ways of doing this, viz., through the personal contacts of the parish priest and curates with members of the clergy of other religious bodies entrusted with pastoral responsibility within the confines of their parish. We have only spoken of this in so far as previous acquaintanceship with these ministers is a necessary precondition for the judicious and prudent organization of « ecumenical gatherings. » But such contacts are of interest and importance in themselves, independently of all other forms of ecumenical action.

It is the spirit governing such relationships that is most important of all. It is in no way a question of individual conquest, of an effort at personal conversion, but rather of common conversion to that higher standard and to that greater effort which God expects from us in the exercise of our ministry. Christian friendship thus entered upon and assuming here a « sacerdotal » colour, can contribute enormously to the removal of reciprocal prejudice and to the intensification of the ecumenical spirit in ourselves and in the flocks committed to our charge.

What we say of the priest must be said *a fortiori* of the bishop in regard to those who assume, in their respective hierarchies, a responsibility analogous to his own.

b) *The Faithful.* — This individual action, as between person and person, between family and family, gives wide scope to those Catholics who have received a sound religious formation, doctrinal and spiritual ; as is more and more often the case among us in these days. Such Catholics will not fail to ask the advice of a priest with the necessary qualifications as often as they find themselves, as a result of these friendships, faced by some difficult problem.

Another form that this individual apostolate can take is the reception in a Catholic home of boys, girls or others who are foreign in nationality or alien in religion. A good opportunity is thus presented of showing them different aspects of the Church's life and of its social, charitable and other activities. In the course of excursions taken in common, ecumenical instruction can profitably be combined with pleasure.

III. THE CHRISTIAN WITNESS WHICH WE BEAR IN COMMON WITH OUR SEPARATED BRETHREN

1. *Justification and Principles.*

The Ecumenical Council of Christian Churches, as we know, resulted from the fusion of two previous ecumenical movements : one dedicated to the search for agreement on the doctrine and structure of the Church (*Faith and Order*), the other to the growth

in collaboration between all Christians in all the tasks of a social
character which their conscience bids them to undertake (*Life and
Action* or *Practical Christianity*). It is interesting to observe that
the traditional liturgical prayer of the Church makes mention of
this double end. Thus in the prayer appointed for *Thursday in
Easter Week*, we beseech God that all those who have been
regenerated (i.e., reborn to a new life) through the grace of baptism may be *united by faith in their minds and by charity in their
actions*. « Ut renatis fonte baptismatis una sit fides mentium et
pietas actionum. »

It is certain, however, that the interest taken in the Ecumenical
problem by Catholics has for a long time been confined almost
exclusively to matters concerning the *faith* and the hierarchical
structure of the Church, because it is here that those problems
are to be found which most pressingly need solution if the restoration of unity is ever to be achieved. Under the Pontificate of
Pius XII, however, an Instruction by the Holy Office, *Ecclesia
catholica*, which we have already quoted, declared explicitly that
its restrictive clauses did not affect

« mixed meetings in which faith and morals are not dealt with, but thought
is given as to how, by joining forces, those concerned can best defend
the fundamental principles of natural law and of the Christian religion
against the combined efforts of God's enemies, or in which questions are
discussed relative to the restoration of social order and similar matters. »

If it is necessary to have permission from the ecclesiastical authorities to take part in ecumenical meetings at which matters of faith
and morals are discussed, there is no such need so far as this other
kind of meeting is concerned, though care must be taken to avoid

« approving or conceding anything which would not accord with Divine
Revelation or the teaching of the Church, even in social matters » (A.A.S.,
1950, p. 145).

Up to the present, little advantage has been taken of this permission. More is the pity. Particularly in view of the fact that, from
his accession onwards, Pope John XXIII gave ceaseless positive
encouragement to contacts and collaboration with our separated
brethren in all fields which may be considered precisely to be *the
proper sphere of the laity*.

The significance of such collaboration from an ecumenic point
of view is double in character :

1) In the eyes of unbelievers it is evidence of the fundamental
community of faith among all Christians, of their mutual love and

of their desire to be of service to all men whom they regard as brothers ;

2) By intimate social contact in the course of a common activity, Christians of different religious persuasions learn to respect each other and to know each other better, prejudices are overcome, and the desire is increased for a deeper union in laity and hierarchical allegiance.

Care must be taken, however, to ensure that what can properly be called controversial matters of faith are not only excluded normally in all these activities, but are not even occasionally touched on. This is the reason for the warning expressed in the instruction *Ecclesia catholica*.

2. *Various Fields of Collaboration.*

A. *All Forms of Charitable Activity and of Benevolence.* — Catholic relief societies have very often set an example in this matter by coming to the help of populations afflicted by some catastrophe. In Greece, for example, recently, gifts that have thus been made have helped towards the reconstruction of Orthodox churches destroyed or damaged by earthquakes. Similar help was given at Constantinople after the riots of 1955.

In connection with this form of collaboration may be mentioned what is known as « le projet Cullmann. » On the occasion of the Week of Prayer for Unity, collections are made in Catholic circles for Protestant charitable works, and *vice versa*, as a sign of practical brotherly love. Whilst encouraging action of this kind, which, however, can scarcely have a psychological effect unless the gifts go to local charities known to the donors, our preference would be for charitable « activities » carried out in common, since these oblige us to make a gift of ourselves, of our time, of our trouble, not merely of our money. For example one would suggest : visits to the poor and the aged, the organization of a meal in common with them, the carrying out of necessary improvements in their lodgings, etc. One would, however, need to be careful to make these sacrifices for the sake of these poor people themselves, not treating these merely as an excuse for ecumenical activity.

B. *All the Great Problems that are Vital Today* and are often presented on a world-wide scale : *industrial peace, international peace, racial strife, the fight against prostitution, against alcoholism, against illiteracy, economic, cultural, political, religious and missionary development of underdeveloped countries.* No doubt large-scale international organisms, often emanating from the governments concerned, have concerned themselves with these different objectives, but they normally have local ramifications and in any case are in need of men of good will if their plans are to be put into effect.

The Ecumenical Council of Churches has taken all these problems to heart and has appointed *specialized Committees* to deal with them. There are analogous Catholic organizations also in existence. The collaboration of the latter with these Committees, which is greatly to be desired, must be brought about by initiatives taken on the Catholic side. *Almost everything still remains to be done in this so important field of collaboration.* It is obviously all-important that, if such co-operation is to prove effective when opportunities arise in the concrete, the respective institutions or organizations capable of taking action should remain in close, not to say permanent, contact with each other.

4

Psycho-Sociological Situations in Face of Ecumenism

Psycho-Sociology of Ecumenism
in the Near East

by Jean CORBON

Professor of Catechetical Pedagogy, University Saint-Joseph, Beyrouth.
Theologian-Interpreter for the non-Catholic Observers at the Council[1]

The Ecumenical situation in the Near East is characterized by a two-fold sociological fact. On the one hand, Christians belong to different, rigorously structured, ritual communities or « Confessions ; » it is the phenomenon of Confessionalism. On the other hand, beneath their Confessional adherence, the Christians are united daily by human ties no less strong within one family, one profession, one nation. The interplay of this two-fold phenomenon, *ritual and human*, influences relations between the Churches, wherever the real ecumenical problem exists.

For the less informed reader, it may be well to state briefly the principal features of the Confessional geography in the Near East. It seems that the region between the Zagros mountains (eastern

---

1. Born in Paris, 1924, Fth. Jean CORBON holds a Licenciate in Theology and Scripture. From 1958-1961 he was professor of methodology at the Institut des Lettres Orientales at the University of Beyrouth. Since 1963, he holds the professorship of catechetical pedagogy there. He has been theologian-interpreter to the non-Catholic Observers at the Council. He is writing some important books : in Islamology, a Koranic exegesis, Bible and Koran; the study of Biblical pastoral in teaching adults; Ecumenical work : Orthodoxy and Catholicism in the Near East; for community development : animation of a research centre on the « values of civilizations » in the Near East. He has already published many articles and collaborated in important books. These titles of articles show his competence in Near East problems : *Le Ramadan au Caire en 1956* (Mélanges d'Etudes Orientales), *Réflexions sur la mort d'une Eglise* (Proche Orient Chrétien P.O.C.), *Pour un œcuménisme intégral* (P.O.C.), *Le monastère orthodoxe de S. Georges-al-Harf* (P.O.C.), *L'expérience spirituelle de l'Eglise à la lumière de l'A.T.* (« Eglise en plénitude » D.d.B., 1962), *L'œcuménisme au Liban* (Istina), *Les valeurs permanentes de l'Orient arabe* (Développement et Civilisations, 14), *La prière musulmane* (Cahiers de l'Oraison), etc. — Address : Couvent des Dominicaines, rue de Verdun, Beyrouth, LIBAN (Editor's note).

frontier of Iraq) and the Mediterranean on one side, and the Taurus range (southern frontier of Turkey) and the Red Sea on the other side, have always known pluralism, ethnic, linguistic, cultural and religious. This has continued in Christianism both for its wealth and its peril. The difficult balance between diversity and unity has appeared here in the historical geography. The Near East is like the typical land where the promises must be tested. Its choice by God in the history of salvation had surely something to do with its natural vocation in secular history.

The Confessional map in the Near East gradually traced itself from the IV century. From the mother-Church at Jerusalem and its extension sprang up two great centres : Alexandria and Antioch, real poles of church development in their respective continent, both for liturgical and spiritual life and for mission work.

ALEXANDRIA gave birth to the *Coptic* rite, then to the *Ethiopian*. When we speak of rite, we do not mean only liturgical form, but also the far-reaching inspiration of the whole life of a local Church. The rite inspires the liturgy, law, spirituality, theology ; it is a complete style of Church life, founded on an originality of race, tongue, culture and territory. The vicissitudes of history have caused territory, race, tongue and culture to be no longer co-extensive with the rite. The Alexandrine rites have probably been the most protected. They have not emigrated, but immigration has caused Egypt to count among her children Christians from other ritual horizons, especially the Greek-Orthodox since the Hellenes are settled in Egypt from Alexandria.

ANTIOCH is the great ritual metropolis of the East. We know the title of the patriarchs of this region of the Near East : « Antioch and all the East » that is, of all the hinter-land towards eastern Asia. In her strictly Semitic territory, Antioch gave birth to two great ritual families : the Eastern and Western Syrian rites. The Western Syrian family branched out later for dogmatic and political reasons into the *Syro-Orthodox*, *Syro-Catholic* and the *Syro-Maronite* rites ; the Eastern Syrian family formed the branch of the « Church of the East » or Church of Persia (*Nestorians*), and after the union of a few bishoprics with Rome, the *Chaldean* rite or the East Syrian Catholic rite. Speaking of the Near East, we need not allude to the Indian branches of the Church of Antioch.

In the non-Semitic area of the patriarchate of Antioch, their rite passed through Cappadocia to Byzantium and into Armenia ; the *Byzantine* and *Armenian* rites are local adaptations of the liturgy on Antioch. The phenomenon of partial union with Rome since the XVI century has cut these two great ritual families into two ecclesiastical fragments : Greek Orthodox and Greek Catholic, Armenian Orthodox and Armenian Catholic.

To conclude the description of the Confessional geography, we must add two analogous elements which have come to the Near East from foreign imperialisms : the *Latin* rite and *Protestantism*.

Thus we obtain the present situation, the result of mixing different rites on the same territory, whereas originally each one lived independently on the territory in which it had taken root :

Ethiopian community in Ethiopia : 5.000.000 (and 50.000 Cathol.).
Copt-Orthodox community in Egypt :   4.000.000.
Copt-Catholic community in Egypt :   75.000.
Syro-Orthodox community throughout the Near East : 70.000.
Syro-Catholic   »   »   »   »   » :   90.000.
Maronite   »   »   »   »   » : 885.000.
Nestorian   »   »   »   »   » : 160.000.
Chaldean   »   »   »   »   » : 170.000.
Greek-Orthodox   »   »   »   »   » : 583.000.
Greek-Catholic   »   »   »   »   » : 330.000.
Armenian-Orthodox »   »   »   »   » : 760.000.
Armenian-Catholic »   »   »   »   » : 175.000.
Latin   »   »   »   »   » :   ?
Protestant   »   »   »   »   » :   ?

This short article can only set down the facts of the problem. We will do this in two sections ; in the first, we will give the principal re-actions of the Christian communities to the ecclesial and social realities, and in the second, we will point out the big common traits of the community psychology which up to now conditions ecumenical relations.

I. SOCIOLOGICAL RE-ACTIONS

So as to give a survey of the Confessional psychology in the Near East, it may be useful to set down the usual reactions of the Christian communities towards the social realities in which they live.

The Nation.

National sentiment in Near East countries developed during the Ottoman occupation and grew steadily during the Mandatory period after World War I. Christians and Mussulmen united in this struggle for independence ; Arab nationalism, especially, became a common factor besides recourse to foreign powers to achieve it. Today national sentiment may vary according to the country, whether the frontiers settled in 1919 are brought forward into question or not, but it seems that regionalism according to men and economics matters more than ideologies of re-groupment. Whatever may be the future of these re-groupings, it is certain that Christians are not strangers in their own country, and they collaborate effectively in the construction of their respective nations, at least where they are not systematically set aside.

The effective collaboration with non-Christian communities at the same time combines with a conscious solidarity among Christians. The lessons of thirteen centuries cannot be forgotten, and in the end this latent tension should turn into favour of religious pluralism in respect for each group. The solidarity of Christians in civic matters is legitimate but is it a Christian solidarity ? it does not seem to really affect ecclesial reconciliation much. Inversely, Mussulmen need not fear that Ecumenism will become a common front against them. In the measure in which national sentiment becomes stronger in the Near East will it become easier to distinguish sociological and ecclesial adherence ; the first will tend more and more to the rite of the Nation, the second more towards that of relation to the Church.

Professions.

Pluralism and solidarity are to be found in various degrees in each country. Lebanon, in particular, based its administrative structure on Confessional division ; from top to bottom of the scale posts are entrusted proportionally to representatives of each creed. In spite of its limitations, the system is wise and prepares a pluralism of equality. But in the private sector, it is usually a matter of competition. Public opinion is denouncing these groups of Confessional pressure who exploit community feeling for their own ends. The Churches do not escape these pressures. Whatever may be the repercussions of this on ecumenical development, it is sure that this state of affairs is unfavourable to it.

Culture.

The Arab Near East is in full cultural effervescence. It is seeking its own path, confronting for the first time itself and the modern human reality. In its present state of evolution, translation is playing an important part : translation of works but especially of living ideas. Confessional pluralism partly covers cultural pluralism. For example, Protestantism is typically of Anglo-Saxon inspiration. Catholicism is fostered more by French religious and human culture. Greek Orthodoxy is more eclectic : Greece, Russia and the American emigration mingle with Franco-German currents. In the Armenian and Syrian communities where the original inspiration is first, exterior cultural influences are very fully welcomed. There lies a very important phenomenon for Ecumenism, in the measure that an original Near East culture is creating itself, both oriental, essentially Arab, and open to the great world cultures. The Near East has always been an exchange ground. But culture helps Ecumenism in inverse ratio of sheer importation and in direct ratio of assimilation. In the first case, experience ends in a fresh partition in the communities ; in the second, there is intercomprehension in a common implantation.

The Communities.

The word is used here in the sense well known in the East of Tâ ifa or sociological group on a ritual basis, like the « Maronite community » or the « Greek-Orthodox community. » It is interesting to note the constants in the reactions of the communities towards one another.

The simplest case is that of the *Protestant* communities. They are essentially constituted, not by the mission towards non-Christians as the first « missionaries » of the XIX century imagined, but *against* the traditional Churches. They are a protest against certain ecclesiastical deformations : neglect of the Word of God, legalism, liturgical formalism, clericalism. They are firstly « conversionists, » and from time to time they glean a few malcontents from the traditional Churches. Against this attack, Catholics and Orthodox unite in the same reaction, either merely defensive and suspicious, or offensive, from within, taking the positive requests of Protestant proselytism seriously. The lines of strength are easy to see : Orthodox and Catholics never feel their brotherhood so much as before Protestants ; Orthodox and Protestants only unite when rejecting the papacy. More deeply, Protestant reaction reveals pure Orthodoxy which is at the antipodes of the Reformation mentality and which shows how much Protestantism is the direct product of the Western Catholic tradition.

Before the *Orthodox* position, Catholic reactions are more varied. Latins who identify the Catholic Church with their own rite are becoming more and more rare but they are still to be found. They have done much to fix the prejudice that union with Rome means Latinization. In varying degrees, it must be admitted that the other Catholic communities have yielded to the temptation of the Latin prestige. Those who have had the merit of reacting most vigorously are the Greek-Catholics, but the Maronites, Syro-Catholics and Copt-Catholics are veering more and more towards « de-Latinization » in liturgy, law and spirituality. The testimony of Orthodoxy is a powerfully revealing factor to promote an authentic ecumenism : it constantly reminds the Catholic communities that they should be both Catholic and Eastern. The Orthodox world has not yet had proof that one can be completely one and the other. This must come before re-union. The orientations so strongly stressed by Paul VI will need time to become facts ; unity is not uniformity but communion in diversity.

Before the *Catholic* position, the Orthodox re-actions are unanimous ; no one wants Roman centralization. The theologian may be convinced that there is no fundamental divergence of faith, and assert that the problem of the growth of the Eastern Churches has been different but not contradictory to the problem of the Western Church, it no less remains a fact that sociologically these Churches feel no interest in the role of the Bishop of Rome. This statement brings to light a two-fold preliminary to Christian re-union. The Catholic Church has some way to go in making some authentically traditional values actual facts (episcopal collegiality, sense of the local Church). The Eastern Churches need to respond to the new demands of the modern world (unity of magisterium, effective and not merely verbal structuration of the local Church and of the local Churches among themselves). It must also be added that the problem differs according to the Eastern Churches. Those which are open to universalism are certainly better prepared for this « aggiornamento »; those of more marked particularism will have to find other paths in order to discover how to reach communion between all the Churches.

Pastoral.

These new paths may appear to concern the pastoral ministry of the Church. The more clear-sighted among Eastern Christians agree that the most urgent problem today is the *evangelization of Christians* themselves. We know that the atheism that blossoms in a Christian atmosphere is firstly a reaction against certain aspects of the Church. It is in this sense that Protestantism in the Near East is very different from the Reformation movement in the West. It can be retrieved here into unity, if the traditional Churches agree to reform themselves, which has a slightly different meaning to what it had in the XVI century. In a wider sense, it is the symptom of a need for re-evangelization of the modern man in the Near East.

The same question arises for all Christians who are gradually becoming aware of their *missionary responsibilities*. Christian division is a preliminary to be solved. Otherwise, the message and the vitality of Christ will always remain hidden from the Moslem world.

It is also certain that it is in daily pastoral circumstances that friction usually occurs between Christian communities and accentuates division. Baptisms, weddings, funerals, Youth and Adult Movements, prerogatives of hierarchs, are the habitual moments of difficulty between communities. We all know that the realities of faith have little to do with these jousts ; the sociological weight of the Churches tells very heavily.

II. CONFESSIONAL PSYCHOLOGY

At the time of Pope Paul VI's pilgrimage, and his meeting with the Patriarch Athenagoras I, a Maronite parish priest in Lebanon went to visit the Greek Orthodox parish priest of the same village. « The time has come, » he said, « for us to be reconciled, to pray more together, and to collaborate in serving the Christians of our village. » The Orthodox parish priest, a kindly old man, listened without a word, and said at last : « I am old, I shall not live very much longer. Listen, brother, let me end my days in freedom. »

These few words describe the psychological atmosphere which still seems to dominate in the Near East. It could be summed up in one word : *mistrust*.

This may be surprising, since real causes for mutual fear are rare. But we forget that a collective memory is tenacious, especially over wrongs. Past centuries were filled with reasons for mistrust. It is often sincerely alleged by Catholics that the declarations of popes and councils have respected the Eastern Churches. They do not know that these declarations were never put into practice. Hence these spontaneous interpretations which are disconcerting : Vatican Council II, say some Orthodox, is only new Roman tactics to annex Orthodoxy ; and they compare Paul VI's advances to the manœuvres of a few priests who would take advantage of the weakness of some Orthodox parish to transfer it to Catholicism.

It is certain that the first awareness to be achieved in the Near East is that of the past, even if it is not to dispute or attribute blame about it. We must understand that the past has inflicted wounds which are not yet healed. It is not the moment for declarations but for facts. The first fact for a Church is to exist, or in psychological terms, *to have some worth*. This legitimate and essential need has been so frustrated that all the traditional Christian communities (Orthodox and Catholic) are on the same psychic level here. The resulting vindication expresses itself in many ways on both sides, but this must be appreciated in order to measure all the distance between vindication and reconciliation.

It must be admitted too that this complex is shared by the Catholic communities themselves, and no one can blame them, unless perhaps those whose Latin sufficiency has never been tampered with. We will never appreciate sufficiently what thirteen centuries of Mussulman domination may have spoiled in the oriental Churches, nor the heroism which has preserved them essentially intact. These Churches are on the threshold of a new era, just as the nations where they dwell are at the dawn of an independence never yet known in history. We must apply to the Near East the general sociological law of the ecumenical movement : ecumenism is a spiritual movement which fits in vitally at a certain level of integral social development. To an economy of mere subsistence there corresponds a fairly particularist sense of the social group. Fresh air only reaches blocked passages slowly, and when they are strong enough. Ideas only reach peninsulas when they have refreshed a continent. The Near East is neither an island nor a peninsula, but a cross-roads between three continents ; the problem of ideological currents here is not that they arrive too late but to make them penetrate. Time is needed.

One of the most frequent manifestations of the need to have worth, too long frustrated, is the famous *inferiority* complex. Its expressions are subtle, especially the one which strengthens itself by referring to what others think. In recent years complaint has been made of the little game of facets in which Catholics and Orthodox exchange depreciated images. It is enough to declare one position Catholic for the opposite position to be called Orthodox and vice versa. Or else, they start from a systematic description of oppositions to return it caricatured still further. Unconsciously, the procedure is helpful : sides become stronger through opposition, each feels assured of its own value and avoids questioning it. Once more, no one has the monopoly of this safety circuit ; conciliar debates have demonstrated the mechanism within the Catholic Church.

But here we touch a reality which surpasses psychology, we are within the mystery of the Church. In other words, if the two poles as close to one another as are Orthodoxy and Catholicism, so easily oppose one another with more sparks or less, it is because they are inseparable complements to one another. The Near East Orthodox may be irritated by Protestant proselytism, but he will not feel the instinctive emotional reaction that he feels towards his Catholic brother. There is the irritating phenomenon of Catholic proselytism, Uniatism, but it seems to have reached its niche ; the Catholic conscience in general has got beyond the Uniate mentality. And yet the *attraction-repulsion* phenomenon at which Orthodox-Catholic relations waver, remains. Is it not partly rooted in the sub-consciousness of both ? While no Protestant Church lays claim to present the whole of Christian truth, Orthodoxy (by definition) and Catholicism (from conviction) claim to do so. Refraining from any relativist acrobatics, let us simply state that on the plane of religious psychology, there lies an authentic heritage of the One and Undivided Church, which our ancestors of the Middle Ages never lost even in the midst of their most violent quarrels. The humble certitude of being in the authentic Tradition can deviate psychologically into a *superiority* complex. Without looking for the mote in our brother's eye, let us admit that the Catholic side has constructed a fine beam ! Is not the first step towards getting out of the safety circuit mentioned above, to become aware of our own superiority complex ? Experience proves that dialogue loses its heat once the Catholic, without compromising his faith, forgets his self-sufficiency. The same relation is verified in the encounters between Catholics of different communities.

Catholic or Orthodox, Christian psychology reacts fundamentally the same way according to the scale of values of the Christian Mystery. But tonalities, approaches, immediate perceptions can vary according to regions. A Russian Orthodox of French emigration is undoubtedly closer to a Catholic French theologian in the logic of his dialogue than to an Orthodox country priest in Greece. This difference within the two great religious families in the Church can help to explain that in the Near East there exists a common way of taking up the real which will influence ecumenical relations. One of the characteristic traits of behaviour before the real here is the *primacy of the emotional concrete*. This trait appears in the structure of semitic languages and is revealed in all social behaviours. It is also one of the most common causes of misunderstanding and irritation for foreigners who live in the Near East. You have an appointment at 10 o'clock sharp, you go there in a car, but you meet a friend on the way. The primacy of the emotional concrete prompts you to talk to him first of all, taking plenty of time, and offering to drive him wherever he wants to go. Time slips by, the appointment came first in itself, but in actual fact the immediate occasion won, because the friend was there in the concrete, and emotionally, it would be an offence to refuse him. All the situations caused by this primacy of the emotional concrete can be imagined, with all its advantages and hindrances in ecumenical relations. Going to extremes, one could more easily imagine Rome and Moscow re-establishing communion than two neighbouring parishes in an Eastern city.

The constant that stands out is that reconciliation between Orthodox and Catholics is much less a question of principles and faith than of daily and concrete charity. Here we touch the real reason of the division ; if we keep to the word schism, in the past, it is precisely because the reality it expresses is a sin against charity. Once more, « let us love not in word only... » it is not words but deeds that Christian unity in the Near East needs.

One other trait, to mention but one, which seems to condition Christian reconciliation is *attachment to Tradition*. As we said earlier about truth, this attachment can be mixed with psychological attitudes which have nothing Christian about them. We know what details our ancestors in the Middle Ages quarreled about : beards and hair-knots for priests, unleavened bread, Saturday fast, etc. Happily we have got past that ; but the psychological attitude thus expressed may still be latent in each of us. The Spirit is at times breath-taking for our heaviness. Spontaneously we call Tradition what we have seen done, and which may be merely a recent deformation. Some Orthodox say jokingly that one of the safeguards of their Orthodoxy has been the fixity to which their historical conditions have condemned them. The same should be said of the Eastern Catholics who endured the same historical conditionings. It is sometimes said that the East is mystical and the West juridical, without realizing that the little game of facets denounced earlier is in full play. There are Easts as there are Wests. That the Russian or Greek East is spontaneously mystical, is quite possible ; that the Semitic East is so too is undeniable in more aspect than one ; but it is equally certain that the Semitic East is naturally juridical. The strength of the law of social practice, of value everywhere, is re-inforced by the deepest genius of the man in the Near East. What a few years have created is not altered in a few years ; what actually exists has the privilege of law. Now if Christian reconciliation must of necessity bring changes, even on the behaviour level only, the flutter its perspective arouses is understandable. The present conflicting views in the Greek Church illustrate this principle, but in the Near East it could be the same, taking into account the emotional concrete which can more rapidly alter situations. Therefore a wise slowness is necessary to achieve full unity. The history of the Church in the East is eloquent enough to remind us that all precipitations have accentuated divisions instead of effacing them.

To pass from the psychological bark to the heart of the mystery of the Church, it must be added that this comparison of traditions is a *test of Catholicity*, an exigency of intimate metanoia to live the plenitude of the Church more fully. When Pope Paul VI thanked the Armenian Orthodox Patriarch of Jerusalem for all the universal Church owed to Armenian tradition it was not mere courtesy or official compliments. It was a sign and a programme. The fulness of communion to which we are tending under the guidance of the Holy Spirit is much more than an organic adjustment of hierarchies ; it is an exigency of spiritual experience by which the whole Tradition of the Church must be lived within a particular tradition. As the local Church is the sacrament of the universal Church, so must its spiritual tradition manifest the total Tradition of the Church. There lies the real theological difficulty beyond the psychological limits in which Tradition lives. As long as we remain in mutual ignorance and defensive mistrust, this theological progress is practically impossible. On the other hand, to rush into an exterior reconciliation while spiritual foundations are still shaky, is to build upon sand, and storms will surely arise and overthrow it.

These few reflections are only some approaches of the psycho-sociology of ecumenism in the Near East. We need to be more aware of what can be called the « sociological religion » of many Christians, and which is without doubt the most stubborn obstacle to an authentic community of faith, liturgy and charity, but this can hardly be set down in a short article. If this one has succeeded in drawing attention to the importance of the psycho-sociological conditioning in ecumenical work and in catechesis especially, it will have attained its end in a certain degree.

BIBLIOGRAPHICAL NOTE

Pierr RONDOT, *Les Chrétiens d'Orient*, ed. J. Peyronnet and Cie. 8, rue de Furstenberg, Paris VI, 1955.

Selim ABOU, *Le bilinguisme arabe-français au Liban*, Presses Universitaires de France, 1962.

Jean CORBON, *L'œcuménisme au Liban*, in the review *Istina*, 1963, pp. 7-38. — *Les valeurs permanentes de l'Orient arabe*, in the review *Développement et Civilisations*, 14 (1963), pp. 101-112. (19, Place du Marché St-Honoré, Paris Ier).

Aspects of Ecumenism
among Orthodox

by Élie MÉLIA

Rector of the Georgian Orthodox parish of Saint Nina, Paris[1]

I. LEGITIMACY OF A PSYCHO-SOCIOLOGICAL APPROACH TO ECUMENISM

Examining the causes of the disruption of unity in the Christian Churches, a distinction has been suggested between the purely doctrinal factors and those which are not theological. Among the latter, one has been called differences of mentality. It may be pointed out that a mentality is à priori difficult to determine, since it is defined as that which is precisely *subjacent* to the procedure of thought or to moral behaviour. If it is not easy to assess an historic figure, how much harder is it when considering a people or a race, and how the task becomes complicated for multi-national religious settings who claim universalism !

Far from being the cause of the disruptions in Christianity since the V century, differences of mentality, as positive facts of human existence, are factors of increased richness and depth for ecclesial cohesion ; we must distinguish between unity and standard uniformity. Unity in diversity is the law of the Church, of her profound being, reflection of the Divine Trinity.

It remains true that we must take into consideration the diversity of mentalities in order to explain the « tensions » which, in the course of history and even from the Apostolic age, have influenced

---

1. The archpriest Elie MÉLIA is at present the rector of the Georgian Orthodox parish of Saint Nina in Paris. He took his Licenciate in theology at the Institut de théologie orthodoxe Saint Serge. He contributes to the periodical « Le Messager Orthodoxe » published in Paris. Address: 24, rue d'Orléans, Neuilly-sur-Seine, FRANCE. (Editor's note).

the collective conscience of the *Una Sancta*, and precisely the general unifying tension special to the Church.

How is it that this fundamentally unifying exigence of the Church has become split up into Confessions of faith and into respective rival structures ?

The limits of this article prevent examination of the doctrinal divergences which, in the long run, are the only serious ones. Here, we can merely disengage some « psycho-sociological » elements of the ecumenical present and future, in the perspective of re-unification.

In this kind of statement, criticism of the action of different Confessions in certain circumstances is inevitable ; if each one does not linger over these, but on the contrary, strives after ecumenical ignoring of even the most well-founded grievances, these criticisms will give no offence, they will even be of use for a better knowledge of the difficulties to be overcome.

As Our Lord Himself said, the Church is in the world but not of it (Jo., XVII, 11-14). We are right therefore, to consider, on one side, this aspect of the Church fitting into historical and sociological actuality, whilst asserting that there remains an aspect of the Church which preserves Her inherent unity and sanctity, *Eph.*, V, 27, which leaves sin no chance of victory. The *notae Ecclesiae* never cease to be existent in the world. We cannot develop this apparent paradox here, but in any case, there is no harm in declaring the « states » of a psycho-sociological difficulty between the different Christian confessions without being accused of sacrilege, it being freely admitted that the blame must be shared.

The historical facts at the base of our observations may seem too distant to some to have any implications now. Nevertheless we all have in us the weight of our historical heritage as we have biological heredity ; our conscience is influenced by it in no small degree. It is particularly true for the peoples of Eastern Europe, where the Orthodox are most numerous, in countries where the sociological evolution was relatively slow until recent years, and who have adopted a Christian confession whose catechesis is largely founded on Tradition. It must be stressed that if the study of the past : history of the Councils, patrology... is chiefly a privilege of men of the Church, these latter, until modern times, have formed not only the religious, but also the cultural and sociological, frame of Orthodox peoples.

II. HISTORICAL CONTENTION BETWEEN
THE CATHOLIC CHURCH
AND THE GREEK ORTHODOX CHURCH

The psycho-sociological contention between « Catholics » and « Orthodox » is very old. It first arose between « Latins » and Greeks, for at that time these two races were the undisputed leaders of the two Churches.

1. *Intentional Depreciation of the Byzantine Empire.*

The first psycho-sociological fact affecting the ecumenical situation and which concerns the beginning of its deterioration was a negative one : the progressive mutual disaffection, the weakening of reciprocal relations between the two halves of Christianity which, except for the Monophysite schism, remained undivided for the first thousand years of our era.

Perhaps the first important manifestation of this process is visible in Charlemagne's efforts to lessen the Byzantine part of the Roman Empire, with a view towards the imperial crown for himself. One of the means used was to question the purity of faith among Byzantines ; the theologians of Charlemagne's court made a kind of ideological banner out of the phrase « Filioque. »

It is but fair to recall that the conflicts between Rome and Byzantium, fairly frequent at the great Councils of the first eight Christian centuries, had accustomed minds and hearts to a certain separateness of Westerns from Easterns, but the dynamism of unity had always prevailed.

Behind the gulf thus created, augmented by the difficulties of communication due to the Norman invasions in the West and Arab invasions in the East, the two halves of Christianity developed along their own lines, regardless of the other. Things drifted apart from then, and the best spiritual efforts on both sides remained fruitless for the other. It was in this ecumenically fragile situation that the fatal interview between Cardinal Humbert de Moyenmoutier and the Patriarch Michael Caerularius took place in 1054. Disputes between Latin and Byzantine theologians now continued on a straight front whereas there had been till then a certain interpenetration.

The confirmed division at the top sent out roots more and more widely, implanting reflexes of loyalty to a side, which finally ended in a *confessionalism* which became a psycho-sociological constant in people's minds for centuries. And yet, in spite of this division, Christianity remained one when facing the same perils for their faith, like the expansion of Islam, a religion which by its very structure confused the temporal with the religious. The advance of Islam, irresistible at first, was checked fairly quickly. But having conquered the whole of the northern shores of Africa and Asia Minor, Islam cut Christianity off from Africa and Asia, delaying its missionary growth in these directions, while the North received the Western mission among the Germanic peoples, and the Slavonic peoples received the Byzantine missions.

2. The Crusades.

Then Providence offered divided Christians an opportunity : the Crusades. We are far from approving the use of force in religious matters. But at that epoch, political and social life, not yet distinct domains in themselves, were inconceivable without religion inter-mingled. Men had no other ideological stimulants to guide them in the complexity of historical facts and interests. Things being as they were, the crusades were at least an ecumenical or interconfessional opportunity. Orthodox and Catholics could work together in a common cause : to break the Mussulman blockade. To achieve this, what they had in common, the Christian faith and the desire to spread it throughout the world, should have been their great motive ; they needed an anxiety for the Church as a whole. Unfortunately the political side took the lead from the start both in the East and West.

The irreparable happened during the fourth Crusade by the capture and looting of Constantinople in 1204, and the setting up over the ruins of its empire of a Latin Eastern Empire which lasted 50 years. The Latins were responsible for the fall of the Byzantine empire and for what followed : centuries of Turkish Mussulman domination.

The collapse of the imperial dream is no longer a political reality. But the results of the historical disaster can still be felt.

3. Councils of Union.

Paradoxically enough at first sight, resentment in the religious domain was fed by the very attempts at re-union made at the

Councils of Lyons in 1274, and of Florence in 1439. There again, the meetings were failures on both sides.

On the Roman side, doctrinal incomprehension was complete ; there was no question of dialogue, but merely of reducing the schismatics to submission. On the Byzantine side, it was only a political venture imposed by the government to try and save the Empire by obtaining military aid, no more than that, from the West by means of religious concessions. Possibilities for negotiation were limited, and facts very minutely circumscribed ; on the one hand, in the West, only the papacy took any real interest in Byzantium, and on the other, Byzantium had nothing politically or economically to offer to the Western monarchs.

Modern Orthodox theologians always insist on the error, from the Orthodox point of view, of these attempts, which have proved the justness of Orthodox ecclesiology based on the unanimity of the entire ecclesiastical body and not on the episcopal collegiality alone, this unanimity being made concrete by the « receptio » (tacit acceptance by the Church as a whole) of Council decisions. In both cases, the « reception » question was soon clear ; apart from those who were actually present at the unionist Councils, no one, in the hierarchy nor in the laity, agreed to ratify the terms of agreement too hastily drawn up. Most of those who signed the documents abandoned interest on the first opportunity.

Unionist councils have thus become theological ground illustrating by contrast, Orthodox ecclesiology. This forms no small part of Orthodox catechesis.

4. *Uniatism.*

The contention between Rome and the Greek Church is further fostered by the *Uniate* question, that is, a Church policy seeking to set up a Greek community, identical in rite to the Orthodox Church, but adopting an entirely and strictly Roman Catholic doctrine. This problem arises in several Orthodox Churches, and we will study it later in connection with the Russian Church, since it is in that area that the problem arose and has reached maximum development. Suffice it to say here that, if this Greek community of « Uniates » is very small, it is supported by the enormous power of the entire Roman Catholic Church, while the Greek Church is reduced to its local resources, given the Orthodox ecclesiastical structure. Hence the anxiety of the Greek Orthodox hierarchy. It is quite different for the Russian Orthodox colossus as we shall see.

It looks as if the Uniates block the ecumenical perspective in Greece in the hierarchy and among the people, at the official level and in the psycho-sociological reality.

III. HISTORICAL CONTENTION BETWEEN
THE CATHOLIC CHURCH
AND THE RUSSIAN ORTHODOX CHURCH

The difficulty between the Catholic Church and the Russian Orthodox Church seems slighter. The colossus of Orthodoxy is a young Church on whom history weighs less heavily.

Catholicism and Orthodoxy in Russia and the Ukraine faced one another in the XVI century over the Orthodox inhabitants of the Grand Duchy of Lithuania definitely under Poland since 1569, and of Galicia or West Ukraine which then came within the frontiers of the kingdom of Poland.

The Orthodox relied, in the measure compatible with loyalty to their sovereigns, on the protection of the Muscovite state. On the spiritual plane, the Orthodox referred to the authority of the ecumenical patriarch (Constantinople); the latter enjoyed privileges recognized by the Polish state nominating or confirming the metropolitan of Kiev and Galicia who held the primacy among the bishops of these regions.

Under pressure from the Polish state, and the Catholic hierarchy there, pressure exerted for nearly a century already, the upper hierarchy of the Orthodox in Poland was led to promulgate union with Rome during the last decade of the XVI century, and in the proportion of four bishops (including the metropolitan) against two. Union was concluded on the following basis : canonical structure, liturgical usages, civil privileges recognized by the State before the act of union were safeguarded, in exchange for recognition of the universal canonical authority of the pope, and all the Roman Catholic doctrine without any restriction.

The act of union was solemnly proclaimed at the Council of Brest in 1596 ; present at it were the four bishops who were abandoning Orthodoxy and the Catholic prelates of Poland. The Orthodox, debarred from the Council, in spite of their efforts to obtain invitations, met together in the same city in another Council, in which assembled two distinct circles, one made up of two Greek metropolitans sent by the patriarch of Constantinople and the two local bishops who had remained faithful, and the other, of chosen representatives of the Orthodox population. In the name of the two Councils the two hierarchies mutually condemned each other. A bitter struggle began then between the two « Christianities. » On the Catholic side, the ideological struggle was led by the Polish Jesuits : sermons, public organized « disputes, » books, especially schools and personal activity towards outstanding Orthodox figures. Catholic propaganda enjoyed the support of the Polish state whose legislation restricted the rights of the Orthodox population. Immediately deprived of many churches and much ecclesiastical property, the Orthodox managed to organize themselves. Led on by emulation and the minority complex, they built schools and churches, and printed books ; moreover, they succeeded in organizing the laity into missionary confraternities. This was a thrilling moment of creative adaptation to an historical situation unfavourable to their faith. It may be said without fear of exaggeration that the strictly ecclesiastical intellectual movement, and school instruction (medium and higher) in Russia sprung from this activity of self-defence.

Later, the historical situation changed with the consolidation of the modern Russian state, and from persecuted, the Orthodox became persecutors in their turn. In the age-old struggle, there have been martyrs who were canonized from both sides.

The unfortunate populations living on the fringe between Poland and Russia passed more than once from one confession to the other en bloc, under pressure, concerted alas, from rival Churches and States. The most recent is due to the intervention of the Soviet police system to liquidate the Uniate hierarchy of West Ukraine in favour of the Orthodox hierarchy ; the Orthodox who are aware of the fact can but deplore it.

Since these unhappy events the words : *unia* (Slavonic form of the Latin word unio), *uniate* (corresponding adjective) and *uniatism* are banished words in the Orthodox conscience. There is no exaggeration in saying that comparison of the two Churches on the ground of uniatism has created a psychological complex both in the Orthodoxy hierarchy and population which must be got over before ecumenical relations can be established between Catholicism and Orthodoxy.

As it was inaugurated in Poland in the XVI century, the *unia* was merely an enterprise of Catholic proselytism, a devise « to measure » made to draw Orthodox away from their Church. Proselytism appears to the Orthodox as the negation of ecumenism. This feeling is certainly a constant of the Orthodox religious conscience, and is a psycho-sociological fact of very general diffusion. The

Orthodox delegates to ecumenical meetings have always made
renunciation of proselytism the touch-stone of the sincerity of ecumenism, and a condition of their participation in the ecumenical
movement.

New Attitudes.

This basic ecumenical exigency has been understood on the
Catholic side by outstanding men in different ways, like Cardinal
Mercier who encouraged with his authority the conversations at
Malines with the Anglicans, and Abbé Couturier who gave the
real impetus to the Week of Prayer for Christian Unity, which
has spread all over the world, and unites all Christian confessions
in common supplication.

More important still : the spirit which ruled uniatism in its
beginnings and long after, seems to have altered ; we can conclude
this from the vigorous proposals of the « unitate » patriarch Maxi-
mos IV at Vatican Council II and many other occasions. The
communities of Eastern tradition in union with Rome can play an
ecumenical role, like all the Churches. They can do so from within
Roman Catholicism, among the enormous crowd of their brethren
of Western tradition, showing that they have a liturgical tradition,
and in some measure an ecclesiological tradition, very close to
Orthodoxy. As for ecumenical activity with Orthodox Churches,
the uniate Churches can only exercise it in so far as they resist the
temptation to proselytism. It must be added that with the Uniates,
the Orthodox authorities retaliate with counter-proselytism.

IV. THE ECUMENICAL SITUATION
IN OTHER ORTHODOX CHURCHES

The Uniate problem exists also in the *Church of Roumania*, the
largest numerically after the Russian Orthodox Church. The question
arose in Roumanian territory long occupied by Austro-Hungarians
who favoured union with Rome.

After World War I, the Orthodox had their revenge. Besides,
a regime of non-separation of the State and the Church of Roumania hardly permitted the Church, had she wished it, to get free
from the national political assimilation followed up by the State in
these regions. The new Communist regime has overturned the whole
question by an official separation of Church and State, which in
reality amounts to systematic persecution of all religions.

The Orthodox Church of Serbia is caught up in the ethnic and political quarrel with Serbs mostly Orthodox, and Croats mostly Catholic ; the two peoples, along with the Catholic Slovenes and other ethnic elements, were welded into one State, Jugoslavia, after World War I. The Serbs were predominant until World War II. As soon as they were able, the Croats broke away and undertook to liquidate physically the Serbian minority who had emplanted themselves in their country ; the Catholic local clergy had their part of responsibility, at least in the sense, that they let this happen, even when they had some influence. That at least is the grievance put forward by the Orthodox Serbs.

The ancient *Church of Georgia* is also faced with the ecumenical problem. According to an old tradition of tolerance the Orthodox majority of Georgians lived peacefully with a small minority of Georgian Catholics and a larger minority of Armenian Monophysites settled in the country ; the same tolerance extended to Mussulmen and Jews. But it was mere co-habitation, with no suggestion of mutual relations. Orthodox Georgia also is neighbour to Monophysite Armenia. In the VI century, the two Christianities were united in Monophysism for some time, but the Georgian Church righting herself, there was a strong Chalcedonian reaction : ideological expurgation of liturgical texts, mutual animosity.

The *Patriarchate of Antioch*, Syria and Lebanon, has its own problems from its existence in a Mussulman setting whose ethnic element is connatural to it. For Christianism took root among the Arabs centuries before the appearance even of Islamism. Besides that, next to Orthodox Arabs live the Maronites in union with Rome, many Monophysite Armenians and a few Protestants. Bringing these together on an ecumenical basis, even a provisional one while awaiting the plenitude of unity, would allow fruitful activity in the Christian testimony before Islam.

Ecumenical effort is particularly urgent in the tiny but honoured *Patriarchate of Jerusalem*, principal guardian of the Holy Places. The dissensions between the different Christian communities, fighting, sometimes coming to blows, to clip off a few inches or a few minutes from ancient privileges inherited from the Byzantine empire, or bought from Turkish sultans, are a disgrace to the Christian conscience, especially in ecumenical activity, and before the Moslem world, disdainful spectator at these degrading squabbles.

V. THE ORTHODOX DIASPORA
IN WESTERN EUROPE AND IN AMERICA

A fresh phenomenon forms a psycho-sociological reality which has a general bearing on Orthodoxy in facing Christianity of Western tradition and the problems of the modern world.

The traditionally Orthodox countries have come late into the world of affairs ; four centuries of Turkish domination kept them apart, with the exception of the Russian Empire. Then, all except Greece, fell under Communist rule and have been prevented from shouldering their own responsibilities. A persecution as wide-spread as it was fierce reduced the Orthodox Churches, like all the religions in Communist countries, to so many « ghettos. » Freedom of worship is hardly tolerated inside the churches. All social activity is strictly forbidden, as is all prayer and preaching outside the church precincts, and catechesis for children under 17 years of age. Personal faith is hunted down by individual coercion.

It is, therefore, when dispersed in the super-industrialized countries of the West, North America and Western Europe, that the Orthodox conscience comes into free contact with the problems of these lands with a Catholic or Protestant majority.

There is no question of giving statistics here or of a sociological study of the Orthodox populations in these countries. The phenomenon we are considering is recent and in process of evolution.

The Orthodox in North America number several millions ; sooner or later they will form one autonomous Church whose entrance into the inter-Orthodox field will surely introduce a new psycho-sociological element, which could eventually contribute towards a better understanding of Western Christianity from within, from a similar field of action. So far this is only a hope, but one that is taking shape ; a Standing Committee has been constituted to co-ordinate the activity of the various jurisdictions in general, and later to unify these jurisdictions on the plane of the internal structure of the Church.

In Western Europe, there are only a few hundred thousands Orthodox scattered in different countries. The activity of the élite counts all the more. In the ecumenical domain, there is the Institut de Théologie Orthodoxe Saint-Serge, where the professors have managed to instil and develop an ecumenical « mentality » in the theologically thinking élite of the considerable Russian emigration, and who have held the indispensable role of reliable Orthodox questioners in the ecumenical dialogue in its beginnings and afterwards. The Association Chrétienne des Étudiants Russes (émigrés) has done the same in larger circles.

An Anglo-Russian Confraternity, the Fellowship of St. Alban and St. Sergius, has developed an ecumenical work between Orthodox and Anglicans, with the approval of high Anglican authorities and of the professors of the Institut de Théologie S. Serge.

*

* *

Under the auspices of the ecumenical See in Europe and America, and especially under the guidance of the present Patriarch, whose pontificate will leave its mark on modern Orthodoxy, the Church of the Greek diaspora has also engaged in the ecumenical dialogue. The primatial See of Orthodoxy has been one of the initiators of ecumenical dialogue, as is proved by the encyclical issued in January 1920 addressed to the heads of the Churches, and it has never ceased supporting with its authority Orthodox participation in important ecumenical meetings. This attitude is a constant in the policy of the Ecumenical See and which befits its primatial vocation.

All the great Orthodox Churches, except the Greek, are now behind the Communist Iron Curtain ; this fact prevents them from developing a normal activity and giving free testimony in the ecumenical domain as in many others. But even this will not limit the ecumenical horizon of Orthodoxy, for Orthodoxy is not held in check by the moment of organization and juridical structure ; its genius reaches far beyond its social aspect. On the other hand, the style of Orthodox ecclesial action is extremely personal. Hierarchs and priests eager for the ecumenical cause do much to inculcate it among believers in the catechetical activity inherent to their function and their spiritual authority. As the Confessional loyalty of the Orthodox refers more to the rectitude of doctrine implicating the quest for divine Truth than to the ecclesiastical Magisterium, the testimony of theologians and thinkers recognized as fully authorized has a sure influence.

It is in this spirit of prophetical testimony more than on the plan of structure that we must think of the meeting desired by H.H. Athenagoras I with H.H. Paul VI in the Holy Land. It was one of these gestures which take root and direct the collective conscience of the Church of God.

CONCLUSION

One last important thought may serve as conclusion : Orthodox Christianity is at a moment of crisis. Nearly all the great Churches are being assailed by « the gates of hell ; » some for more than forty years, others since World War II. All « structured » ecclesial activity, all social activity, be it only testimony, is absolutely forbidden by the Communist State, except the testimony of blood and the longer one of prisons, concentration camps or Communist re-education. No one knows, under these conditions, how much, in what, or how this state of things will alter these Christian Churches which constitute three quarters of the Orthodoxy.

This brings once more into question the picture of the ecumenical situation in the Orthodox world as we have tried to describe it. But is it not a general ecumenical problem ? In spite of relentless repression, cries of anguish are reaching the West, these Christianities preserved by God in their freedom, not in a bleeding participation with their brethren who are visited by Christ crucified. There is a more poignant cry still : the silent appeal. To hear this silence is perhaps the most probing ecumenical test of our time. at any rate it is the most urgent duty.

The Child's Conception of His Religious Identity

by David ELKIND

Child Study Center, University of Denver [1]

Every child who is exposed to religious teaching eventually arrives at an understanding of what it means to belong to a particular religious group i.e., a conception of his religious identity. The question arises, however, as to whether this conception of religious identity is entirely due to the effects of religious instruction or whether its formation is determined, at least in part, by maturational factors. According to the Swiss psychologist, Jean Piaget, for example, conceptions develop in a necessary sequence of stages that are related to age. At each developmental level, in Piaget's view, the form of thought is determined by endogenous factors whereas the content of thought is determined by experience. Piaget, however, has never explored the growth of religious conceptions and the influence of maturation in their development remains to be demonstrated.

It was the need for such a demonstration that led the present writer to study the growth of religious identity conceptions among children of different faiths. Three investigations were carried out, one with Jewish (Elkind, 1961), one with Catholic (Elkind, 1962) and one with Congregational Protestant (Elkind, 1963) youngsters. If Piaget's view of conceptual development holds for religious conceptions, then one might expect a similarity between the forms of thinking but differences in the content of thought for the three denominational groups. In general the results of the studies were in agreement with the Piaget position and the development of religious identity conceptions seemed to mirror both the influence of endogenous maturational and of exogenous, environmental factors. The purpose of the present paper is to summarize the results of the three investigations and to elaborate on some of their implications for religious education.

---

1. Address : « Child Study Center, » University of Denver, Denver, U.S.A.

Method of these Studies.

Before summarizing the results of the studies, however, a brief description of the method by which they were obtained may help orient the reader for what is to come. The method employed was the semi-clinical interview devised by Piaget (1929). It will be recalled that this method requires a set of novel questions — designed to elicit spontaneous thought — which serve as the starting point for an interview type discussion aimed at clarifying the child's initial responses. The questions used in the religious identity studies were formulated on the assumption that such an identity consists of at least four components : a) a conception of the extent of membership in the child's religious group ; b) a conception of the external signs by which religious group members may be recognized; c) a conception of the common property or properties shared by all religious group members and finally d) a conception of the possibility of multiple (non-religious) group membership.

In order to explore the child's thought in each of these four areas of conceptualization, the following six questions were devised. Of these questions two dealt with the extent of religious group membership : a) are you a ...., is your family ...., are all boys and girls in the world .... ? and b) can a cat or a dog be a .... ? To disclose the child's awareness of external signs of religiosity the following questions was asked: c) how can you tell a person is a .... ? Of the remaining three questions two dealt with the properties common to all members of a particular religious group : d) what is a .... ? and e) how do you become a .... ? The final question dealt with the problem of multiple group membership : f) can you be an American and a .... at the same time ? These questions were the starting point for a discussion in which the examiner encouraged the child to amplify and clarify his answers.

Close to eight hundred children participated in the investigations and with the exception of some of the Protestant children all the subjects were individually interviewed by the writer. Of the 790 children seen, 210 were Jewish, 280 were Catholic and 300 were Congregational Protestant. The Jewish children ranged in age from 5-11 : the Catholic children from 6-12 and the Protestant children from 5-14. With the exception of the 5-6 year old subjects among the Protestant children there were at least thirty children at each age level within the age ranges indicated.

The results of the interviews were evaluated by means of Piaget's (1929) criteria for determining a true developmental sequence.

These criteria were : a) uniformity of responses among children at one or more adjacent age levels ; b) the presence of adherences (remnants of ideas appropriate to young children among the older children) and anticipations (suggestions of ideas appropriate to older children among the younger subjects) ; c) movement with age in the direction of more abstract and adult-like conceptualization. All of these criteria were met by the replies given by each denominational group and the replies were therefore classed according to developmental stages. In what follows each stage will be taken up first from the points of view of the four components of religious identity conceptualization and then from the point of view of denominational group differences.

STAGE I (USUALLY AGE 5-7)

At the first stage children had a global, undifferentiated conception of their religious identity. These youngsters knew that denominational terms referred to persons and that such terms related to the God concept. But when they were forced, by the examiner's questions, to break down this global conception and to state its particular referents, they chose at random among national, racial and ethnic qualities. This global, undifferentiated quality of thinking permeated all four components of religious identity conceptualization.

Extent of Denominational Group Membership.

Children at the first stage already had an idea that denominational terms were not all inclusive categories but, when they were forced to rationalize these ideas by the examiner's questions, they erected racial, national and geographic boundaries.

Bob (6-5). Are all boys and girls in the world Catholic ? « No. » Why not ? « Some are Irish and some are Russian. »

Lin (5-10). Are you Jewish ? « Yes. » Is your family Jewish ? « Yes, well all except my dog, he's a *French* poodle. »

First stage children's awareness of the limited inclusiveness of denominational terms was also shown by their response to the « dog and cat » question. As with the first question, however, their rationalization of this limited inclusiveness revealed their confusion as to the specific referents of denominational terms.

Lee (6-2). Can a dog or cat be a Catholic ? « No. » Why not ? « They are not a person, they are animals. » How are animals different from people ? « They walk on four legs. »

Mar (5-1). Can a dog or a cat be a Protestant ? « No. » Why not ? « Because it's a dog. » But why can't it be a Protestant ? « It goes bow wow. »

It is clear from these replies that first stage children judge that a particular denominational term did not refer to all persons nor to any animals. First stage children were, however, unable to correctly rationalize or explain their judgements.

External Signs of Religious Group Membership.

In general first stage children had little or no idea as to how a Protestant, Catholic or Jew might be recognized. They either said that they did not know or gave fanciful answers :

Bob (6-3). How can you tell a person is Catholic ? « I don't know. »

Hal (5-0). How can you tell a person is Protestant ? « The way they talk. » How do you mean ? « They have a little black cup sorta. »

These replies gave further evidence of first-stage-children's confusion regarding even the most concrete referents of a denominational term. This confusion was present despite the fact that these children knew the term applied to a limited number of persons and not to animals.

The Common Property
Connoted by Denominational Terms.

The replies to questions dealing with the property common to denominational group members complemented those already obtained. Once more the young children demonstrated their awareness that denominational terms referred to people but also their confusion about specific referents of the terms.

Jay (6-1). What is a Catholic ? « A person. » How is he different from a Protestant ? « I don't know. »

Sid (6-3). What is a Jew ? « A person. » How is a Jewish person different from a Catholic person ? « Cause some people have black hair and some people have blonde. »

A new facet of denominational conceptions was revealed by children's answers to the question about becoming a member of the group. Replies to this question indicated that even at the first stage children already associated denominational terms with the God concept.

Lon (6-1). How do you become Catholic ? « God makes you it. »

Tom (6-1). How do you become Jewish ? « God makes you Jewish. »

First stage children knew that a denominational term pertained to God but they regarded God as the « Maker » of their denomination as if it were some real object or quality.

Awareness of Multiple Group Membership.

Replies to the question regarding multiple group membership made it at once clear that the first-stage-children did not distinguish between religious and non-religious class designations. And, as in the answers to the previous question, they displayed a kind of nominal realism and seemed to believe that denominational terms had physical existence. Consequently these children argued that multiple group membership was impossible for physical reasons, namely, that one thing couldn't be two things at the same time.

Lea (6-2). Can you be a Catholic and an American at the same time ? « No. » Why not ? « I don't know. » Are you a Catholic ? « Yes. » Are you an American ? « No. »

Ed (6-12). Can you be a Jew and an American at the same time ? « No. » Why not ? « You can't have two (names). »

For these children there was both a lack of differentiation between national and religious designations but also a reification of the terms. As one child expressed it, he could be both at the same time « only if we move. » At the first stage, then, the conception of religious identity was global and undifferentiated without clear awareness of the specific referents of denominational terms.

Denominational Group Similarities and Differences.

Despite the quite different backgrounds and experiences of the children, the uniformity of responses at this age level was striking. There were, nevertheless, group differences even at this early stage. For one thing the Protestant children were far behind both the Catholic and the Jewish children in awareness of denominational group membership. This may be due, in part, to the fact that the term Protestant is a second order (including many subclasses) concept whereas the terms « Catholic » and « Jewish » are both first order concepts. Inasmuch as second order concepts are more difficult to learn than those of the first order, this conceptual difficulty might account for the identity lag among Protestant children. It should be said, however, that when Protestant youngsters were asked whether they were « Congregational » (a first order concept) they were equally at sea. The delay in the Protestant child's awareness of his denomination is thus probably not entirely due to difficulty in conceptualizing it. In addition this delay may reflect a fundamental difference in the age of onset of religious education between the denominational groups. In this regard it needs also to be commented that at this age level it was the Catholic and Jewish children who displayed the largest reservoir of religious knowledge.

STAGE 2 (USUALLY AGES 7-9)

By the age of 7-9, some rather remarkable progress was made in the conceptualization of religious identity. This progress can best be measured in comparison with what was known at the first stage. In contrast to the first-stage-child who knew only that the denominational terms referred to persons, the second-stage-child knew *what* persons were designated. The second-stage-child accomplished this differentiation because he had abstracted certain concrete referents, primarily actions, characteristic of different denominational groups. It was the abstraction of concrete referent properties of denominational terms that was the outstanding characteristic of the second stage.

Extent of Denominational Group Membership.

The awareness of the limits of denominational group membership among second-stage-children was reflected in their spontaneous use of other denominational terms in response to the first question.

Hal (7-8). Are all boys and girls in the world Catholic ? « No. » Why ? « Some are Jews and some are Protestant. » Anything else ? « No. »

Paul (7-3). Are all boys and girls in the world Protestant ? « No. » Why not ? « Because some are Catholic and some are Jewish. » How do you know ? « They live in my block. »

Answers to the dog-cat question revealed a similar differentiation only now with respect to concrete behaviors in addition to the differentiation between denominational terms revealed by the answers to the first question.

Herb (9-20). Can a dog or a cat be a Catholic? « No. » Why not? « Because he can't go to church or receive the sacraments, stuff like that. »

Stu (8-3). Can a dog or a cat be a Jew? « No. » Why not? « They are not human. » What difference does that make? « They can't go to the synagogue or say the prayers. »

It is interesting to note that the spontaneous use of different denominational terms appears at the same time as evidence for the abstraction of criteria for discriminating between their referents. This correlation would seem to reflect the close connection between thought and language i.e., a child will spontaneously use a term when it has meaning (a reference base) for him.

External Signs of Religious Group Membership.

Second-stage-children used religious actions not only for excluding animals from religious group membership, but also as distinguishing signs of particular religious group membership.

Will (8-2). How can you tell a person is Catholic? « If you see them go into a Catholic church. »

Nor (9-4). How can you tell a person is a Protestant? « The way they act. » How do you mean? « You can tell by the church they go to. »

These children had, it was clear, arrived at a concrete means of recognizing membership in a particular denomination.

The Common Property Connoted by Denominational Terms.

As might be expected from the foregoing discussion, second-stage-children regarded particular actions as the property shared by all members of a particular denomination.

Herb (9-12). What is a Catholic? « He goes to mass every Sunday and goes to Catholic School. »

Al (7-9). What is a Jew? « A person who goes to Temple and to Hebrew School. »

The same action emphasis appeared in response to the other common property question.

Will (8-2). How do you become a Catholic? « You get baptized, the priest throws water over you (sic !).»

Beth (7-1). How do you become a Protestant? « By going to a Protestant church. »

Concrete action thus permeated the religious thinking of these children and served as a source of answers to all religious questions.

Awareness of Multiple Group Membership.

Second-stage-children, in contrast to youngsters at the first-stage, were able to grasp the notion of multiple group membership. But the understanding of this notion was built upon the awareness of actions as the distinguishing feature of categorical terms.

El (9-7). Can you be a Catholic and an American at the same time ? « Yes. » How is that possible ? « Because I live in America and was baptized. »

Pr (7-8). Can you be a Jew and an American at the same time ? « Yes. » How is that possible ? « Because you live in America and are an American Jew. »

For second-stage-children the discovery and abstraction of religious actions was the magic key to the understanding of religious terms and was sufficient for recognizing the extent of denominational membership, for recognizing individual members of a denomination, for giving meaning to the denominational term itself and for recognizing the compatibility of multiple group membership. The limitation of the action criterion, however, will appear when the responses of the third-stage-children are considered.

Denominational Group Similarities and Differences.

Once again the similarities between the groups were more striking than the differences. There was one difference, however, which deserves to be noted. It appeared in responses to the question « How do you become a .... ? » Far more Jewish than either Catholic or Protestant children said that they were Jewish because their family was. Christian children, on the other hand, attributed their religious identity to some form of church activity. This difference may reflect the emphasis, in the Jewish religion, on the importance of ritual observances carried out in the home.

STAGE 3 (USUALLY AGES 10-12)

Children at the third stage displayed a new level of thinking about their religious identity. If the second stage could be characterized as one in which action held sway, then the third state would have to be designated as one of *reflection*. At the third stage, children no longer looked for manifestations of religious identity in the person's outward behavior but rather they sought it in the evidence of his innermost beliefs and convictions.

Extent of Denominational Group Membership.

It was noted earlier that the spontaneous use of certain terms coincided with the awareness of the meaning of those terms. This was true in relation to the child's use of the term « religion » which did not appear spontaneously until the third stage coincident with the discovery of belief as the core of religious identity.

Bob (11-12). Are all boys and girls in the world Catholic ? « No some belong to other religions. »

Jeb (10-6). Are all boys and girls in the world Protestant ? « No. » Why is that ? « God made all different religions. »

The other side of the reflective coin is revealed in the responses to the dog-cat question.

Bill (12-0). Can a dog or a cat be Catholic ? « No because they they didn't have a brain or an intellect. »

Sid (11-4). Can a dog or a cat be Jewish ? « No. » Why not ? « Because they are not human and would not understand a religion. »

The use, by third stage children, of the terms « intellect » and « understanding » indicated that they had abstracted their own mental processes and used such processes as the criteria of religious identity. At the same time this higher level of abstraction also permitted the formation of the third level class conception of « religion. »

External Signs of Religious Group Membership.

In contrast to second stage children, many third stage youngsters said there was no (external) way you could tell that a person was a Catholic, a Protestant or a Jew. This reflected their awareness that religious identity was an inner and not an outer manifestation. The answers of those children who did reply to the question pointed in the same direction as the negative answers.

Claire (11-7). How can you tell a person is Catholic ? « Well you could ask him. »

Fred (14-2). How can you tell a person is Protestant ? « Because they are free to repent and to pray to God in their own way. »

The Common Property
Connoted by Denominational Terms.

After the foregoing discussion of the third stage it might be expected that children at this stage would find the property shared by all denominational group members to be such things as beliefs and convictions. This was in fact what was observed.

Bill (12-0). What is a Catholic? « A person who believes in the truth of the Roman Catholic Church. »

Sid (10-4). What is a Jew? « A person who believes in one God and does not believe in the New Testament. »

A similar theme ran through the replies of third stage youngsters to the other question under this category.

Tom (11-7). How do you become a Catholic? « You gotta study your religion, study the catechism, receive communion and first confession. »

Beth (12-5). How do you become a Protestant? « Well you are baptized first and worship in the Protestant way and follow Protestant rules. »

At this stage religious membership meant more than attending church and signified thought, study and the observance of a moral and an ethical code.

Awareness of Multiple Group Membership.

As one might anticipate third stage children were often amused by the question regarding multiple group membership. The level of their explanations was in keeping with the high level of abstraction that has already been demonstrated as characteristic of this stage.

Bob (11-12). Can you be a Catholic and an American at the same time? « Yes. » How is that possible? « They are two different things — American is a nationality, Catholic is a religion. »

Bert (12-5). Can you be a Jew and an American at the same time? « Yes because in America you have the right to be any religion you want. »

At the third stage the lines between religion and nationality are clearly drawn but not, as at the second stage, on the basis of behavior but rather on abstract categorical grounds.

Denominational Group
Similarities and Differences.

Once more the similarity in level of conceptualization among the three groups has to be remarked on as evidence of a maturational factor in religious identity development. On the other hand there were group differences. One of the most interesting of these was the way in which children answered the question, What is a .... ? To this question the Catholic children often replied by stressing the practices and creeds of their church. Protestant children, on the other hand, often defined their identity negatively by placing themselves in opposition to Catholic doctrine. The same was frequently true for Jewish children who often defined themselves in contradistinction to Christian dogma (i.e., the New Testament). Put differently, this suggests that Protestant and Jewish children conceive their religious identity relatively, in contrast to other religions whereas the Catholic children conceive their identity absolutely and within the confines of their own church.

IMPLICATIONS FOR RELIGIOUS EDUCATION

The results of the present study have shown that before the age of 11-12 most children are unable to understand religious concepts as they are understood by adults. In addition the results have shown that children spontaneously give meanings to religious terms that are beyond their level of comprehension. For example, one little girl was overheard reciting the Lord's Prayer in the following manner « Our Father who art in New Haven, Harold by thy name » and many children go to the zoo expecting to see the « Consecrated cross-eyed-bear » they heard about in Church. Such examples could be multiplied but should, together with the evidence presented in the preceding pages, suffice to show that most children fail to understand religious expressions prior to adolescence and that they interpret such expressions within the limits of their own level of comprehension.

Does this mean that the child should not be exposed to religious teachings so as to avoid his forming erroneous ideas ? Even if such an implication were warranted, it would be impossible of fulfillment. The child picks up information about religious matters from many sources other than religious school. He hears about it from his older brothers and sisters, from his friends and from the mass media including books, radio, television and the movies. So it is inevitable that children will be exposed to religious ideas before they are ready to assimilate them and that they will form erroneous religious conceptions.

Fortunately, however, the child gives up these erroneous ideas as easily and as spontaneously as he constructed them. Piaget (1929), for example, has shown that animistic and artificialistic notions are gradually replaced by objective concepts in areas where children receive little if any systematic instruction. The same held true for the global and concrete conceptions described in the present paper. Although most of the children had probably never thought about animals and religion, their ideas in this regard underwent a spontaneous transformation with increased maturation and experience. The child's erroneous ideas about religious matters need, then, be no cause of concern since they are spontaneously given up as the child's thought becomes more socialized and objective.

The question still remains, however, as to whether religious instruction is worth the effort if the child will only misinterpret what is taught him. Even if these misinterpretations are later overcome, is there any sense in teaching religion in the first place? Such a question has point only if religious education is conceived as a purely intellectual enterprise. But true religious education feeds the emotions as well as the mind and it is the child's emotions that are ready for religious training. Contrary to popular belief, the child is most like the adult in his feelings and least like him in his concepts. As a consequence *the child can experience religious emotions before he can entertain religious thoughts.*

What this means, or at least so it appears to the writer, is that the child must be shown and not told about religion. He must participate in Church services, perform religious rituals, take part in religious customs, truly celebrate religious holidays and be treated with respect and consideration during such activities. It is the writer's strong conviction that children ought not be separated from their parents during the Church service but rather that the family worship together. Furthermore, it is an idle and unfounded fantasy to believe that religious emotions will be built within a child who is sent to religious school while his parents avoid Church attendance. For children, religion is first of all feeling and action within the sphere of Church activity. But such feelings and actions are seldom really incorporated within the child if they are not sanctioned by the parents. The Church can provide the form of religious identity but only the parents can give it substance.

5

Principles and Methods in Ecumenical Catechesis and Pastoral Activity

To be Men of Reconciliation

The Testimony of a Monastic Setting

by Frank VAN HET HOF

Brother of Taizé [1]

A New Current.

Christ's prayer for unity is resounding in an ever increasing number of Christians of all confessions, and is opening the doors of our greenhouses in which we have cultivated for centuries what we imagined to be exclusively our own. The fresh air entering here sometimes reluctantly, elsewhere like a wind upsetting everything in its path to purify our vision of christian life and the life of all men.

Christians today are underway towards a new epoch which some are already calling the post-modern era. The transition between two such widely different periods is symbolized by the pontificate of John XXIII, the Pope of the Council and of the encyclical « Pacem in terris. » The first steps on an unknown road are still difficult to discern and we must go forward by faith. But we are discovering that for Christians of all confessions there is only one path, one example to follow.

The greatest strength is in brotherly love, nourished by common prayer, possible in spite of our divisions. Our eyes are opening more and more to the signs of the times, because, in learning humility, we are trying to listen attentively. In order to renew our heritage of traditions and institutions we have received, we are seeking to discover the essential in them.

Our patience is often put to the severe test, because our capacity to change our way of thinking and our way of life develops so slowly. But patience persists ardently while sustained by a great hope.

---

1. Brother Frank VAN HET HOF is Dutch. He became member of the Community of Taizé in 1960. The Brothers of Taizé are living a monastic life in the Churches of the Reformation and praying and working for the unity of Christians. — Address : Communauté de Taizé (S.-et-L.), FRANCE (Editor's note).

In thinking over innumerable questions together, Christians of all confessions are seeking answers to these questions which a rapid changing society presents to everyone in the same way. It is not a question of giving ready-made answers. We are simply asked to be consistent with our christian vocation so that our life may conform with our words. We are asked that the words utilized to express our relationship to God be authenticated by a life visibly engaged in the Church and in the world.

The gulf that often exists between our words and our actions has become more intolerable than ever in the world where non-baptized millions and non-practicing baptized millions challenge Christians. The world expects us, the Bearers of the name of Christ, to leave the surface of ourselves (Bernanos declares that most men live on the surface of themselves) and to live dangerously today as committed men and women.

Our dedication may seem poor in our own eyes when we discover our incapacity to dialogue with an un-believer or to bear a brilliant testimony of the risen Christ. Or still we may consider ourselves too plain and ordinary Christians for this effort of renewal to pertain to us. Let us bear in mind that the engagement for reconciliation has as first distinctive feature this renewal which pertains to every Christian. How can we consider this engagement other than obedience to Christ ?

As we advance along the road which will one day lead us to visible unity, « that the world may believe », we discover that ecumenical engagement is summed up in this : convert our own heart to « the love we let gradually grow and develop in sympathy for all men in the Church and in the world. » [1]

Passion for the Unity of the Body of Christ.

To come out of oneself to seek reconciliation and to turn in the direction of the life of other men, demands a revision of life. Instead of judging men from the exterior, it is necessary to allow a new mentality to grow within in order to grasp what animates other men from within so as to see them as they are and not as we want them to be.

This new mentality means : rendering an authentic content to the faith, hope and charity professed by our lips. To witness a faith which is confidence and engagement. To open oneself to the sense of the universal which man needs if he wants to find a place in tomorrow's world so incongruous to the size of man. To bring

---

1. Roger SCHUTZ, Prior of Taizé, *Living Today for God.*

hope to men who live in a poverty without love, who have lost the meaning of life, who look for a truth to cling to, when everything around them is collapsing. To live every day from a charity which « beareth all things, believeth all things, hopeth all things, endureth all things. » Fundamentally nothing else than to observe with an ardent heart Christ of the Gospel, to carry over into daily life the demands of Christ Himself.

From the beginning the Community of Taizé has wanted to labour through prayer and in common pursuit for a reconciliation between Christians and between all men. He who seeks Christ and wishes to lead all men to Him, can but open his own heart to reconciliation with his nearest brother as with his most distant.

One does not talk about reconciliation ; it is above all an act to be carried out. We do not wait for the other person to come first to us. Reconciliation goes forward and commits each person individually. Every Brother who commits himself in the cenobitic life at Taizé carries in himself the passion for unity of the Body of Christ, the dominant note of the Community's vocation.

How does this ecumenical vocation fit into our daily life ? « We are expected to be consistent with the ecumenical vocation : to be men who seek unity in everything, to manifest brotherhood in their daily life. If we wish to call all Christians to visible unity, let us begin with ourselves, let us achieve unity each day within us and between us. » [1] « Every quest for unity among men implies first of all that a man who is engaged in it is careful to see that he has this unity in his own person. It would be putting the cart before the horse if one wished to inverse this order. Just in so far as we can overcome the disintegration which threatens us day by day by such inner unity of ourselves, so it becomes possible to work for unity between men and to wait eagerly the visible unity of all Christians in one Church. » [2]

Common prayer and individual prayer may transform a Christian, and make him an instrument of reconciliation, peace and unity. It is not a state reached once and for all, but a continual combat in a life that encounters tensions, like any Christian life. « Unstable men, we cannot maintain perfect peace in everything. But if tensions are not allowed to sustain conflicts, and if we are always factors of fraternal unity, that will constitute much in the path towards reconciliation. » [3]

1. *Directives spirituelles* following the Rule of Taizé, pp. 107-108.
2. Roger SCHUTZ, Prior of Taizé, *Unity, man's tomorrow*, p. 16.
3. *Directives spirituelles*, p. 113.

The first step to take is to be a sign of brotherly love in the Church and in the world, a sign of unity fully lived, a sign of love and loyalty one to another achieved in daily life. Thus a new mentality is created, open to dialogue with members of other confessions or with those unable to believe. Then it is possible to bring a spirit of reconciliation to others, either by going to live among them, or by inviting them to the communal prayer of the Community, which is an element of ecumenical training, that prayer which ceaselessly implores God « to pour out, in His Goodness, the grace of unity that he wishes for the Christians. » [1]

Church of the Reconciliation :
Place of Pilgrimage.

The thousands of visitors, of all confessions and non-believers, come to Taizé to pray with the Community and to seek reconciliation. The Church of the Reconciliation, built in 1962 by young Germans sent by the Action Sühnezeichen, permits visitors and pilgrims to join together in the Community's Office or go aside for personal prayer.

The church is a place of pilgrimage for unity and reconciliation of father with his son ; husband with his wife ; believer with one who cannot believe ; Christian with his separated brother.

The communal prayer which three times a day, morning, noon and evening assembles the Brothers together in the church, is the source of all ecumenical life. In the presence of God, interior renewal is effected with a view of unity. « How can each person respond individually to the ecumenical vocation ? By feeding the flame lit for unity all throughout the world. By remaining in the presence of God ; alone or in communal prayer together ; kneeling, standing, seated, no matter ! We are certain that unity is God's supernatural work and that all our activity only has value in so far as it continues this prayer and renders it true. » [2]

Pilgrims discover or rediscover in the Office, the essential of all ecumenical effort : communal prayer, adoration, praise and intercession. Christians of all confessions, Catholics, Orthodox, Anglicans, Protestants, meet there daily, living already from unity.

The communal prayer forges a profound unity between the catholic and the protestant seated one next to the other, or between Christians from different nations. The prayer of the Office helps

---

1. *Office de Taizé, La prière pour l'unité des chrétiens.*
2. *Directives spirituelles,* p. 109.

one to discover that in a world of indifference and atheism, a common task has been confided to Christians, that is to orient the heart and the mind of men toward the Mystery of God's reconciliation with mankind.

Madame Smirnova, a Soviet citizen who declares herself atheist, wrote to her newspaper, the Izvestia : « Does atheism make you happy ? People need to know that man is a friend and a brother to man, this is what religion teaches. » [1]

For one who lives in loneliness and despair, the prayer of a Christian Community carries a sign of hope. Participating in the Community's prayer makes one conscious of the fact that one and the same mission was confided to all Christians : to give a hope for life to the sick, the lonely, the hungry, to proclaim Christ our hope, to men.

Communal prayer leads everyone to radiate reconciliation among the members of his parish when he returns home. All who come to Taizé are called to commit themselves in the heart of their respective confessions or in the heart of the human milieux deaf to the Gospel, partly owing to the inconsistency of our Christian separations, to live reconciliation day by day, to be a leaven of unity. Reconciliation in the family, with a view to true conjugal unity so that the married couple may become a household of light ; reconciliation at work ; reconciliation in the parish community so that all may have but one heart and one soul.

The Church of the Reconciliation is in one way a place of ecumenical education. People come there as pilgrims. They leave their good Confessional conscience behind, in order to go out to meet other Christians, their separated brothers, to pray with them and grow in unity. They go away with elements of an ecumenical and liturgical spirituality, with the intention of becoming men of dialogue and reconciliation.

Throughout the year, young people come to stay at Taizé to gain some ecumenical training, to make a spiritual retreat, and for working camps. An ecumenical group of young men help the Community to receive the pilgrims.

On the hill of Taizé there is the presence of a fraternity of Franciscans, and the perspective of an approaching Orthodox presence extending the sign of unity set up at Taizé round the Church of the Reconciliation.

We are only at the beginning of ecumenism. Much research is needed. To feed the flame lit by Christ Himself we must have

---

1. Cf. *Informations Catholiques Internationales,* 14 April 1964.

our eyes open for the signs of hope God gives us. It is essential
to remain open to the universal with continuity and ardent patience.
We shall only keep the passion for the unity of the body of Christ
alive in our hearts on the condition we remain attentive to the
masses of men without bread, without hope of life, without Christ.

« Opération Espérance »,
Concrete Gesture of Reconciliation.

From the outset, a modest exposition on hunger in the world
had been installed in the Church of Reconciliation. An appeal was
made to all visitors to be attentive to the needs in underdeveloped
countries and Latin America in particular. How could prayer for the
reconciliation of all Christians not result into a concrete gesture
of solidarity with those who suffer ?

In Latin America, where Confessional tensions are increasing,
where the demographical upsurge is creating an imbalance which
nothing can check, bishops have taken courageous initiatives to
come to the aid of the very poor. For the Protestants at Taizé
stretch out a hand of reconciliation to support these bishops was
in the same spirit as the ecumenical collection organized in the first
century by St. Paul.

The first collection supported the project of a Latin-American
bishop. The contacts made at the Council by the Prior of Taizé
where he assists as Observer, are the foundation of a larger effort
« Opération Espérance ». It is not really for a cenobitic community
to undertake such a venture. But as the Prior of Taizé said : « We
are being bold during this year of hope, which is the year of the
Council. John XXIII, a providential man, this great witness to
faith, hoping against hope, has truly set in movement a processus
of reconciliation. » As John XXIII wrote in his Spiritual Diary :
« this feeling of belonging to all men should inspire and prompt
my mind, my heart, my actions. » [1]

The « Opération Espérance » is also a means of ecumenical
apprenticeship, of openness to the universal. Does not openness to
the universal pass through openness to what is human ? « Bringing
hope to men who have none, or who no longer have any, has a
value of which we are all aware. And it is precisely those people
who bring a reason to hope to others that they themselves became
more authentic because they are more human. One may say that

---

1. *Journal Spirituel de Jean XXIII*, 29 Nov. - 5 Dec. 1959, Retreat at Vatican.

« Opération Espérance » is as important for those who give as it is for those who receive. » (The Prior of Taizé).

Christians of different Confessions deepen their unity by working together in the service of others, in the service of those who are suffering. Certainly these are the men who are truly our separated brothers.

By this common *diaconia* we realize more acutely the common mission of all Christians in the world. Doing this we advance on the road of reconciliation. And along this road we can make concrete gestures, erect visible signs which will give rise to others.

In this way, we form within us a spirit of reconciliation ; by communal prayer keeping ourselves in the presence of God in the eager expectation of the grace of unity, and by the common service of men, our brothers. Thus we become men and women of reconciliation, artisans of Christian unity and the unity of all men in Christ.

Catechetical Orientations
for the Inter-ritual
and Inter-confessional Setting
of the Near East

by Jean CORBON

*Professor of catechetical pedagogy, Institute of Religious and Catechetical
Instruction, University Saint Joseph, Beyrouth,
Theologian-Interpreter for the non-Catholic Observers at the Council*[1]

In proportion to its population and territorial area, the Christian
near East is inter-ritual to the extreme : Egypt includes seven rites
(Coptic, Byzantine, Armenian, Syriac, Maronite, Chaldean, Latin),
Lebanon and Syria have six (the same as Egypt without the
Coptic), Palestine, two chief ones (Byzantine and Latin) and Iraq
two (Syriac and Chaldean). With the exceptions of Maronite and
Latin, all these rites divide in two Confessions, the Orthodox (the
most important) and the Catholic (Eastern « united »). One can
form some idea of the Confessional pluralism by adding the many
Reform communities which have built themselves up in the last
hundred years by gleaning from the traditional Confessions.

At the catechesis level, this pluralist situation raises different
problems according to whether it concerns school age or adults. At
the school age, there are some rare strictly Confessional schools.
Usually the Christian schools contain all rites and all creeds.

We find more and more official or Government schools providing
lessons of religion for both Mussulmen and Christians. Outside
school, parish catechesis exists, rare for children by right but also
rare in fact for adults. The more privileged of the latter receive
catechesis at their own level in various Movements or associations
according to the initiatives of their rite or creed.

---

1. See biographical note, p. 611.

Up to now there is no inter-Confessional collaboration over catechesis. There is a certain convergence among the Catholic rites, but the efforts at re-planning catechesis with consideration for the Christian pluralism, are only beginning. To describe briefly the inspiration of the Confessional catechesis, we might say that with the Reformers, it is the Bible, used in a devotional or rationalistic manner, according to the individual teachers ; with the Orthodox, the Biblical revival is at the service of an essentially liturgical catechesis ; with the Catholics, the various modern revivals (Bible, Liturgy, Fathers, Pastoral) are still cramped by a pseudo-theological frame-work, inherited from little Catechisms and imported from the Latin West.

And yet the necessity for a new catechetical orientation in which ecumenism is not one chapter among others, but a basic inspiration is most keenly felt. The first reason is the Near-East Christian himself who belongs to his country and to Christ before he is marked by his creed or rite. Nothing is more similar to a good Christian Greek Orthodox than a good Christian Maronite. The second reason comes from the new exigencies of Mussulman governments who cannot enter into all the subtle shades of Christian divisions, and want to impose one Christian syllabus in the State schools. On the other hand, the unavoidable de-Christianization is raising questions common to all Christian catechesis. Lastly, if the re-union of Christians must be a renewal of communion in faith, sacraments and charity, and not simply an agreement among hierarchs, it must have remote preparation at the level of catechesis for the faithful.

To trace the outlines of such a catechesis, a preliminary purification seems imperative : what catechesis should no longer be in the pluralist setting of the Near East. Then we could set out in the paths of a renewed catechesis.

I. PRELIMINARY PURIFICATIONS

The catechete who addresses listeners of various rites and creeds together must pass through a double purification for the Message to be transmitted in all its purity. The first concerns himself : he must overcome several temptations. The second concerns his listeners more : pluralism easily leads to a sociological religion and this tendency must be resisted.

1. *Temptations to Overcome.*

Facing pluralist Christian listeners a whole list of temptations threaten the catechist ; by overcoming these he already discovers the positive orientations of an authentic catechesis.

Syncretism is the temptation of the easiest way when we wish to be at the level of all. But it means disloyalty to the Message and to those who receive it ; it deceives the latter and betrays the former. Faith cannot be a cause of division in itself. The result of syncretism is practically agnosticism, as several institutions in the Near East show : Mussulman, Druse or a Christian of any shade goes into these establishments and comes out vaguely theist and in practice atheist.

Minimalism has more respect for the Message and its listeners, but it still betrays Christ by reducing Him to simple material data, like the logic of Descartes. Its most obvious failure has been typified by the textbook of Christian instruction put forward in Egypt a few years ago on a basis of the most elementary Protestantism : God the Creator and Rewarder, the example and teaching of Christ long ago, the believer's answer of faith. This reduces catechesis to a moral code based on the teaching of Christ.

Nominalism changes the accent from eagerness for charity to eagerness for truth, but with a fixed attachment to formulas. It is the temptation of Protestant missionaries who repeat the words of the Bible or Creed without explaining them (that would be doing theology !) ; it is also that of Catholics for whom the words of the little Catechism are demands less open to demonstration than the words of the Gospel. The lack of comprehension and the resistance of the Orthodox among the audience can be imagined.

Triumphalism pushes the previous tendency still further, especially over the historical presentation of Christianity. It is so sure of possessing the truth, that the events of Church History prove that we are always right and others always wrong and in fault. It can be said that Catholics are not the only ones to yield to this temptation. A few dates may suggest at what occasions it occurs : 451, 1054, 1204, 1438, XVI century, 1854, 1870, 1950.

Lastly, the direct opposite to syncretism is the temptation to *proselytism*. In the last century Christian teachers have often fallen into it in the Near East. The school has been their principal field of action and at the end of their efforts the Church is still more divided. As with the preceding temptation, there is the same mistake : that of God's gift, gratuitous and free, that of the liberty of the child and its parents.

2. *The Tendency to Resist :
from Sociological Religion
to the Community of Faith.*

All catechesis in the Near East must remember that Confessionalism has debased the Christian mystery into sociological religion. A preliminary change of mentality is needed, so that the facts of the Message may not be received « according to the flesh. » We mention some characteristics of this dominant religiousness ; they are perverted Christian values which need re-conversion.

Because *Confessionalism* results from an authentic sense of the local Church, catechesis must stress especially the true nature of the mystery of the Church in the local Church. Spontaneously the people are anticlerical and the priests anti-espiscopal ; catechesis must emphasize the true meaning of ministers, bishop, priest, deacon, laity. The Christian community is on a territorial basis, but sociological conditions have changed since the Middle Ages. This territorial community is centred round the Eucharistic celebration ; let us stress the role of the parish and especially the Eucharistic Assembly's demands for truth.

The community of rite or creed is often only a husk devoid of substance ; the people are Christian because that is their rite. Here we need to combat *formalism* of rite for a real sense of the Liturgy as sign of faith. Catechesis of faith before that of sacramental practice — this vital order must be respected today more than ever.

Parents and pastors naturally seek an ally in the Christian law. The *moralism* of their teaching finds the commandments easier than the theological virtues. If the learned discuss among themselves whether preference should be accorded to the morality of the virtues or to that of the commandments, experience could convince them of the need for the first. The revolution of modern mentalities in the Near East urges the necessity of a theological catechesis.

Those who want to liberate their search for God from the fetters of moralism and legal formalism fall into a vague *devotionalism*. This is the whole attraction of Protestantism in the Near East, far removed from the primitive demands of the Reformers in Europe. It arrives in the East via North America with all the force of efficacity and sentiment. These offshoots of Confessionalism can only be won back by catechesis with historical, community and sacramental dimensions.

Those whom devotionalism has not drawn away from the Church, stay there with a little religious philosophy of their own. It is distressing to see that most Christians live much less by faith than by religious *rationalism*. In this sense, they are faithful to the catechesis they received ; everything was proved to them, especially the existence of God, and they were prepared to meet objections from other creeds. It is time for the Near East to go further than the XIX century textbooks, and to bring apologetics back to its function in theology.

Finally, if sociological groupings are so important to sustain Christian life, is it not because catechesis is marked with *unrealism* ? It does not direct life. Here again discussions over the legitimacy of separating dogma and morals, sacraments and « sacred history » are belied by the facts. Since we have practised vivisection in catechesis, we cannot be surprised if Christians are more united by sociological ties than by a community of faith and liturgy.

II. A RENEWED CATECHESIS

The Word of Life which catechesis must transmit is always the same, but He is in progress of growth in the history of salvation. The man of the Near East, whatever his rite, has remained the same for centuries but today he is changing. This two-fold need must inspire the renewal of catechesis in the Near East. In the light of preliminary purifications, let us try to outline its principal orientations.

Above the temptations of the catechete and the deformations of setting, *we must proclaim the MYSTERY in all its fulness*. This Mystery is revealed and given us according to a divine Economy : the double mission, always joined together, of the Word and the Spirit, throughout history, which becomes entirely the history of salvation. The Economy of salvation is both the object, the frame and the pedagogy of all Christian catechesis. It is « maximalist » and can be accepted by all. It is unifying, because it places itself before any division ; but it is also exacting because it leads along the road that goes beyond all divergences. It is in this sense that the Catholic inter-ritual catechetical committee of bishops at Beyrouth is working at the elaboration of a general programme, and from now at the training of specialized catechists.

*
* *

But if we consider what the classic Catechisms say [1] — or do not say — about the mystery of the Holy Spirit, and then what He represents in the liturgical, doctrinal and spiritual development of the East, it looks as if the *catechesis of the Holy Spirit* in the history of salvation should attract more attention. This does not necessarily mean that a materially larger place should be given to the doctrinal expositions on the « procession » and mission of the Spirit, or to spiritual developments on the personal life, but above all to the action of the Holy Spirit whose role is « to reveal » the Word and to fulfil it. Such catechesis should be chiefly Biblical (the stages of the history of salvation) and liturgical (the present economy of salvation). All that is inseparably doctrinal, historical, liturgical and vital. To our mind, this catechesis of the Spirit is the basic test in the Near East. Our « classic » Catechisms are heavily stamped by a certain cultural development proper to the West of recent centuries, but which lacks universal value of itself. Catechesis is rationality's effort in the service of faith, but the oriental has his own type of rationality : concrete, emotional, cosmic, community and historic. His sense of things and of God dislikes partitions : he is unifying, existential and vital. The Bible is fundamentally Semitic, made Hellenistic later ; so are all the mother-liturgies. The Holy Spirit follows a mode of action that has affinities with this oriental genius, and every Christian should be a « spiritual Oriental. » It will be seen that this is not a material part of catechesis to be revised, but its basic inspiration.

*

* *

The classic catechesis does not capture the Oriental genius, it produces Christians who become strangers in their own Church. If we want to no longer alienate the Eastern Church, we must revivify another inspiration of its traditional catechesis : the *Liturgy*. Orthodoxy, which has escaped directly, if not in reaction, the Latinizations of the last centuries, is the most striking proof of this. The « true faith » is not so much a theological system as the riches of the Mystery preserved intact in the Liturgy. For centuries, hundreds of Christian generations have known no other catechesis than the Liturgy. Why ? The East does not see the sacraments as means, the sacramental world is above all a new ontology, the existential

---

1. Cf. G. DELCUVE, S.J., *What the Catechisms say about the Holy Spirit,* *Lumen Vitae*, XVII (1962), pp. 241-278.

novelty of the Risen Christ ; it is in this world that we live, and
it is there that the Spirit, through the Church, is leading history
to its consummation. The sacraments are the « master-pieces of
creation, » said St. Seymeon the Neo-theologian ; all is fulfilled in
the mysterious anticipation of the new world.

*

*   *

The catechetical inspiration from this is *mystagogical*, as the
Fathers preached. There they inseparably placed the history of
salvation and the individual and community experience of the
baptized soul. If it were not too bold for some, we could outline a
full syllabus of catechesis, spreading out over the school years, the
centre of which would be the Eucharistic Liturgy ; the first cycle
would be the three sacraments of initiation, the second, the liturgical year, the third the other sacraments, the fourth the history
of the Church as a sacramental event, the fifth Christian anthropology as humanism of the Transfiguration, and the sixth the world's
becoming as cosmic Liturgy. Partisans of theological vivisection need
not fear ; everything would be there, but with what ecclesial power
of life and community of faith ! As long as catechesis in the Near
East is not formally inspired by the Holy Spirit and the liturgical
mystery, we shall only proclaim without unity some religious instruction just as the same class-rooms witness any other school subject
being taught.

*

*   *

What has been said may seem satisfactory for Orthodox and
Catholic students, but what about the Protestants ? Experience has
convinced us that this catechesis cannot be rejected by the Reformed
Churches, because it brings out *the mission of the Word of God* in
its fulness. The requests of the Reformation are authentically
Christian ; only negative polemics have distorted certain expressions,
such as the dis-incarnation of the Word outside the ecclesial community or the disinclination to liturgical life. But the present
researches of the real Reformed Churches (the East knows chiefly
the marginal phenomenon of sects) are going precisely in the direction of a re-discovery of authentic Tradition, beyond mere anti-
Catholic polemics. To re-introduce the Holy Spirit and the Liturgy
into catechesis would lead to placing the Tradition of Scripture
accurately into the whole Tradition of the Word Incarnate. « This

is my Body *delivered* for you... » : it is the whole Economy of the Alliance between God and men. But this presupposes a re-discovery of the Biblical dimension of catechesis, not only as educational instrument but especially as sacramental universe of the Risen Christ. Put in another way, the « spiritual » reading of the Bible is inseparable from the liturgical event, which brings us back to the unifying centre of catechesis.

*

*   *

It is from this centre too that the value of *particular traditions* can be re-integrated into a Near East catechesis. These traditions are linked up with rites and creeds, it is a fact and a mystery, that of the catholicity of the One Church. Not to consider this is the minimalist temptation, catholicity is maximalist. In the pluralist setting of the Near East, Christian catechesis can experience this unique grace of revealing concretely the catholic countenance of Christ's Church. Catechetical effort must first aim at the accurate knowledge of the originality of each of these traditions. But it should go further. It must go back to their common source and explain their complementarity : the vitality of the Church is finally the fruit of their interaction. Now since rites are first specified by a liturgical tradition and a spiritual tradition incarnate in the Liturgy, we can see that catechesis must always start from the same unifying centre : the action of the Holy Spirit in the history of salvation, made actual in the sacramental event. It is here that a patristic training is indispensable for the Eastern catechete probably more than any other. This shows the need for a catechesis which transmits the Mystery completely : traditions within the total Tradition of the mystery of Christ.

*

*   *

This return to sources may give rise to a certain archaeologism which modern Christians reject with a slight feeling of inferiority. There is no question of returning to the style of church life in the IV century ; just when Latin is at last giving way to living languages we shall not revive Syriac or classical Greek. Here more than ever, catechesis cannot be retro-spective, it must be pro-spective. The real problem for « traditional » catechesis, as defined above, is to bring back the Eastern man of today into contact with his sources, *to make him really become himself*. We are at a growing-crisis ; in order that the Near East Christian may develop his life of faith according to the call of his modern mission, he must be much more deeply rooted in his ecclesial humus. The problems of the young Churches in Africa and Asia are similar ; but whereas for them, it is more the past human culture which is waiting to be vitally integrated into the life of the Church, here it is the Christian patrimony which is neglected compared to the development of human riches. The « sign of the times » in the Near East is that of the oldest Church where the spiritual spring is behind the new blossoming of human vitality. One of the imperatives of catechesis is to be attentive to this start-off. The re-integration of Tradition must aim at the renewal of the Church in a development harmonized to the human group in which it comes to life. It is then evident that this catechesis attentive to the mission of the modern Christian cannot but attract consent from the creeds that witness it. In fine, one is only ecumenical for the mission.

*
*   *

And yet we must not hide divergences in a cheerful optimism. It remains a fact that in a certain Orthodox college one-third of the pupils are Catholics, and in the neighbouring Catholic establishment there are the same percentage of Orthodox. Can one teach all the year round skating over what seems to divide us ? The most sincere solution found up to now is to say to the « minority » of the class : Here is the question, and here is the answer provided in our Church ; consult your own priests and pastors for the answer given in your Church. Can we go further than this minimum without falling into either polemics or proselytism ? We think it is possible.

The new step demands from the catechete a fairly rare sense which one might call a *super-intelligence of doctrinal formulations*. The cases however are limited : nature and person at the Council of Chalcedon, purgatory, merit, nature of the sacrament, papal infallibility, universal jurisdiction of the Pope, sacerdotal ministry, episcopal ministry, priesthood of the faithful, the Immaculate Conception, Assumption... Avoiding all relativism or syncretism, the catechete must be attentive to three demands of the Message. First, to what the East calls « apophatism » or negative theology ; the West also spoke of the « via remotionis, » but many catechists seem to have forgotten it. Let us say : *the sense of the Mystery* and the powerlessness of human words to express it. The East has more confidence in liturgical expression, where the event is lived, than in the doctrinal expression which always runs the risk of nominalism. This first purifying step prevents dead-lock over a word as sine qua non of integral faith, and obliges us to pass on to the reality. Thus an Armenian pupil could accept catechesis on the mystery of Christ : he firmly believes that Jesus is truly God and truly man, but he is repelled by the words nature, person, which belong more to Greek conceptualization than to the concrete facts of the Gospel.

Then the second demand : know how to discern the *theological elaborations and data of Revelation*. In the usual catechesis on Purgatory, this discernment is easy to guess. But an Orthodox who refuses the theological formula of the West on this point, does not refuse, in the name of his « true faith, » to take part in a Liturgy for the dead. He lives on the data of Revelation and Tradition but he rejects its theological elaboration. Must not catechesis first explain the revealed data ? and at this level divergences should be able to be settled.

Finally, the super-intelligence of doctrinal formulations must take into account the *disparity of growth* of local Churches within the universal Church. This fact is fundamental in ecumenical dialogue and cannot be ignored in a catechesis for inter-Confessional settings (it is very desirable everywhere). This disparity of growth is in no way exclusive from communion in faith. Who would venture to claim that it does not exist within the Catholic Church too ? Christ has not the same age in all his members. Let us take an example of an Orthodox catechist. We know that the Orthodox theological and spiritual developments on the role of the Holy Spirit are much more advanced than among Catholics, and yet their fundamental faith is the same. The Orthodox catechist can quite well present the faith of his Church without misunderstanding the level of growth reached on this point by his Catholic brethren. The reverse would be the case over the ministry of the Bishop of Rome, or for Protestants over Mariology [1] and it will be realized that a basic catechesis, respectful of standards of growth is not at all minimalist.

A particular consequence can arise from this, especially for the use of Catholic catechists : *know how to distinguish the juridical and the mystery*. This holds good for all the aspects of the mystery of the Church, both for the sacraments and the ministries properly speaking. We know quite well, from the Council especially, that the juridical conceptions of Catholic ecclesiology are only one aspect of the growth of the Catholic Church, but an aspect relative to the mystery of the Church. If the usual mentality of the Church's

---

1. Cf. Max Thurian, *Marie*, éd. Taizé, 1963.

catechesis draws inspiration unilaterally from the concept of society, it is to be feared that there will never be complete understanding either within the Catholic Church or with our brother Christians. A catechesis for inter-Confessional settings demands purification and deepening.

*

*   *

This suggests one last observation about general orientations. *We need to re-awaken slumbering possibilities.* The Council is beginning to do so for episcopal collegiality. Catechesis must not await the Council for other traditional talents which more recent traditions have helped to bury.

We mention by way of example : the meaning of the Church, One and Undivided, the meaning of the local Church (bishop, priests, Eucharistic assembly, parish, ministry of the faithful), the meaning of the Church in solidarity with the world and substituted to it in the work of redemption, the bond of the Liturgy and of the Christian life as « mystical, » the meaning of the Resurrection of Christ, the meaning of Christ's baptism in the sacramental economy and the transformation of the world...

We are not concealing the fact that it is not enough to lay down a few large orientations to see them pass immediately into our lives. It is easier to make a new Catechism than to train catechists in this spirit of ecclesial renewal. In this sense, we must not omit to point out by way of conclusion that fresh catechetical orientations inspired by the ecumenical fact will remain a dead letter unless integrated into a general pastoral. The first necessity remains the training of seminary students, but intensive sessions, like the Council sessions, would sometimes be very useful for the Bishops. Lastly, at parish level, a truly ecumenical pastoral, not as a sector along with others, but as formal inspiration, is still awaiting pioneers among priests, nuns and the faithful. [1]

---

1. On this subject in general the following books can be read :
— I.H. DALMAIS, *Origines géographiques, historiques, doctrinales de la diffé-renciation des rites orientaux*, in *Union et désunion des chrétiens.* Desclée De Brouwer, 1962, pp. 27-40.
— also in the same collective volume, *Problèmes œcuméniques en Liturgie*, pp. 41-55.
— J.CORDON, *Nouvelles perspectives œcuméniques au Proche-Orient*, in *Proche-Orient Chrétien*, XIV (1964) fasc. 1 and 2.

The Ecumenical Effort in Catechesis among Protestants

Pastor of the Reformed Church,
Professor of Protestant Religion at the École Européenne, Brussels [1]

It may be well to begin by recalling the major interest always taken by the Reformed Church in catechetical instruction, the promotion of a « universal priesthood » of believers, adults and those in charge, and constant Biblical return to sources.

« We must recognize (wrote the Oratorian Louis Bouyer in his recent theological dictionary) that Luther has the merit of compiling the first manual to win a very wide popular success, with his Little Catechism (on the Decalogue, Creed, Our Father, sacraments of Baptism and Eucharist, appendix on Penance) accompanied by a Larger Catechism, a master's key similarly planned. Openly copying his method, St. Peter Canisius, S.J., drew up books of the same kind containing fully Catholic doctrine, which also had great success. » [2] How do things stand now ?

After a very brief historical survey in order to understand the present evolution better, we give some significant texts from the Catechisms most in use now in our churches (Catechisms for children) and some indications for adult catechesis. We conclude with a few authorized testimonies showing that the most obvious

---

1. Pastor Gaston WESTPHAL is son and grandson of pastors, cousin of the President of the Protestant Federation of France. He studied theology in Paris and Geneva. He has served parishes in Ardèche, in the suburbs of Paris (Asnières), in La Haye (Holland), the Walloon Church, and Verviers-Spa (Belgium). He has spent a year at the Protestant Catechetical Centre of Villemétrie (La Ferté (S. and O.), France, and 8 months at the Oriental Benedictine Abbey of Chèvetogne to draw up the tables of the well known review Irénikon.

Thesis of his Licenciate : *Opposition entre la théorie de la prédication chez Alexandre Vinet et la parole de Dieu prêchée de Karl Barth.*

He has written articles and accounts in various papers and reviews. St. Paul's Editions will soon publish : *La Piété Protestante.* At present, Professor of Protestant Religion at the Ecole Européenne, Brussels. — Address : 119, avenue Coghen, Bruxelles 18, BELGIQUE (Editor's note).

2. Louis BOUYER, *Dictionnaire Théologique*, Desclée, 1963, p. 23.

ecumenical effort in catechesis among Protestants today is undoubtedly that of ecclesial deepening.

I. THE PROTESTANT CATECHISMS
HISTORICAL SURVEY

If catechesis was once flourishing in the Church (Augustine, *De
catechizandis rudibus*, Catechisms by Cyril of Jerusalem, Origen of
Alexandria), it looks as if, at the dawn of modern times, ·the confessional replaced catechizing [1] with textbooks used in preparation
of souls for Communion by Penance (see Gerson, *De parvulis ad
Christum trahendis*), and that it would be for the Reformation to
give a great impetus to religious instruction of which « the Catholic
Church hardly took any more notice » (Melanchton, *Apologie de
la Confession d'Augsbourg* VIII/14 : apud adversarios nulla
prorsus est κατήχησις puerorum). [2] Most of the Reformed Catechisms are still used in our parishes :

— *Calvin's Catechism*, the sub-title of which ran : « Formuloire d'in-
struire les enfants sur la Chrestienté, fait en manière de dialogue où le
ministre interroge et l'enfant respond :
— *Heidelberg Catechism* — the 400th. anniversary of which was solemnly
celebrated last year, and which came out in 1563 with the title « Cate-
chismus oder Christlicher Underricht, wie er in den Kirchen und Schulen
der Kurfürstlichen Pfalz getrieben wird, » and is one of the books symbolic of the German Reformed Church. Composed by pastors and laity,
it is a Catechism for adults.
— *Luther's Little Catechism* also used in Reformed parishes (it was
used in the parish of Ardèche which I once served).
— The *Westminster Catechism* (1648), (for the presbyterians in Great
Britain), divided into two, one for pastors, compiled according to the
« Compendium theologiae » by Professor J. Wolleb of Bâle (1626), the
other for the people, the « Shorter Catechism » very like Calvin's (without
the « Decretum reprobationis ») and which begins, in very popular style,
in the same way : « Man's chief end is to glorify God and to enjoy Him
for ever. »

Some years ago, the Anglican Church brought out a separate
Catechism. [3] Until then, every « Book of Common Prayer » contained

---

1. Lukas VICHER, *La Confirmation au cours des siècles*, Neuchâtel, Delachaux
and Niestlé, 1959, p. 42.
2. See also the « Ecclesiastical Ordinances of Wittenberg (1533) of Wurten-
berg (1553) which insist much on this point.
3. For further details see *Baptism and Confirmation*. A report submitted by
the Church of England Liturgical Commission, London, 1959 (Broad Church
tendency).

a catechism or « instruction everyone must learn before being presented to the bishop for Confirmation. » Let us say in passing that this Catechism is very short. In the « Prayer Book, » each child gives his own name, and declares that it was given him by his god-parents, who promised three things in his name : 1) that he would renounce the devil, the world, etc., 2) that he would believe all the articles of Christian faith, 3) that he would keep God's Commandments. Explanation of the Creed, the commandments, the summary of the law, the Lord's Prayer and of the two sacraments.

At present they are reviving these catechisms of the XVI century urged by the Neo-Calvinist [1] and Neo-Lutheran [2] movements, and also by the Trinitarian and ecclesial return to sources largely due to Karl Barth, who practically brought Protestantism out of the crazy sentimental individualism into which it had almost sunk : instruction often left to the improvisation of each pastor, without reference to a « norma normans » (the full inspiration of the entire Scriptures and the ancient creeds of the ecumenical Councils). Pastor Eugene Bersier writes : « The great catechetical movement inspired by the Reform was taken up again in the XVIII century under the impulse of Spenser and Francke. They helped to remove from catechesis the dogmatic character which it was given chiefly during the XVII century, and gave a larger place to the psychological method and historical study of the Bible. Unfortunately this salutary reform was compromised by the rationalism of the XVIII century which saw catechetics chiefly as a method of moral instruction much more than as communication of revealed truth. In Germany and French Switzerland these effects were markedly felt and their influence is visible in the successive and posthumous editions of the Catechism by the devout Ostervald. » [3]

From that time on, instead of simply exposing the faith, the law and the means of grace as did Calvin and his successors, these Catechisms insist on the historical side of Revelation, with the following plan : natural religion, necessity of revelation, primitive then patriarchal then Mosaic revelation, the law, prophecy, Jesus Christ, His Person, His work, the Holy Spirit and the Christian life, explanation of the Law, the Christian's duties towards God, his neighbour and himself.

---

1. Pierre Marcel, *A l'Ecoute de Dieu.* Modern edition of Calvin's works.
2. P. Lovy and Th. Suss, *Positions luthériennes.* Complete re-edition of Luther's works.
3. Eug. Bersier, *Encyclopédie des Sciences Religieuses*, Lichtenberger, t. 2, p. 698. The Catechism by J.F. Ostervald of 1702 contains about 310 pages.

My grandfather, professor of theology at Montauban gave a
Biblical catechesis according to psychology and history, fairly wide-
spread : « Jehovah, the stages of Revelation. » My father, a missionary in Africa, gave me a Christocentric catechism, of Methodist
origin in three parts : Jesus, announced by the prophets (study of
the Old Testament), Jesus in His own times (the Gospels), in the
Church (Acts of the Apostles, epistles, the Holy Spirit) ; the decisions
of the four first Councils were considered as surpassed.

II. THE ECUMENICAL EFFORT IN THE CATECHISMS MORE RECENTLY IN USE

At present the tendency is to make catechetical instruction uniform both for adults (Centres of Christian Training under the
control of Faculties of Protestant theology) and children, so as to
submit souls less to the personal experience of their pastor — which is
always necessary however — than to the traditional teaching of the
Reformed Churches and, though still timidly, of the ancient Fathers.
Tradition is being solidified with less prejudice for studying the
history of the Church between the Acts of the Apostles and the
Reformation, in spite of Harnack and others. Besides the cate-
chumenate properly speaking, the « Schools on Sundays and Thurs-
days, » the religious courses in schools (when there are such) include
in their syllabus no longer the Bible only but Church History before
the Reformation. [1] It is true that it is studied preferably in its sympathetic figures like Saint Francis of Assisi and Joan of Arc, while
it is often wondered if these were not « evangelicals » before their
time. [2]

We will give a few examples from the catechisms most in use
now in our French-speaking churches, in order to detect the ecumenical effort under the doctrinal aspect, for the training of adolescents
from 13-17 years. With us, Catechism, after the children's Sunday
School, normally starts at about 12 years of age, and lasts 2 or
3 years preparing for the confirmation of baptism and first communion towards the age of 16, 17, more and more according to
this plan : First year : knowledge of Holy Scripture. Second year :
doctrinal catechism. Third year : problem of life, dedication,
question-box. Here are four examples :

---

1. *Histoire de l'Eglise.* 50 cards. P. Chrétien et Derforge, Paris, Soc. Ec. du
Dimanche, 1963.

2. *Histoire de l'Eglise*, Société Centrale d'évangélisation, 47, rue de Clichy,
Paris.

A. *Je suis le Seigneur ton Dieu*,[1] 8th. edition. Reformed Catechism for the 2nd. year (Pasteur de Pury, Chapal, Jeanneret), being a sequel to the 1st. year Biblical Catechism « L'argile et le maître potier. » In the Notes at the end of the book, after the four parts : Revelation, Confession of Faith, Obedience of Faith, the Sacraments (a fairly « Barth » plan) we read (p. 106) :

> « The Reformers neither invented nor discovered anything new. They simply went back to the great news which had been more or less asleep in the sanctuaries of their Church, as it had often been dormant in the Ark of the Alliance at the time of the prophets. The Reformers never meant to found a new Church. They only wished to remain the true Catholic and apostolic Church, towards and against the Church that had rejected them, as the apostles wished to remain the true Israel towards and in face of the Israel that rejected them. There was the same kind of rupture between Rome and the Reformers as there had been between Jerusalem and the Church. In fact, it was not rupture but an unforeseen continuity and a miraculous revival forth of God's Word. The Reformed Church therefore, simply must not be a new Church, but strictly the *Catholic Reformed Church, vivified, purified, simplified* by the apostolic testimony to which the Holy Spirit has given His full authority. »[2]

B. *Doctrinal Catechism by Pastor Espaze*.[3] It is again in an appendix, but longer this time, that under the rubric « Life of the Church » (p. 73), we find four pages on the various Christian Churches.

On the subject of the Orthodox Church we read :

> « The Church of the East, separated from the Church of the West in 1054, takes the name of Orthodox Church, because she considers she holds the correct doctrine. The separation took place for reasons of doctrine, discipline and political rivalry. In reality the Orthodox and the Catholic Church have very similar doctrines. »

Concerning the World Council of Churches (p. 74) :

the Churches who belong to the World Council know that if they draw nearer to Christ, they also draw nearer to one another. They therefore seek together a greater fidelity to their Lord, awaiting the day He will re-unite them.

---

1. R. DE PURY, *Je suis le Seigneur ton Dieu*, Librairie Protestante, 140, Boulevard St-Germain, Paris VI.
2. For further explanation of this attitude, see *Qu'est-ce que le Protestantisme ?* by the same author, Paris, Les Bergers et les Mages, 1961, p. 16 ss.
3. A. ESPAZE, *Catéchisme doctrinal*, 28th. thousand, Sté. Centrale d'évangélisation, 47, rue de Clichy, Paris IX.

After some statistics showing fairly objectively the importance of the different Churches, the question is asked :

« Why do the Reformed Churches exist ? (Pages 77, 78 give a short comparative analysis of the Catholic and Protestant positions on tradition, the Sacraments, the clergy, the Saints and the Virgin Mary, wih a broad conclusion): « other aspects of the Roman Church could be considered ; such a Church believes that she alone *is the Church of Christ. She is confusing God's glory with her own.* She seeks to be powerful. On occasion she thinks she ought to use violence against those who disagree with her... The Word of God is read and meditated in the Roman Church. For that we can thank God and rejoice. But their popular piety delights in stories of miracles, in the power attributed to certain images and objects, in the veneration of saints, and in certain practices which are almost superstitious. The Reformed Churches wish to proclaim that the Scriptures are the only means of knowing the Saviour. »

At the bottom of the same page, we read the reflection: « Are not members of the Reformed Churches often tempted to commit the same errors as the Roman Church ? »

Let us hope that these rather severe critics will take more and more into account the Catholic parish revival so vigorous since the Council.

C. *Catechism of the National Church of the Canton of Vaud.* [1]

There is always an appendix, seven pages this time, on Roman Catholicism and the Reformed faith, in the tonality of « the pastoral letter from the Reformed Churches in Holland » [2] which is already a bit old (the Mass is still spoken of as a repetition and not an actualization of the unique and perfect Sacrifice of Our Saviour); right in the middle of the Catechism, there are two pages (100, 101) on ecumenism, under the Biblical title : « There will be one fold, one shepherd » (John, X, 16), and the final definition : « ecumenism is the movement which endeavours to restore Christian unity. »

We quote a few paragraphs :

a) « The breaking up of Christianity hinders God's plan ; it is unnatural for the Church, making her look like a disjointed body, with disordered movements. »

b) « In the divided Churches nevertheless, Christ's prayer to His Father has never been completely forgotten : ' That all may be one, so that the world may believe that Thou hast sent me ' (John, XVII, 20, 21). »

---

1. *Catéchisme* (National Evangelical Reformed Church of the Canton of Vaud). Vevey (Switzerland), 1961.

2. *Lettre...* Paris, Les Bergers et les Mages, 1957.

In the XX century a movement has begun which endeavours to re-group
the Christians of the whole World. This movement is called « ecumenical, »
a term derived from a Greek word meaning « all the inhabited earth. »
 c) ... We must pray and work for the regrouping of our separated
brethren and for the re-union of the various factions of the Universal
Church.
 In the questions following the lesson, we find :
 — « Begin by agreeing among yourselves » — is this taunt flung at
the Churches justified ?
 — Why does the Roman Catholic Church not join in the ecumenical
movement ?
 — At what time of the year is there a week of prayer for Christian
unity ?
 The chapter concludes with the prayer from the Didache.

A picture which often illustrates the « ecumenical » chapter (in
the school books this time) shows Christ as the Good Shepherd as
the Christians of the III century liked to depict Him, carrying a
lamb which is looking at the cross, sign of salvation, and around
which are visibly grouped : A Protestant Church among the Eski-
moes, Notre-Dame de Paris, the Anglican cathedral at Mombassa,
a temple at Tananarive, a Russian basilica, the Frauenkirche at
Dresden, the church-spire of Ulm, Saint Paul's in London, and Saint
Peter's in Rome. [1]

D. *Appartenir à Jésus-Christ.* [2]

It is in the reformed catechism of J.J. von Allmen that the
ecumenical orientation is most striking. Promoter of the *Vocabulaire
biblique* and many theological brochures in the Delachaux and
Niestlé series which has just completed its pre-arranged number
of fifty, organizer of the famous biblical camps of Vaumarcus, and
member of the dogmatic commission in the World Council of
Churches, the professor writes the introduction to this catechism
compiled in collaboration : « The content corresponds to the traditional matter for catechesis in the Reformed Churches : the
Apostles' Creed, the Lord's Prayer, the decalogue, sacraments. The
arrangement, Faith, Hope, Love is not original either since, whether
in this order or not, it has been suggested by St. Augustine, by
the Moravians, by the Muscovite Orthodox tradition, [3] etc. What
may be considered original is that we have given up one particular
chapter on the sacraments, in order to speak of baptism as sacrament

---

1. Cf. *Histoire de l'Eglise*, S.C.E., *op. cit.*, p. 123.
2. Catechete's text-book and (pupil's) answer-book. Delachaux, Neuchâtel, 1960.
3. Cf. the famous Orthodox Catechism by Platon (Paris-Klincksieck).

of Faith, and of the Holy Supper as sacrament of Hope. If one
particular chapter on the sacraments has been abandoned, it is in
order to follow the New Testament which does not know the
concept « sacrament » as such » (Introd. p. 1).

In Section I (Faith), in the explanation of « I believe the holy
universal Church » we read :

What is the Church ? The Church is the people that Jesus Christ has
chosen, that He groups, loves, protects and leads faithfully to eternal life.
Are there several Churches ? As there is only one Lord, there is only
one Church.
This unity was both given and ordered by Jesus Christ. It must be
received with faith and sought with perseverance : the divisions in the
Church are disobedience to God and a scandal to the World.
How is the Church universal (= catholic) ? Because she bears witness
to all men and throughout the centuries that Jesus Christ is the one
Saviour and one Lord of the world.
(Thesis no. 1 of the Reformed World Alliance, catholicity as a function
of testifying to Christ. « A Church lessens her catholicity when she
diminishes her testimony to the Saviour. »)
Where is the Church ? The Church is where God's Word is preached
in truth, where the sacraments are faithfully celebrated and Christ's
ordinances are taken seriously. It is in my parish that I must seek her
(cf. *Confession of Augsburg*, Melanchthon).
The ecumenical questions are approached in the course of the Catechism,
with the following dictum : « The Church has not remained united. The
great Christian divisions occurred in 1054 (division between the Churches
of East and West) and in 1521 (division in the Western Church, which
largely did not accept the Reformation). In our time, chiefly owing to
the World Council and the missionary effort, we are slowly, painfully,
returning to Unity. God grant that I may be a worker and not a wrecker
towards Christian Unity. »

Statistics list about 15 % Orthodox, 40 % Anglican-Protestants,
45 % Rome.
In the description of the marks of the Church (holiness, apostolicity...) we can detect the depth of ecclesial renewal, as in the
explanation of « I believe in the communion of saints, » where the
following advice is given :

« It is important to bring to life an action of grace, a real ecclesial
consciousness : I, a poor little catechumen, because I belong to Jesus
Christ and am a member of my parish, am with Abraham and Moses,
with David and Elias, with St. Peter and the Virgin Mary, with St. Paul
and the martyrs, and the Fathers, and St. Francis and the Reformers etc.
(in time), and with the Queen of England, newly-baptized Africans, the
Christians who suffer in Eastern countries, etc. (in space). We must

cultivate this consciousness, not only by intercession but also by information : reading ecumenical news in the religious press, etc. » (p. 52).

The Holy Supper (Eucharist) is spoken of as :

« A sacrament of communion with Christ and the Church, sacrament in which, through the elements of bread and wine, the sacrifice of Christ is made actual once more, in which the joy of the future Kingdom dawns already » (p. 70). « If the Lord is « offered » in the Eucharist, He is offered to the Church (the Holy Spirit gives Christ !). The Church, also, through the Spirit, gives herself to Christ and dedicates herself to His service. This permits us to recognize the Biblical and patristic interpretation of the Eucharist, sign of the nuptials of the Lamb, of the bridalsong Christ-the Church (*Eph.*, V, 25, 30). Contrary to the idea of Rome and of symbolism, we cannot explain the real presence : *we can only declare the fact of this adorable mystery.* »

Concerning marriage, included in the explanation of the 7th. commandment [1] (Section III : Love) we find :

« It demands a life of fidelity and holiness, for it is a reflection and demonstration of the Unity between Christ and the Church. Every human couple has a mission (the nuptial blessing [2] consecrates this mission): to reproduce in the concrete fact of conjugal life the mystery of the Love of Christ-the Church. That is why divorce is condemned : it denies this mission (no one could imagine a divorce of Christ from His Church), it deserts the position given by God » (p. 87).

It is probably because of our Eucharistic non-intercommunion that the sacrament of the Holy-Supper is placed in the section « Hope, » rather than in the one « Charity » which would seem more logical to us, but at least we can rejoice over the stress on baptism which cannot be exaggerated, and which recurs in the author's [3] conclusion to the Catechism :

« If by this catechism we have managed to make catechumens feel that belonging to Christ is entering a new world — they will have their whole life-time to become aware of this baptismal transplantation — we have not worked in vain, because then the catechumens will become men and women who « love the Lord's coming » (*II Tim.*, IV, 8) in St. Paul's lightning definition of a Christian, and who can say of themselves and joy and humility : « We are not the children of withdrawing unto perdition, but of faith to the saving of the soul » (*Heb.*, X, 39).

---

1. The 6th commandment for Catholicism, which unites the first two, a source of dispute with Protestants who greatly stress the 2nd. : (Thou shalt not make any graven thing... etc.). But on this point see the adjustment in J.Ph. RAMSEYER, *La Parole et l'Image,* Presses de Taizé, 1963.

2. Remember that marriage does not rank as a « sacrament » with Protestants.

3. The Catechism most used in Belgium, but perhaps because it was sent free from Neuchâtel and there are many Swiss pastors among the relatively few Protestants in Belgium.

III. ECCLESIAL DEEPENING

The ecumenical effort among Protestant which is the most obvious seems to be a striking ecclesial deepening. Dean Lestringant, for many years Professor of practical Theology at the Faculty in Paris (Protestant Faculty), wrote justly : « ... thus, Catechism and Liturgy both declare the doctrine professed by the Church.

« Nothing is more logical, since catechesis directs the believer towards a conscious, thoughtful and personal insertion. in the Church. When the study is over, he will no longer be the disciple of Pastor X... but will approach the holy table, to share the one bread with his brethren. The Church will have accomplished her most ecclesiastical function for the new communicant. » [1]

We all know how much K. Barth has centred the whole life of the Church on Preaching (in the wide sense, that is Word and Sacrament, the Holy Supper, necessary seal of preaching). In this perspective he writes, « catechism has no other aim than to prepare children to understand preaching. It is a kind of technical frame, very simple preliminary instruction. It is the teaching of what the Church has known and recognized till now as being the true Faith ; till now, that is, till the appearance of this new generation, called in its turn to form part of the Church. The catechism makes known to the child the principal elements of *tradition* to which present-day preaching is attached. [2] Naturally the religious lesson must sometimes be turned almost imperceptibly into worship for the young. But at all costs, this must not be done to the detriment of the necessary distinction between the two activities. Catechism's proper work is to teach not to convert. Its role is not ' to provoke a decision, ' that is to preach. » [3]

Pastor Voeltzel, of the Faculty of Theology at Strasbourg, stimulator of the syllabus of Protestant religious instruction for the secondary cycle in Alsace, writes : « ... On the doctrinal plane, we could approach frankly the differences which separate Catholicism and Protestantism, the characteristics of the various families of the Reform, the significance of « Sects » and the efforts undertaken in the domain of ecumenism. » [4]

---

1. Pierre LESTRINGANT, *Le Ministère catéchétique de l'Eglise*. Paris, Je Sers, 1945, p. 124.

2. Cf. J.L. LEUBA at the conference « Faith and Order » in Montreal, July, '63. Section Scripture, traditions and Tradition — « Sola Traditio » et non « Sola Scriptura » he cried !

3. K. BARTH, *Dogmatique*, Geneva, Labor et Fides, vol. I, Tome I, 1, p. 49.

4. R. VOELTZEL, *Petite Pédagogie Chrétienne*, Presses de Taizé, 1960, p. 141.

In spite of some risks of secularization [1] we must mention the important ecumenical effort in the youth movements for all like the Scouts, YMCA and the Christian Students Federation. Catholic Bibles are perhaps not given to children, but adults and catechists use them (notably the Bible of Jerusalem). The coming Second version will have a well-developed glossary and theological notes regain their place in the Book itself, according to the present general orientation.

New methods are being brought out : catechesis by socio-drama acted by the children (Oud-Polgest Leyde ; Darmstadt and the Marienschwester). Instruction by schematic posters « History of the Church in 30 posters » (very up-to-date, made by theological professors, Dean Lods, Prof. Stauffer etc., and Lutheran-Reformer pastors : Delforge, Chrétien).

Centres of « Christian education » are being opened in connection with Faculties of theology, with regular correspondence courses, and the ecumenical note is not lacking. Protestant communities like Grandchamp, Pomeyrol, Villemétrie, [2] Taizé give para-liturgies before the Offices for all-comers, and has not Frère Max Thurian written : « the privileged place of catechesis is the liturgy itself, and especially the liturgy of the Holy-Supper » ? [3]

We would mention also that we are coming out more and more from our partitioned isolation. At the European School, for example, religious lessons are sometimes in common. In the last two years Protestant and Catholic pupils have momentarily united to hear and question pastors and priests, who must reply in « spiritual emulation. » To teach the XVI century Reformation to the children, a Catholic teacher yielded his place for 4 lessons to a Protestant teacher in the Religious Course for the older pupils, and more particularly during Unity Week. The priest in « clergy attire » and the pastor with « the collar » helps this needed compenetration, and in the meetings of the teachers of religion, a

---

1. Danger of a certain deism with Baden-Powell, of a sentimental « Jesus-latria » often found in the YMCA, of an intellectual snobbishness (as Bultmann at the moment) at the Fédé (otherwise a real cultivation-centre of ecumenical staffs of the *World Council of Churches*).

2. Proposes (like many « Evangelical Academies » or « Centres for encounter and research » started after the war 1945) to help the layman in the testimony of his professional life. There are about a hundred in Europe, U.S.A. and Australia, federated in Europe into the Association of Institutes for Lay Training, which would need a special study (cf. the weekly « Réforme » for 8/1/64).

3. M. THURIAN, Neuchâtel, *La Confirmation, consécration des laïcs*, 1957, p. 86.

colleague of another faith can receive loud applause, in spite of
the very hostile textbooks still current on both sides when referring
to other religions. How many textbooks are no longer suitable for use!

CONCLUSION

We hail with joy and a holy envy the catechetical renewal in
the Roman Catholic Church, apparent in these last twenty years,
and which is attracting our attention more and more, precisely in
the measure that catechism is becoming Biblical and seems to engage
the whole Church and not only the priest. As Reverend Father
Delcuve has so aptly written : « from being clerical, the catechetical
movement is becoming ecclesial. » [1]

For our own part, coming out of a non-community individualism
and a strict Bible-ism, into a complementary movement, we are
regaining the ecclesial savour, and are converging all together
towards this thesis : « The catechetical ministry belongs to the
Church ; those who have the duty, do not discharge it instead of
the community but with it ; not in excusing the community from
this duty, but in ceaselessly reminding them of it. » [2]

We still have to rediscover, besides the position of the Mother of
God in the Son's work of salvation, the value of the traditional
schema of the Church : the internal apostolic succession, the episcopate, not only as « bene esse » of the Church, an idea which is
growing, but also as « esse plene » of the Una Sancta ; what is
the collegiality of bishops and the Petrine privilege, [3] moderated by
the charismatic dimension of St. Paul who, without being one of
the appointed Twelve, is an « absolute » apostle « ultissimus inter
pares » (*I Cor.*, XV, 9) : May institution and event combine to
promote a more beautiful Church !

Hebrew sessions, deeper thought on the mystery of Israel, revealed
in the recent pilgrimage of Pope Paul VI, strengthen our conviction [4]
that we must trust God and continue our intercession.

---

1. G. DELCUVE, S.J., Religious Pedagogy in France: Some Present Trends, in
Lumen Vitae, 1956, p. 205.

2. A. ESPAZE, *Aspects contemporains d'une catéchèse de l'enfance au sein de
l'Eglise catholique romaine*, Thèse de doctorat, Montpellier, 1960.

3. Cf. O. CULLMANN, *Saint Pierre, disciple, apôtre, martyr*, Delachaux and
Niestlé, 1952. In preparation: *Saint Pierre et le Pape*.

4. Cf. the Pope's very important reply, 17 October, at the reception of 66
Observers, for whom Doctor Skydsgaard spoke, of « the role of a Biblical
theology concentrated on the study of Salvation in the Old and New Testament » : « ... A true Christian never remains stationary... To these developments
you hope for « a concrete and historical theology, » « centred on the history of
salvation, » we willingly ascribe for our own part, and the suggestion seems
to us most worthy of study and closer attention... » (I.C.I., 1-XI-63, p. 15).

Two Conceptions of Ecumenism

Schema of Catechesis for Young People and Adults

by Marcel VAN CASTER, S.J.

International Centre for Studies in Religious Education, Brussels[1]

The existence of disunion between Christians raises a problem, which is not only very important for the Christians themselves, but is becoming especially urgent from the fact that Christians are more directly in contact with non-Christians in the world of today.

I. ORIGIN AND HISTORY OF THE QUESTION

1. *The Facts.*

The *two great schisms*, between Western Catholicism and Eastern Orthodoxy in 1054, and between the Roman Church and the Reformers in 1521, need to be correctly set in their very complex historical setting. Then two truths stand out ; first, that the ways of acting and of argument which influenced them belonged very much to the mentality of their epoch, and of those in the different groups. *In the course of the centuries that followed,* we notice a general movement towards centralization in the Catholic Church, and a phenomenon of ulterior dispersion among the Orthodox and still more among the Protestants.

On the other hand, in recent years, the disadvantages which both these movements entail, when not counter-balanced by other tendencies, have given rise to an active desire for a better equilibrium. The Protestants take the initiative of an Ecumenical effort (Söderblom 1910 ; Week of Prayer 1907 ; Congress of Stockholm 1925; World Council of Churches 1948) which must establish more union among them, and which even raises the question of a possible re-union with Rome ; the Orthodox joined this movement (1961). The Catholics have already made great efforts too in prayer and

---

1. Address : 184, rue Washington, Brussels, BELGIUM.

study (Père Portal, Dom Lambert Baudouin, Cardinal Mercier, Père Congar); in 1962 Pope John XXIII convoked a Council which is preparing better conditions for dialogue with non-Catholics; especially the sense of the collegiality of bishops which is in another line than that of centralization. These efforts at mutual understanding and interior reform are explicitly placed within the frame of prayer in common (Abbé Couturier).

2. *Ways of Interpreting these Facts and Considering the Problems they Raise.*

These points of views have been most clearly described by Père Y. CONGAR (*Aspects de l'œcuménisme*, pp. 8-21), who sees in them various stages. We can summarize them.

First, we start spontaneously with *analytical polemics*. Objections are made, and immediately answers must be found to these. The theoretical and vital context is neglected. Then controversy develops on the *plane of general theology*. The general expositions disagree, but both sides acknowledge a certain unity of theological context.

The next stage is to situate the body of doctrine into the *psychological, sociological and anthropological context* (types of mind and sensitivity to values). Thus we discover that realities on the human plane (not theoretical, but rooted in the structures of life) have played an important part in Christian divisions. Père Congar even says : « Without minimizing the question of doctrine, we are convinced of the determining character of differences of anthropology... » (l.c. 16). See the exposure of these differences in our next paragraph.

Finally we reach the *fully religious plane* which is that of the plenitude of the Church. The problem then encircles the *totality of divisions* and its extension all over the world. At this moment the word « ecumenism » is born. And the sense of its extent favours the sense of its duration. We realize that the ecumenical question is not settled in one short encounter, but demands a lengthy maturation. This *maturation* also will permit transformations later in the manner of stating the problem.

On the ecumenical plane itself, the first encounter brings up a divergence of view between the Catholic Church and non-Catholics. According to the Roman conception, and before the maturation of which we shall speak, it was simply a question of « return to the unique Church. » Whereas for the Protestant and Orthodox communities, all the groups, including the Roman Church, should consider themselves on an equal footing, and find the best form possible of the « reunion of all. »

II. THE PRESENT POSITION OF THE PROBLEM

The present position must take into account the transformations in progress ; and yet it understands a difference in points of view as a permanent reality.

1. *Points of View with Incidence on Doctrinal Positions.*

One of the ways of presenting the diversity of points of view stresses the difference existing between two types of mind (see *Lumen Vitae* **XIX**, (1964), no. 1, pp. 52-57).

The first type sees the reality under the *angle of continuity*, the second type under the *angle of discontinuity*.

This difference entails the following *choices in the manner of conceiving the Church.*

Either the accent is placed on uniform unity, on fixed and general institution, on authority, on the sacrament as an exercise of power ; or the accent bears on pluriform unity, on the varied (charismatic) gifts, on liberty in accord with personal inspiration, on the Word of God and a sincere answer in the interior attitude of one who prays.

On one side we insist on what the Church has already effectively received as redemption, beginning of eternal life, and as efficacious institutional organization ; on the other side we stress what remains imperfect in every man and in all human history ; God's gift is, above all, promise of perfect salvation in eternity ; God's intervention is actual for each one in view of the future. In other words : choice between stressing institution or event ; choice between the possession of truth entirely revealed and the deliverance from sin considered as perfect in the constituted Church, although imperfect in knowledge and effective charity in the members, on one side — and the persistence of sin in Christians, the necessity of growth in faith by openness to all God wishes to say, when and how He wishes, on the other side. Or again : the instituted Church and thus the « already instituted community » which those outside must join, and those within become more and more united ; and the Church, « community to be made in faith and charity. » Or once more : a unity which the Church already possesses, and a unity which is only made by the ever new and more complete gift of God, and which Christians should pray for with perseverance.

This very difference means analogous choices in what concerns communion in the Divine life and the personal transcendence of God ; between the mediation of Christ acting through « participation » (sin excepted) or acting by « attribution, substitution, absolute unicity, » etc., and finally what is perhaps the clearest crystalizing of this divergence in points of view : the way of looking at not only the content of faith, but the *act of faith* itself in its functioning and role.

2. *Attitudes concerning these Points of View.*

If we recall the history of the ecumenical question, we know that there was a tendency *to harden* opposition for a long time on both sides. This prevented any dialogue.

At present some are inclined to avoid the problem by *minimizing differences*, by advocating a minimum of doctrine, furnishing a kind of « common denominator » for Christians, uniform and identical for all. This can serve as an intermediate position in a common non-religious activity ; but if such an attitude is taken as definite on the religious plane itself, it will work against the progress of faith and real unity.

The truly useful attitude lies in seeking a *pluralist synthesis*, which allows real dialogue in which all the riches of God's supernatural gifts and anthropological diversities can develop. This pluralism cannot be absolutely nothing but the result of dispersion caused by human defects. It contains some elements of uniformity ; the diversity must base itself on the diversity of God's action, and the patience He has with us, in order to give us time to correct our defects.

To obtain a synthesis of elements between which there has always existed a certain tension, we must reduce exaggerations and unjustified exclusivisms, and recognize that there is some good in a difference of accent.

Let us notice from the outset that the choices we have described above may offer clear resemblances with Catholicism on one side and with Protestantism on the other, but they cannot be attributed indiscriminately to one or the other. There are different spiritualities [1] within the Roman Church ; and some Protestants have a natural tendency to put the accent on positions very close to the Catholic ones.

Let us notice next that present circumstances and especially the action of the Holy Spirit in these cases urge both Catholics and Protestants to recognize more and more that points of view formerly foreign to them have some value.

---

1. *La Rédemption*, « Etudes religieuses », n. 764, Pensée catholique, 1964, pp. 25-36. Redemption, Paulist Press, 1965.

We can therefore hope for substantial progress in this direction. But we must not hide from ourselves that progress remains difficult, and that for reasons belonging to three orders of reality. Notably that of doctrinal interpretations of common sources (infallibility, divorce); that of psychological dispositions, innate or received from a setting, which cause people to have a certain type of mind ; and that of moral dispositions : true charity demands the renunciation of some ways of acting too often considered as belonging to a necessary prestige ; it will never be easy to make respect for truth, humility, fidelity and charity accord perfectly together.

If at present we must interpret these facts — notably the different points of view and the search for a synthesis — we need criteria to determine a competent choice.

III. REFERENCES PERMITTING
THE ELABORATION OF A SOUND JUDGMENT

We can lay down some criteria under the form of principles. But then we must refer to more living sources both to justify these principles, and to be guided in their application.

The *principles* concerning the unity of the Church must express, in stating it precisely, the tension that exists between the aspects complementary to each other.

They should be formulated — either combining these aspects, presenting a paradox ; or in mentioning the complementary aspects alternatively — in which case, the paradox will appear in the whole.

References should chiefly be to the Bible, the synthesis of Tradition in the past, and to present « figure-heads. »

1. *The Bible.*

The Bible shows us the grouping of the people of God, that is, its unity developing according to certain permanent elements and profound transformations.

We see there the tension between event and institution, between charismatic gifts and authority, especially between particularism and universalism, based on a community of faith, hope and charity.

Jesus Christ made the unity of the new people in His own life and His personal function as Head, chiefly understood in the sense of « vital principle, » as the sap is for the branches ; and understood, in the second place in the sense of « constituted power » especially of teaching authority.

To make the members share in this fundamental unity, Christ did not first resort to an institution but to preaching which engendered faith ; then and chiefly to the saving and sanctifying action of His Death-Resurrection followed by the gift of the Holy Spirit ; yet Christ did not neglect the institution which consists chiefly in authority and in the sacraments.

Saint Paul, making the theology of the Church, explicitly indicates several characteristics of its unity. One may say that implicitly he admits others, by analogy. Thus the liberty received from Christ is *already* present in Christians, but chiefly in the state of growth ; we live *in libertatem gloriae* (*Rom.*, VIII, 24); in the same way the Church lives, already one, but chiefly *in unitatem gloriae*.

2. *Tradition.*

The Tradition of the past presents an evolution of the ways of conceiving the tension between the living community and institution, between collegiality and primacy, uniformity and diversity. These varieties of conception concerning religious unity are clearly under the influence of the variety of conceptions of secular unities, like political, philosophical unity, etc. See a typical example quoted by P. CONGAR : *Aspects,* pp. 62-63. This relation and relativity are also verified for the transformations in recent years. It is fairly lately that this historical sense (a very important sense of relativity) has found its way generally into modes of thought.

Besides, the history of the Church makes us see a difference between unity by right and unity of fact, between the *invariable doctrinal data* of this unity and its *changing situation* which is that of a *broken unity* (the two great schisms and their consequences) and a *unity ceaselessly in process of re-establishment* and perfection. And that by an always necessary reform within the Church, concerning not the essential of the gift made by God, but the situation in which men welcome God's gift.

3. *The Figure-heads.*

The figure-heads of present ecumenism are to be considered as much in the domain of *action* as in the domain of *thought*.

For the official position of the Catholic Church in doctrinal thought the most important document will be the *schema on Ecumenism* of Vatican Council II.

This document must be interpreted in its full context. Then we must refer as well *to the words and deeds* of Popes John XXIII and Paul VI, to the activity and commentaries of Cardinal Bea ;

to the meetings and opinions of Catholic theologians and persons belonging to other ecclesial communities.

On this subject see *Documentation catholique*, especially no. 1420, March 15, 1964.

Several reviews have either special numbers or articles on present ecumenism, *Parole et Mission*, no. 266 and no. 273 (1963); *Lumen Vitae*, XIX (1964), no. 3 and 4.

These references present the elements of *maturation*.

Christ is present and the Holy Spirit is at work in the whole world. This can be observed in a special way not only among individuals but also in the Christian communities which are not in perfect union with the Catholic Church.

Since the schisms, knowledge of the faith, practice of prayer and of the Christian life have developed in different ways according to the communities. That is why every Christian and every community has something to learn from the others and something to give them.

But this development has not been positive only ; in all the communities there is some lack of openness to truth and charity which calls for reform.

The *paths of union* then are to be seen as different kinds of steps towards a point for encounter « ahead. » At the same time this point of arrival is first settled by fidelity to the starting-point, that is, to Christ Himself as the Gospel reveals Him in His work and person. According to this fidelity must the interior reform of each community be made.

IV. MEANS OF PROMOTING
THE BEST ECUMENICAL SPIRIT

1. *Attitudes Based on the Principles.*

To promote the ecumenical spirit and thus help towards a closer approach, several basic attitudes are necessary :

To know oneself truly ; to abandon prejudices ; to resist sectarianism.

To banish distrust ; believe in the other's good faith ; correct our own real or even apparent defects which give rise to distrust in others, especially self-sufficiency or inversely, lack of seriousness (total relativism or insincere diplomacy).

To reform oneself at ecclesial level. By a return to sources : a better knowledge of the Bible in its context. By a knowledge of history also, which recognizes the faults which have crept into the community to which we belong, and also acknowledges the religious riches which have been developed among others.

To meet together in different ways :

— in *prayer*. Praise and intercession in common. Meditation on God's Word in common. Pilgrimage to the sources ;

— in *acts of charity situated beyond divisions*. Mutual assistance, gifts in common to those in need ;

— in ecumenical *dialogue* properly so called. For there to be genuine dialogue, it is most important to avoid two imitations of it, a succession of alternating monologues and a confusion of all points of view.

2. *Ways of Proceeding Motivated by Opportunity*.

Let us notice that opportunity can run in two opposite directions : that of *urgency* which incites to action without delay, even taking risks ; that of *temporizing* which avoids all precipitation. Real « prudence » takes both into consideration, imitating the insistence and the patience of God. In the application of this prudence to the ecumenical movement, we may point out :

— a distinction between *two periods of encounter* : the first, provisional, when each is finding a footing of equality with the others ; the second, definitive, when each, with the necessary reforms, has taken their normal place in the unity of all.

— a distinction between the *people best prepared* for encounter and others who will only be able to encounter after later preparation ; preparation aided by their own progress in the ecumenical spirit, and by a *better arrangement of terrains for encounter*, which more specialized people are working at now.

See the information given by Père Dumont and published in « La Semaine Religieuse de Paris ; » with the author's permission considerable passages have appeared in *Lumen Vitae*, XIX (1964), no. 3, pp. 520-532.

These distinctions do not hide the urgent necessity for all Christians, in a world where the masses tend to become a huge non-Christian multitude, to collaborate with Christ to achieve the end He expressed in His prayer to the Father : « *That all may be one... in Us, so that the world may believe that Thou hast sent Me* » (John, XVII, 21).

Ecumenical Training in Seminaries and Houses for Theological Studies

by Gustave THILS

Professor at the Catholic University, Louvain [1]

A good pastoral training is eminently ecumenical in itself. We need to agree over what we mean by « pastoral » and « ecumenical, » hence this brief article which is more of an outline for reflection, than a fully elaborated programme.

The two first sessions of Vatican Council II have revealed a deep ecumenical intention, sometimes very enlightened, always full of charity, among the Fathers. This is a new factor which will assuredly mark pastoral training in the future. The Instruction *Ecclesia catholica* of December 1949 was already some progress. The creation of the *Secretariate for the Unity of Christians* has placed the Church in « structure of dialogue » as the expression goes, since it is an ecclesiastical organ set up for contact with non-Roman Christians. Cardinal Bea, President of the Secretariate, has announced that a general Directory will be elaborated, when possible, to serve as a basis for regional Directories promulgated by episcopal Conferences. In a word, a new era has been inaugurated, thanks to the fearless intuition of John XXIII. The whole Church is already

---

1. M. le Chanoine Gustave THILS was born in Brussels in 1909. He did his ecclesiastical studies in the Seminary at Malines from 1926-1931, and theology at the University of Louvain from 1931 to 1937. Doctor in Theology and aggregated Master of the Faculty, he was professor of Holy Scripture at the Major Seminary, Malines, 1937-1947, and from that year, he has held the Chair of Fundamental Theology at the University of Louvain. Chanoine Thils has been summoned as expert to the Second Vatican Council. His works are both valuable and numerous: *Théologie des réalités terrestres, Théologie des réalités sociales, Tendances actuelles en théologie morale, Mission du clergé et du laïcat,* etc. A list of his principal publications up to 1953 was given in *Lumen Vitae,* IX (1954), no. 3, p. 493, French edition. We can add to it: *Sainteté chrétienne. Précis de théologie ascétique,* Tielt, Lannoo, 1958, *La théologie œcuménique. Notions, Formes, Démarches,* Louvain, 1960. *Histoire doctrinale du mouvement œcuménique,* Louvain, 2nd. ed., 1963. — Address: 39, rue Léopold, Louvain, BELGIQUE (Editor's note).

deeply engaged in this movement ; with one accord she sees it as an invitation from Divine Providence ; in its essential idea, the ecumenical spirit can be considered as a definitive acquisition.

Spiritual Approach.

The central element of training in ecumenism is this : the ecumenical approach is *spiritual*. The separations we regret are not divergences of theologians but ruptures of fraternal bonds of communion in Jesus Christ. They affect the very manifestation of the mystery of the unity of all in Christ, and according to the forms desired by Him. This « mystery of unity » certainly remains impenetrable to theological reflection. Who would dare to foretell if and when the history of salvation is to know this day of unanimous remembership ? Who would dare to guarantee that dissensions will not spring up, from age to age, until the day of the Lord ? The theology of « the time of the Church » is still so little known. But, whichever way it is, it is on this plane of « the mystery of unity » that every ecumenical step must be situated. All deep ecumenical training must insist on it, for prayer, study, pastoral, all depend on it.

Prayer and Worship.

Ecumenical *prayer*. Whatever the concrete orientation given to ecumenical prayer, it is indispensable to place it in the very heart of Christ's own prayer. For only Christ's prayer can fully express God's Will for His Church. We cannot do better than allow His Spirit to prolong in us His ever-present prayer for His Church and its unity.

Our prayer is also an expression of the unity already existing between disunited Christians ; we speak of separated « brothers. » This means that the question of prayers « in common » will arise more and more. The Instruction *Ecclesia catholica* (1949) foresees already that duly organized ecumenical meetings may begin and conclude with the recitation of the Our Father or a prayer approved by the Catholic Church (AAS, 42, 146). And there are so many approved prayers in the inspired Writings and patristic literature ! At present, all ecumenical encounter must be engaged in prayer ; all agree about that.

But that is not all. Ecumenical directories should also foresee mixed meetings with the object of a celebration of worship, more or less official, with an officiating minister. The existing norms actually in force on the « communicatio in sacris » will surely be revised, especially concerning meetings of Orthodox and Catholics.

Whatever is fixed by Canon Law and the ecumenical Directories would have to be followed in this matter.

Training for these shades of conduct concerning prayer and religious meetings is very delicate. We need to be very extended in charity and understanding, but to keep our heads clear, with a sense of discretion, avoiding offence with those who might be « scandalized. » If apostolic παρρησια is very far from premature initiatives, servile timidity is also far removed from the Gospel prudence,

The ideal would be for future pastors to take part occasionally in these re-unions for prayer, during their period of training, so as to experience their spiritual vigour and perceive the problems that arise, which they can discuss with their professors.

Doctrine and Study.

Theology also should feel the repercussion of the call to ecumenism. First of all, it should strive to be more Biblical, patristic, historical, and especially in a better way. Biblical, not by an accumulation of Scriptural quotations, but because it brings out from it and expresses the most fruitful doctrinal tracks. Patristic, not by some passages passing from one textbook to another, but by assimilating the spirit of the Fathers, their sense of the analogy of faith, their creative boldness steeped in tradition and actuality. Liturgical also, because theology loses some of its savour, if it does not feed on the life of worship of the Christian community, as an indispensable, vital setting.

Teaching, to be ecumenical, should also be attentive to all the problems which touch it from the fact of separations. By returning to sources, the master should try to regain an explanation, a guiding-line for encounter, elements of dialogue. This holds good in all dogmatic treatises, in whole and in detail : faith, revelation, tradition, Scripture, magisterium of the Church, the laity, grace and works, redemption and merit, sacramental rites and the Word, ecclesial mediation and the One Mediator, etc., etc. This holds good too in the exegetical disciplines : for it is on this basis that the Reformed Churches and ecclesial communions lay their affirmations and positions. It is also the case with Church History ; so many chapters touch either moments of dissension and separation, or periods of revival and renewal. The history of non-Catholic doctrines, people and facts must be taught with enlightment, sound documentation and fairness. One could write a whole book on ecumenical incidences affecting all the disciplines of instruction in seminaries and Houses of study.

But there is more than that. Ecumenism supposes doctrinal *encounters*. Theological students should be well informed on the directives of competent authority on this point ; and they find out, if they take the trouble, that the concrete possibilities for encounters are usually much greater than they think. It would be an excellent thing if on occasion, the young could take part, with experienced masters, in an encounter of this kind. They would find out de visu, the sincerity of the participants, how far they are from indifference and confusion, and above all, how much knowledge and competence is required to make these encounters useful. Such experience would be a fine stimulus for study and research.

Finally, *dialogue* must be set up at these encounters. They must be capable of dialogue, which is not a natural gift with everyone. Authentic dialogue implies many not common qualities, which would be useful to ecclesiastics on several other occasions besides ecumenical encounters. To set up dialogue, one must first know how to be silent in order to understand and grasp accurately and from within the ideas and behaviours of the other party. To set up dialogue, one must be solidly firm in one's own doctrinal position, and also unhampered by the categories and formulas in which it is expressed. To set up dialogue, one must be alive to the real and not to schematism only, obedient to truth rather than to school routines, ready for research and not afraid of what might demand greater precision. Such intellectual plasticity is only acquired by contact with very gifted masters.

Pastoral and Action.

Above all, ecumenism should be used in pastoral life and all its concrete implications.

The first thought is collaboration, already recognized by the Instruction *Ecclesia catholica* (1949) on the social and charitable plane with all its branches. This is becoming more and more usual, as the schema *De œcumenismo* of Vatican Council II suggests. Here especially theological students can learn to work with disunited Christians, so as to discover the balance which makes the most of the common quality of Christian, without injuring what is specific and unique in Catholicism.

The pastoral aspect of ecumenism does not stop there. Far from it. The chief aim of ecumenism, as the schema *De œcumenismo* declares, is to examine oneself and see to it that the physiognomy and interior balance of the Catholic Church are more faithful to God's Will. In practice that means that the whole *Catholic* life should be a point of questioning, of examination of conscience, so that in preaching, devotion, activities, in Catholicism in a word, non-Catholics may always see that perfect image of Christianism as Christ willed it ! Ecumenical work thus imposes a care for equilibrium, for perfection in the whole of pastoral life which requires a tireless ascetism of mind and action ! To answer this demand of ecumenism, the preparation of theological students needs to be very strict and rigorous and in all directions.

In Seminaries and Houses
for Theological Studies.

To the foregoing considerations, which are very important in spite of their general character, we may add a few more precise suggestions.

In the life of prayer. — Everyone knows the « week of universal prayer » which should be proposed — this is vitally important — in a genuinely ecumenical spirit. The ecumenical intention can be renewed on various occasions : in some spiritual conference, on the feasts of Apostles, as a sacramental penance or special intention. The end of the encyclical *Mystici Corporis* speaks of this very appropriately.

In various activities. — When we celebrate the « Day for the East » asked for by Pius XI in his encyclical Letter *Ecclesiae Decus* (AAS, 1944). Or in occasional Lectures, especially during the week January 18-25. Nowadays, meeting and interview with people filled with the ecumenical spirit have become so easy !

In studies. — It is possible to give a survey of the ecumenical work of different popes. Or to provide some descriptive elements on the spirituality of the Churches and Christian communions. Or again, explain more clearly some point of history of the Great Schisms, their causes and their authors. Give some informative lessons on Ecumenism, its history, problems, method, its incidence on theology, on the pastoral it calls for ; here, possibilities are considerable.

At University Level.

The most opportune suggestions for universities have already been made several times. It should be possible to introduce a course of Introduction to the theology and life of Eastern Christians — this was asked for some time ago by Pius XI in *Rerum orientalium* (AAS, 20, 284) — and of the Christians who follow the rulings of the Reformation.

Then, in the best equipped universities there should be a « Centre for ecumenical research » or an «Ecumenical Foundation » even a « Chair of Ecumenism »; the questions are sufficiently numerous to authorize the creation of a special organ, although to become idealistic for a moment, it would be preferable for all the disciplines to be given by professors alive to the requirements of Ecumenism. The Libraries too, primordial necessities in all serious work, should be more plentifully stocked, not so much with books on ecumenism as with basic works on the history, doctrine and life of the different Churches and Christian communions. It is also in the universities especially that theological encounters could be organized. These are more easily brought about in the academic settings. It is for the universities to take the initiative in this domain which is a delicate one in many ways.

Conclusion.

These suggestions are very fragmentary. They should be compared with the schema *De œcumenismo* of the Second Vatican Council, and with the Directory which the national meetings of bishops will have to elaborate. Such as they are nevertheless, we hope they will be useful.

BIBLIOGRAPHY

General bibliographical information, selected and classified : *Éléments de bibliographie sur l'œcuménisme.* Lyon, Unité chrétienne, 8, place de Fourvière, 1963, 62 p.

Documentary, spiritual, doctrinal and practical Introduction to Ecumenism : M. VILLAIN, *Introduction à l'œcuménisme,* 3rd. ed. Casterman, 1961, 324 p.

Outlines of the history of the Ecumenical ideal in the XIX and XX centuries : G. TAVARD, *Petite histoire du mouvement œcuménique.* Paris, Éd. Fleurus, 1960, 235 p.

Study of the Pontifical documents relating to the separated brethren : G. BAUM, *L'unité chrétienne d'après la doctrine des Papes, de Léon XIII à Pie XII.* Paris, Éd. Cerf, 1961, 247 p.

Doctrinal documents and prayers for each day of the Week of Prayer for Unity : R. AUBERT, *Unité.* Bruxelles, 11, rue Brialmont, 1959, 94 p.

History of the World Council of Churches and theological problems of ecumenism : G. THILS, *Histoire doctrinale du mouvement œcuménique,* 2nd. ed. Paris, Desclée De Brouwer, 1963, 338 p.

Small directory of encounters : C.-J. DUMONT, *Pastorale des rencontres œcuméniques.* Paris, « Semaine religieuse », 1963, 24 p.

6

Presentation of
Some Doctrinal Themes in an
Ecumenical Perspective

God Speaks to Us

by Jean GIBLET

Professor at the Catholic University, Louvain [1]

All the documents which have fixed Biblical tradition proclaim one decisive fact over and over again : God speaks to us. The Epistle to the Hebrews even sees the whole of the history of salvation as a word from God. « God who at sundry times and in divers manners, spoke in times past to the fathers by the prophets, last of all, in these days, has spoken to us by his Son, whom he has appointed heir of all things, by whom also he made the world » (*Heb.*, I, 1, 2). It is this word which is fixed by Scripture, it is proclaimed now by the Church, and it is through the function of this word that Christians live their faith. It is important first of all to grasp the different aspects under which it is presented to us while discerning clearly what unites these aspects in the end. [2]

The Prophetical Word.

Men had probably been talking to each other for a very long time, before some sage began to marvel at the fact and tried to explain its conditions. Thence they began to outline a philosophy of language to which many of our contemporaries are devoting their

---

1. Born at Nivelles in 1918, Chanoine GIBLET is a Doctor of Theology of Louvain University, with Licenciates in Philosophy and Biblical sciences. He lectures on the New Testament at the University. The author of a thesis : *L'image de Dieu chez Philon d'Alexandrie* (Louvain, Studia hellenistica), Chanoine GIBLET has directed the compilation of *Grands thèmes bibliques* (Paris, Feu Nouveau), English version : *The God of Israël. The God of the Christians*, New York, 1961, and he collaborates in several reviews. — Address : 7, avenue de Croij, Héverlé, BELGIQUE (Editor's note).

2. L. DÜRR, *Die Wertung des göttlichen Wortes im Alten Testament und im antiken Orient* (Mitteilungen der Vorasiatisch-ägypt. Gesellsch., 42 Band) Leipzig, 1938 ; T. BOMAN, *Das hebraische Denken im Vergleich mit dem Griechischen*, Göttingen, 1954 ; DEBRUNNER, KLEINKNECHT, PROCKSCH and especially KITTEL, art. *Logos* in the *Theol. Wört. z. N.T.*, t. IV, pp. 69-140 ; TOURNAY, BARUCQ, ROBERT, STARCKY, art. *Logos*, SDB, t. V, col. 425-496.

best energies. More than ever, we are realizing the complexity of
the fact, and the groping character of our explanations.

In the same way, ancient Israel noted that God spoke to them
long before they began theological reflection. This was to stay at
the opening stage and it may be for our epoch to advance it further.
At the outset, we must point out the Semitic idea of the principal
function of language.

The verb *davar*, we know, belongs to a root which evokes what
is at the bottom. Some have concluded from this that the mono-
syllable ' word ' suggests the expression of the essence of things.
But it is more probable that the verb signifies a movement coming
forward from behind ; perhaps this was meant to evoke the speech
which comes from the heart and passes through the lips like a
stream. Other writers, while retaining the same etymology, have
thought to detect the dynamic character of the human word that
sets in motion those who hear it. Is this last interpretation the
right one ? We cannot be sure, but it certainly reflects an essential
aspect of the Hebrew notion of the word.

While the Greek *logos* is essentially the fruit of the activity of the
reason which has grasped series of similar data in the mass of things,
the Hebrew *davar* is first addressed to some one and normally aims
at producing an action. That is why the word is closely linked to
action, it arranges, rouses, directs and expresses the act. Hence the
human word should be considered as a force, more exactly, its force
will vary according to the force of the man uttering it. « The
word, » remarks Pedersen, « is the bodily expression of the content
of the soul... behind the word lies the totality of the soul who has
created it. If the speaker is an energetic soul, his word will express
more reality than a weak soul... » [1]

It is in the experience of the prophets that is first found the
consciousness of what the word of God implies. The prophet feels
constrained to speak for God, to transmit the Lord's will to the
people of the Alliance. He speaks human words which express
the will of God, and which are powerful from the very power of
God. An ancient oracle attributes these words to David : « The
spirit of the Lord has spoken by me : and his word by my tongue »
(*II Kings*, XXIII, 2). All the prophets were aware of being the
mouth piece of God. In the transmission of this will which they have
perceived (which at times goes against their own feelings) they put
something of themselves ; their personality, sensibility, imagination,

---

1. J. PEDERSEN, *Israel, its Life and Culture*, London-Copenhagen, 1946, t. I-
II, p. 107.

poetical gift, are involved. Yet it remains that they do not speak
on their own initiative, that the message sometimes runs counter
to their personal feelings. The more we advance the more we stress
unilaterally the part of God (as with Ezechiel). This word from
God is endowed with power, it acts, it achieves what it utters
(*Deut.*, XVIII, 15 ss ; *Is.*, LV, 10, ss). It stands for ever, whereas
man is but flesh and passes away like the flower of the field
(*Is.*, XL, 8).

It is the consciousness of this fact that explains, to a certain
degree, the setting down in writing of the prophetical oracles. On
principle indeed, the prophetical words were essentially addressed
to their contemporaries, concerning a very concrete and unique
historical situation. But they also place events in the thread of the
history of salvation, between the basic events which the word of
God fulfilled and those which must happen at the end according
to the same word of God. Thus it was realized that the whole
movement of history is conditioned by the word of God. This concrete word for a given situation is an expression of the Will that
leads the whole of history. Therefore it has value, light and power
for later generations. The presence of glosses, additions, the existence
of very long passages like the Deutero-Isaias or the Deutero-Zacha-
rias, prove that the texts were read and re-read again, with the
idea that they threw light from God on later situations.

After the Exile, the Torah was fixed, and prophecy seemed to
decline. It was the epoch of scribes and commentators. But other
forms of proclaiming the word appear, notably in the apocalyptical
writings. We also see developing the doctrine of the word creating
the universe : « He spoke and they were made » (*Ps.*, XXXII, 9);
« God said : Be light made. And light was made » (*Gen.*, I, 3).
Then we see a comparison of Wisdom and the word being outlined.

And the Word was Made Flesh.

That Christ was seen as a prophet, linking up with the great
prophetical tradition is a fact that no one thinks of questioning,
but its importance is not always grasped. [1] He speaks openly unlike
apocalyptical writers, but he does not come forward as a commen-
tator or interpreter of the Law ; He is on another plane to the

---

1. Cfr R. Asting, *Die Verkündigung des Wortes in Urchristentum* dar-
gestellt an den Begriffen « Wort Gottes, » « Evangelium, » und « Zeignis, » Stuttgart, 1939; E. Repo, *Der Begriff « Rhema » im Biblisch-Griechischen,* 2 vol.
(Annales Academiae Scientiarum Fennicae B-75), Helsinki, 1951-1955.

scribes and doctors who, discomforted, will end by leaguing against Him. Moreover, His message, extremely positive, proclaims the actual presence of the long hoped for Kingdom. He speaks with authority, not hesitating to affirm that He goes further than Moses. He feels invested with absolute authority concerning His role of Sovereign of the new Kingdom just beginning. The Son of Man has authority over the earth. His word is therefore endowed, in a unique and definitive way, with the power of God. Much more, it is by His word that Christ, like a sower, inaugurates the fulfilment of the eschatological Kingdom ; His word is a seed which must grow in secret, according to the quality of the adherence and correspondence of those who welcome it with faith (Mark, IV, 14-20). Thus, Christ is not a simple intermediary ; if He appears as a prophet, He is decidedly more than a prophet, for He promulgates with authority. The quality of His word is linked up to mystery of His person. The more we understand what He is, the better will we measure the unheard-of extent of the word of God which thenceforward reaches us through Him. More still, in the measure in which the Kingdom is closely bound up with what He is and that He lives among us, we are set in the road of the great declarations made by St. John.

The Gospel according to St. John gives a very large place, as we know, to the idea of the word. Throughout that Gospel we find a series of notifications offering a very rich and varied vista. [1] But there is more : the prologue sees Christ and the eternal Word who took flesh. The question of the origin and meaning of this formula has been discussed at great length and the debate is not yet closed. We know how apt is the Johannine tradition to integrate elements of various origins into his new and profoundly unified synthesis. Personally we think that as regards notion, we must see here certain conceptions dear to the philosophical milieux of Hellenistic Judaism. Christ is the Son par excellence, He who, God, is in the bosom of the Father. This unique condition on which the Gospel throws light under several aspects, includes a perfect resemblance : He is the image of the invisible God (*Col.*, I, 15), the brightness of the divine glory (*Heb.*, I, 3). The prologue uses the term *Logos* ; it is the very expression of the Father. The Word is not uttered for time ; He is with God, or better, towards God, ordained entirely to God. But if, as actually happened, the Word was made flesh, all that appears of Him will be perfect manifestation of the Father's glory. « And the Word was made flesh and dwelt

---

1. J. GIBLET, *La théologie johannique du Logos*, in *La Parole de Dieu en Jésus-Christ* (Cahiers de l'actualité religieuse 15). Tournai, 1961, pp. 85-119.

among us, and we saw his glory, the glory as it were of the only begotten of the Father, full of grace and truth » (John, I, 14). And this contemplation is itself active : « And of his fulness we have all received : and grace for grace (John, I, 16). Such are the affirmations which will dominate Christian theology ; no text will be more often quoted than this prologue, which has often been considered as the quintessence of the Gospel.

The Christian Discovery : Saint Paul.

All apostles and Christian preachers have been aware that they were carrying on, with an increased efficacity, the works of the ancient prophets, and that the message the Risen Christ had entrusted to them really bore salvation for all men whosoever, ready to welcome it with faith. [1] « We also give thanks to God without ceasing, » wrote Saint Paul to the Thessalonians, « because that when you had received from us the word of the hearing of God, you received it not as the word of men, but as it is indeed, the word of God, who works in you that have believed » (I Thess., II, 13). The apostle is primarily a servant of the word (Luke, I, 1 ss), and Saint Paul could assert : « Christ sent me not to baptize but to preach the gospel... Woe unto me if I preach not the Gospel » (I Cor., I, 17 ; IX, 16). That is why an apostle like Paul expresses his condition in meditating what concerned the ancient prophets (Gal., I, 15 ss ; Acts, XXVI, 16 ss). Much more, this preaching which constitutes the Church, which is, in union with Her Lord, the pure oblation, appears to him as a sacerdotal gesture (Rom., I, 8 s. ; XV, 16).

But the apostle goes much further than the ancient prophecies. Closely associated to the Risen Christ, he achieves, in function of his mission, in the community which binds him to the other labourers for the Gospel, the last times. Christ had indicated it (Matth., X, 7, 15 ; 40-42). Paul knows it, as from experience : « Thanks be to God who always makes us to triumph in Christ Jesus and manifests the odour of his knowledge by us in every place. For we are the good odour of Christ unto God, in them that are saved and in them that perish. To the one indeed the odour of death unto death ; but to the others the odour of life unto life » (II Cor., II, 14-16).

---

1. J. DUPONT, La parole de Dieu suivant saint Paul in the same work La Parole de Dieu en Jésus-Christ.

Closely linked up with Christ (*I Cor.*, II, 2 ; *II Cor.*, IV, 1 ss), this preaching of the word draws all its efficacity from the fulness of the gift of the Spirit bestowed on the missionaries. The preaching of the Gospel is not done by word only, but it is accompanied by power in the Spirit and an abundance of all kinds (*I Thess.*, I, 5). The new ministry is superior to that of Moses for it is accomplished in the abundance of the Spirit (*II Cor.*, III, 8). A charismatic function, apostolic preaching is also an ecclesial function ; carried on in the cohesion of the Body (*I Cor.*, XV, 3, 11), it aims at grouping and building up the Church (*Eph.*, IV, 12).

There came a moment when certain sequences of this word were set down in writing ; there were the collections of matter which ended in the Gospels, there were Letters, the Acts of the Apostles, the Apocalypse. Faced with deviations and the erroneous tendencies of the gnosis, the Church soon insists on the normative importance of these writings which share in their own way the inspiration of the apostles. But these writings cannot be considered as containing as such the entire word.

Theology of the Word.

In the course of this progressive discovery we have met many different aspects. How can we grasp them in their right order and unity ? It is clear, though it has not always been seen, that everything must be centred on Christ Jesus, the Risen Lord seated at the right hand of the Father. [1] He is the Word Incarnate in whom are all the treasures of wisdom and knowledge (*Col.*, II, 3), to whom all power has been given (Matth., XXVIII, 18-20). Wherever the word is manifested it is finally in function of the Word and the Word Incarnate. We cannot insist enough : Christology conditions ecclesiology, and notably all that concerns the apostolate and problems relating to Scripture and Tradition. If we lose sight, in practice, of this centre as source and reference, there is danger of insisting on one or other aspect, with excellent intentions, but thereby losing to a certain extent, a well-balanced sense of the whole. Every word meriting to be called word of God is related in some way to the Word Incarnate.

Christ's Church is conditioned, if we may so express it, by the proclamation of the Word. She is constantly assembled, then built up by the word of the apostles, members of the apostolic college,

---

1. H. Urs von Balthasar, *Die Schrift als Gotts Wort*, in *Schweizer Rundschau*, t. 49 (1949), pp. 428-442.

and those who, for divers reasons, are associated with them. The Christian community, to begin by the liturgical community, is one in which we listen together to the proclaimed Word. The teaching function is primordial in the Church. The periods when real preaching has been more or less neglected are the darkest in the Church's history. Like her Lord, and in function from Him, the Church must bring the truth to the world where those who are of the truth will listen to the word (John, XVIII, 37). Through Her it really is the very word of Christ that reaches the world bringing the only salvation and the true life. And since this preached' word constantly refers to the Lord Christ, it will be in constant conformity with the written word, the Scriptures. Not that we should return to the mentality of the ancient scribes for whom everything was so perfectly written that it sufficed to interpret the texts. Privileged means of reaching the foundational events of our salvation and of our ecclesial community, the Scriptures only take on their full meaning when read in the living and structured community which is the Body and the voice of the Lord.

Thus then the preached word refers to the written word and is only thus fully active. The preached word especially refers constantly to Our living Lord as the totality of the lights from the Holy Spirit permits us to perceive Him. That also forms the bond between the word and life in the Church. What is most important finally is not to unravel texts with perhaps the danger of vainglory (John, V, 40 ss) but, by proclamation which faithfully refers to the Scriptures, to encounter Him who is the Word by His whole being, who reveals to us the will and action of God which will transform our whole life. Now we can grasp the intimate link between proclamation of the word and celebration of the sacraments, especially the Holy Eucharist. From Origen to the Curé d'Ars, it has been stressed (too rarely in the West) that in the liturgy, the Lord broke simultaneously the bread of the word and the Eucharistic bread. We have no right to choose according to our own preferences.

Our whole soul must welcome these gifts of God so closely connected. We must receive the Word with the same reverence as the Holy Eucharist. This was already declared by Origen.

It is a fact that in spite of the exhortations of the Council of Trent, the Catholic Church has neglected the Word to a certain extent. In how many places hardly anyone preached a hundred years ago... and even today... When they did preach, how much did they really refer, through Scripture, to Christ the Word incarnate ? How many sermons were merely human eloquence !

To my mind, the Council's decision, in the Constitution on the
Liturgy, to impose a homily at the Sunday Mass and encourage
them more frequently, is immensely important. It means reviving
concretely and practically, a method of preaching based on Scripture
and thus more conscious of its condition of Word, having its source
and power in Christ, Word of the Father. [1]

Obviously, passing a decree is not enough, we must conform with
it. This adherence can only be effected at the price of great effort
at several levels. For we cannot just limit ourselves to expatiating,
as they say, on subjects more or less connected with the texts in
question. Reviving the homily presupposes discovering once more the
complex exigences of integral Christian hermeneutics ; it also
demands a very vivid sense of this sacrament [2] of the Word of
which the priest is the celebrant by vocation and consecration. Anyone can see how this revival of the great tradition of the early
centuries but in the conditions of today, even if arduous, will
contribute enormously to this union of Christians which is at the
heart of all our hopes.

---

1. Cfr the collective volume *Le Prêtre, ministre de la Parole* (Congrès national
de l'Union des œuvres catholiques de France, Montpellier, 1954), Paris; A. GÜN-
THER, *Die Predigt*. Theoretische und praktische theologische Wegweisung, Frei-
burg B., 1963. — E. FOURNIER, *L'homélie selon la Constitution de la Sainte
Liturgie*, Bruxelles, Ed. Lumen Vitae, 1964.
2. K. Barth has developed at length a theology of the Word which has many
remarkable elements. But one would say that he has not sufficiently grasped
the whole range of the Incarnation of the Word and its sacramentary consequences.

Christ and the Church

by Édouard BEAUDUIN

Director of the Œuvre d'Orient, Brussels [1]

I. THE HISTORY OF SALVATION

1. *The New and Eternal Alliance.*

« God, who at sundry times and in divers manners, spoke in times past to the fathers by the prophets, last of all in these days, has spoken to us by his Son, whom he has appointed heir of all things, by whom also he made the world. Who, being the brightness of his glory and the figure of his substance, and upholding all things by the word of his power, making purgation of sins, sits on the right hand of the majesty on high » (Heb., I, 1-3). Thus in his prologue, the writer of the Epistle to the Hebrews sketches the whole history of salvation, God's eternal purpose, and mentions the time appointed for its fulfilment. God spoke first « at sundry times and in divers manners. » These were the beginnings of His redemptive action. By a succession of events, God marks the existence of His people and stirs up in some way the progress of its history through the voice of the prophets. He renews His promises and makes His calls more insistent. From the Exodus to the Captivity, from Abraham to John the Baptist, were so many breathings of the Spirit which re-assembled the spiritual people each time and revived their faltering faith. This first and ancient Disposition had this characteristic : the Eternal touched historical time at successive and isolated points, fixing the moments when, as Ruskin expresses it, « He deigned to let down his ladder. » Another feature marked this ancient Alliance : everything was promise and concerned the future. Events like the spoken words were prophetic. This people, so often delivered, was dimly hoping for a quite different liberation ; after the word heard so often, they

---

1. Canon Edouard BEAUDOUIN was born in Waremme (Belgium) in 1907. Doctorate in Philosophy and Theology, he worked as Professor at Saint-Hadelin's College from 1931 to 1940, then, from 1940 to 1956, he has been teaching religion at the Royal Atheneum in Liège. Since 1956, he is Director of the « Œuvre d'Orient » for the Ecumenical Movement. His articles has been published in several periodicals as *Irénikon, La Revue Nouvelle, Lumen Vitae.* — Address: Œuvre d'Orient, 8, rue Marie de Bourgogne, Brussels 4, BELGIUM(Editor's Note).

awaited one which would spell freedom, the coming of the Just One, Servant of the Eternal God. Time in which their history was unfolding, time belonging to a tangled and fugitive world, which God occasionally touched « with his finger, » was preparing a completely different time, new and definitive : the fulness of time. At last this time comes : the Event occurs which is to fulfil all things. The Holy Spirit forms the humanity of the Word of God in the Virgin's womb. The Son of God, consubstantial with the Father, by whom all things were made, united himself to man for ever. The new time, which is indeed « the last, » has been inaugurated. It is not only an historical fact, but the event of the end of history, which nothing can surpass, the beginning of a world that catches and takes possession of the whole future. [1] From it human time takes on the value of eternity, man is promoted to God. It is the new and eternal alliance.

2. *The New Time, the New Race in Jesus Christ, in the Spirit.*

Nothing is more central or fundamental in the message brought by the Gospels and Epistles and the commentaries on them by the earliest Fathers, than this narrow, substantial relation between the humanity of the Son of God and the definitive establishment of the new man.

Christ, through his humanity exactly like our own is the eternally active and effective cause of our deliverance from sin and of our life in God. It is in this perspective that we hear faith in the authentic human nature of Our Lord proclaimed by our Fathers at the Council of Chalcedon : « One and the same Christ, the Son, Our Lord, the Only Son, whom we recognize in two natures, without mingling, transformation, division or separation, without the union altering the difference of natures, on the contrary, the two natures keeping their own character all the more clearly, to meet in one person. » We must try to understand this taking up of sinful humanity in Christ, this divinizing influence of the Word of God upon the substance of generations, from His human life and His earthly sojourn in the flesh. It is from Scripture, testimony made ever present and living by the Spirit, that we can hear what Christ does and what He is « yesterday, and today and the same for ever. »

---

1. *Gal.*, IV, 4; *Heb.*, IX, 26; *Eph.*, I, 10; Luke, XXIII, 43; John, I, 29; *Apoc.*, V, 6-7; *I Pet.*, I, 19-20.

The Word of God revealed Himself in the flesh. The whole Gospel story testifies this, from His birth to His glorious ascension. And yet two modalities of this revelation are clearly discernible. Up to the cross, the Word is hidden under the veil of His humanity. All Christ's actions during those thirty-three years, His obedience, the choice of His own, His encounters and conversations with men, and the free oblation of His death, certainly were the acts of His eternal, divine Person working through His nature of man, but His divinity was not perceptible to bodily eyes. Only the spiritual vision of faith could catch a glimpse, beyond the human form, of Him who was Light of Light, true God of true God. Except for His Baptism and Transfiguration, the two theophanies of His mortal life, Our Saviour's divinity was concealed from human eyes. Was it not for having no greater insight, that the disciples of Emmaus heard the words : « O foolish and slow of heart to believe in all things which the prophets have spoken ! Ought not Christ to have suffered these things and so to enter into his glory ? » With the Resurrection of His human body, the reality and truth of the Word flashed upon the world. What had been hidden and only mysteriously perceived, was now unveiled and manifest. Not that, during those glorious forty days, the life of the Risen Christ was less authentically human. It is not a spirit that appeared to the women and the disciples ; nor was their meeting with the Lord a vision. The same Gospel goes on : the very man whom they had known and touched is among them in the joy of a meal in common and the intimacy of conversation : « See my hands and feet, that it is I myself. Handle and see ; for a spirit has not flesh and bones, as you see me to have... Have you here anything to eat ? » (Luke, XXIV, 39). And to Thomas : « Put in thy finger hither and see my hands. And bring hither thy hand and put it into my side. And be not faithless but believing » (John, XX, 27).

That was certainly a man living in the flesh, but a flesh in which is manifest, thanks to the Holy Spirit, the sovereign Lordship of the Word. This same Spirit who had fashioned the body of the Saviour, has now raised up His flesh, as He will raise up all flesh. « And if the Spirit of him that raised up Jesus from the dead dwell in you ; he that raised up Jesus Christ from the dead shall quicken also your mortal bodies, because of His Spirit that dwells in you » (Rom., VIII, 11). « Christ being put to death indeed in the flesh but enlivened in the spirit » (I Pet., III, 18).

That is why it is written : « the first man, Adam, was made into a living soul : the last Adam into a quickening spirit » (I Cor., XV, 45).

Thus the Spirit completes the work begun at the Incarnation ; for Christ, glory and triumph ; for the whole of humanity, through the Risen Christ, inauguration of a new world. With the light of Easter morning human time, dominated by sin and death, is transformed : it is the end of history, and the beginning of a new creation, of an eternity. The humanity of Christ Glorified is for ever in the Father's Kingdom, and by the same token places ours there. Through Him time and eternity meet and are inseparably joined. In this eternal Alliance, it is no longer like the old one when God from his infinite height touched human history by successive points, but in the Risen Christ, the whole man is drawn up and placed on His right hand.

The Risen Christ is therefore present in all future history. « Behold I am with you all days, even to the consummation of the world. » This sentence expresses clearly both Christ's will and the full reality of this presence. « I am... » His ascension to the right hand of the Father will not change this reality. It is not a presence outside and above time and history, but like His earthly existence, it is incarnate in this time and history. He has wished that every Christian may be able to meet him, His very Self, to touch and be touched by Him, as it happened to the disciples of Emmaus, to Thomas. What He is for us, what He has done for us, all the redeeming acts of the glorified God-Man are actual and strictly contemporaneous reality for every generation of all time. This presence of the glorified Christ in the future humanity, His acting power which transforms our sinful and mortal lives, to place them on the plane of eternity, leads us to the centre of our subject : the concrete and living bond which unites the Risen Christ and the Church. For there is permanent and deep union, reaching substance. Without such a presence of Christ in the Church, His sojourn here below would only be an historical event, the passing along of a proclaimer of the divine, a prophet, a leader by way of example, but not of the Mediator, of Him in whom all things are renewed and established ; we would still be in the period of promise and not in that of the fulfilment of time.

This great plan of Salvation, the proclamation of New Time and its definitive inauguration by the death and resurrection of Our Lord Jesus Christ, is the basic declaration of the faith, it is also the essential message borne by all Christian Churches, the reason for their existence and mission as Churches ; they share this message in spite of divergences, and historical, ecclesiastical or Confessional separations, and this under pain of betraying and suppressing themselves as Christian Churches.

Their divergence will appear in the modality with which they understand this presence of Christ in the world through the Church until the end of time, modality which will affect their theology of the Church (ecclesiology), and also indirectly their theology of Christ (Christology). Thus, according to the tendency of the Reformation, the Church will be considered as a community of believers, in which the saving Word of God is proclaimed, in order to arouse, by the strength of the Spirit, faith, conversion, life in Christ, eschatological hope ; as a setting, whose role is to be a mirror reflecting this message of salvation confided to Scripture, rather than a ministerial mediation assuring the presence and efficient application of Christ's saving action in the generations of time.

This brief synthesis of the relations between Christ and the Church does not allow us to go into the details of these divergences and their implications ; it seeks to re-assemble and illustrate slightly all the aspects of this ineffable union in its plenitude, and according to the faith we testify, that of the undivided Church, of Scripture, of the Apostles, of our Fathers in the faith. May it help each Christian to meditate the depth and extent of the mystery, to realize their own infidelities, and to grant to their brother the justice and praise he deserves.

II. THE MYSTERY OF THE CHURCH :
THE UNION OF CHRIST
AND HUMANITY THROUGH THE CHURCH

How is the Risen Christ present to each individual, to each generation, with this active and concrete presence ? He teaches us, He heals us, He accompanies us to transform our lives and conform them to His, but how ? What is His mode of existence among us now, as at each period of history as it comes ? Under what form does His presence act in the reality of our lives ? He is present really as during His mortal life in the past, but « in mystery » — in mysterio — the mystery of faith and its sacraments. The sacramental mystery grasped in faith is our place of encounter and contact with Christ, the setting of his permanence and sanctifying efficacity. The mystery of our belonging to the eternal Christ in the faith and its sacraments is precisely the mystery of the Church.

That in the Gospel story, the forty days after the Resurrection appear as the chief moment of the foundation of the Church is full of significance. Except for the holy women and Mary Magdalen mentioned only the first day, the apostles exclusively are favoured

with the appearances of Our Lord, as receivers of His last words
and wishes. The ecclesiological character of the discourses after the
Resurrection stands out clearly in the synoptics, and more clearly
still in St. John's narrative. First, the apostles are sent out into the
world : « Peace be to you ! As the Father has sent me, I also
send you » (John, XX, 21). And the triple question to Peter :
« Lovest thou me ? » — « Feed my sheep » (John, XXI, 15,
17). « Go into the whole world and preach the gospel to every
creature » (Mark, XVI, 15) : « All power is given to me in heaven
and on earth. Going therefore, teach all nations, baptizing them in
the name of the Father and of the Son and of the Holy Ghost...
and behold I am with you all days, even unto the consummation of
the world » (Matth., XXVIII, 18, 19). More significant still, is the
sending of the Holy Spirit in close connection with the command
to teach. « When he had said this, he breathed on them ; and
he said to them : Receive the Holy Ghost. Whose sins you shall
forgive they are forgiven them » (John, XX, 22, 23). « And I send
the promise of my Father upon you ; but stay in the city until
you be endued with power from on high » (Luke, XXIV, 49).
And His last words before the Ascension : « You shall receive the
power of the Holy Ghost coming upon you, and you shall be witnesses unto me in Jerusalem and in all Judea and Samaria, and
even to the uttermost part of the earth » (*Acts*, I, 8).

And there was the Spirit who renews and transfigures the earth.
After the Son's Ascension, Pentecost continues Easter and completes
it in mortal humanity. The Holy Spirit, through whom each divine
act had been accomplished up to now, is sent as had been promised, and henceforward His mission takes on an official and personal character : to maintain the presence of the Risen Christ in
humanity. « Go and teach all nations... baptizing them... he who
believes and is baptized shall be saved... » On leaving the Cenacle,
Peter preaches, baptizes, and the people are converted. The Church
of Christ is founded. Instruction, priesthood, conversion to the faith,
triple work achieved by the Spirit in the Church continuing Christ.
We still have to look more closely at these three actions of the
Spirit, and to show how by their mutual connection and intimate
conpenetration is built up, structured and increased one living
organism, the Church, the Body of Christ.

1. *The Church, Setting of Faith.*

« What do you ask from the Church of God ? » « Faith. » This
opening question and answer gives access to the baptismal rite and

bring the new-comer into the participation of the Christian mystery. Faith is the first aspect of the mystery in which, as we have said, the Risen Christ appears to the believer. « Faith is the substance of things to be hoped for, the evidence of things that appear not » (Heb., XI, 1). Enlightening the faithful soul, in spite of its veil of obscurity (« We see now through a glass in a dark manner » *I Cor.*, XIII, 12), it bases its confidence on the sovereign power of the Risen Christ and His redeeming act, its unshakeable certitude of salvation. This mystery of faith by which Christ manifests Himself to the believer is not situated first of all within individual conscience ; in its basic reality, it is neither dependent nor subject to the original and variable modalities of this conscience, it subsists first of all above it. Faith is a Gift — the Spirit's gift to the Church. Before being a personal gift to each conscience, as will be stated further on, it first animates the Church as its total conscience. This total conscience, which is the Church, is not separated from individual consciences, but neither is it the addition nor the result of them.

It is the Church that believes and hopes. In proposing her faith, she is not a screen putting herself between the believer and Christ, on the contrary, she is the setting, filled and enlightened by the Spirit, in which Christ makes heard his Word of salvation ; she is the eternal Christ « made objective » at the level of our earthly humanity.

To achieve this end, to give this setting of faith its vivid brightness in the misty eddies of history, Christ has endowed the Church with organs and functions with defined properties and closely connected, which the Spirit animates and directs according to their order. Of these organs, the first in nobility is the Scripture. Formed and gathered together by the Spirit and intended for the Church, Holy Scripture is the concrete expression of God's redeeming action invading history, of the divine revelation in act. Incarnate word, it is an integrant part of the total incarnation of the Divine Word. From this fundamental source the Church draws knowledge of the mystery of Christ ; she explores it without ceasing, and makes known its breadth, height and depth. Her primordial function is to draw out the full significance of the Scriptures for the generations as they journey on. Scripture is a collection of words and signs, but its essential value consists in the supernatural reality signified by these. It is for the Spirit, who brought together these Sacred Letters, to explain through the mouth of the Church all that must be understood in these texts. To do this the Church has a structure and appropriate functions. The great moment when this takes place is the very prayer of the Church, her sacred liturgy. The Church has Christ's sentiments, she feels with the Spirit of Christ. Prayer taught, and teaching « prayed » ; living commentary of the inspired text, the liturgy is the presentation, the paraphrase and the active sacrament of God's word. In this ecclesial teaching, the hierarchy has a very definite office, a normative function. The episcopal body, continuation of the Apostolic group, in union with Peter's successor, centre and guardian of the faith, must watch over the integrity of the deposit, check errors, correct deviations, prevent encroachments, so that no path may be closed to the passage of the Word in its full richness. The whole Christian people has its part in proclaiming the message of salvation. The faithful soul lives by the law of Christ. Member of His Body, animated by the faith of the Church, the Christian proclaims to the world the works of Christ, making his life conformable with Christ's.

Aware of the needs of this restless world in which he is immersed, knowing its expectation and eager cravings, the laity can make the light of the Gospel shine in it, it can support the pastor's vigilance in leading the flock, it can radiate the beams of this light in the total conscience of the Church, which will answer the more efficaciously the questions of man in a given historical context. Thus by the living faith of the whole ecclesial organism, Christ is present to the world, in all the dimensions of time and space.

2. *The Church,*
Setting of the Sacraments of Faith.

To this presence of Christ in the mystery of faith, is added a mode of existence, and of more closely actual presence, which makes faith itself real. The Risen Christ unites us to Himself in the sacramental mystery. By His sacramental existence, the God-Man communicates to us every moment the supra-temporal effects of His triumphant mediation. The whole existence of the Word Incarnate, the entire work of His life among us, are made actual in the succeeding ages of life here below. The sacraments are re-presentations in the Church, of the earthly existence of Our Saviour and His redeeming acts ; they are the mysteries of Christ fulfilled in us. His obedience, His prayer to His Father, His baptism, the gift of His Body and Blood, judgment and pardon through His cross, His attaining to glory, become strictly actual for us through the sacraments. The existence of the Risen Christ in glory and His sacramental existence in the Church on earth are inseparable. [1]

---

1. « The author of the sacraments matters more to us than the sacraments. »

In the Eucharistic Banquet, the whole life of Our Saviour, His Passion, death, resurrection and ascension, is offered us, placed before us and for us ; what was the unique event of human history becomes, through its institution, the permanent, ceaselessly renewed event, made present for the whole duration of history. Here again it is the Spirit who gives to the Church's sacramental signs, the sanctifying virtue of the presence of Christ. It is the Spirit who vivifies the priesthood of the Church. Just as He confers on ecclesial structures, apparently fixed, their interior vitality and spiritual dynamism, so through Him, do the matter and sacramental words — the water of baptism, the Eucharistic bread — receive a mysterious and supernatural destination, a profound substance, a vital power which transcends their own nature. The Spirit of Christ is the Lord of the Sacraments.

3. The Church, Setting of Life in Christ.

This double mystery of faith and of the sacraments of faith has but one aim : to make Christ real within us, so as to build up the total Christ ; it is entirely directed towards the presence of the Risen Christ in the life of His members. Through Him the new humanity forms but one body, and enters into intimate communication with God. « You are the body of Christ and members of member » (*I Cor.*, XII, 27). « From whom (Christ) the whole body, being compacted and fitly joined together, by what every joint supplies, according to the operation in the measure of every part, makes increase of the body unto the edifying of itself in charity » (*Eph.*, IV, 16).

A member of Christ, each Christian lives by Christ's life, his acts become Christ's acts. United in Him, Christians become members one of another, animated by the charity of Christ, the love of the Father and of their brethren. The new man lives by Christ's law ; Our Lord's life is the pattern of his thoughts, feelings and actions. This conformity of each Christian with Christ is again inspired and made concrete by the Holy Spirit, who thus crowns the whole of His personal work. For it is not a question here of a pattern abstractly proposed like a general rule of action. This free adherence of man to Christ's law must be raised to the highest degree of liberty, the liberty of Christ Himself... This principle is the Holy Spirit. He stirs conversion within us — the « metanoia, » the basic

---

In this perspective of the sacramental mystery, this answer from the Abbess at Port Royal de Montherlant is erroneous, and devoid of meaning (Montherlant, Port-Royal, p. 126).

change in the whole heart and soul which makes us open to the love of God, to universal charity. It is He who, in the practical situations of life, inspires our choice, our will, our action. If in Our Lord's life there was a particular moment for everything, as in every human life, as the Scripture says, « a time for planting, a time for uprooting, a time to weep and a time to rejoice, a time to be silent and a time to speak, » a time to pray and a time to act, a time to lie hid and a time to come forward, it is the Spirit who prompts us in what we must do, with Christ, when the time comes.

« Spiritum nolite extinguere » (*Thess.*, V, 19). Sanctifier of all the faithful, the Spirit raises up among them and for all the Church, saints and prophets as the time requires ; for He breathes wherever He wishes. During the various epochs of the Church, the great saints are the concrete answer, born into history, to the world's queries and worries, the living tradition, the manifestation of the *vertical* action of the Spirit of the Risen Christ within His permanent and *horizontal* assistance in the Church.

These three modes of the presence of the Risen Christ are inseparable, because they form one mystery. The edification of the total Christ in our pilgrim humanity pre-supposes their mutual reference and implication. The sacramental mystery is connected with the mystery of faith since the sacraments are the operative signs of it. The double mystery of the faith and of the sacraments, of social and impersonal character, is essentially directed towards the personal sanctification of each Christian in the Spirit. Inversely, if the Spirit breathes in each soul as He wishes, if He raises up prophets and saints in the Church, it can only be in the pattern and according to the structure of the whole Body ; for the Spirit is one. If the sacred Word tells us : « The Spirit breathes where He will and thou hearest his voice, but thou knowest not whence he comes and whither he goes. So is everyone that is born of the Spirit » (John, III, 8), it also says : « The Spirit of Truth... shall not speak of himself, but what things soever he shall hear, he shall speak » (John, XVI, 13). That saints like Bernard or Catherine of Sienna judge those who are of the Church, and these, from the angle of Christian responsibility and life, must feel legitimately judged by them, all this spiritual zeal is employed in the faithful belonging to the Church of Christ, and under its rule. And Peter sums up this great mystery of the Church of which Christ is the corner-stone : « Coming as to a living stone... be you also as living stones built up, a spiritual house, a holy priesthood, to offer up spiritual sacrifices, acceptable to God by Jesus Christ » (*I Pet.*, II, 4-5).

4. *The Church, Prophetical Setting.*

To render Christ present to men, to proclaim, manifest and give Him to all, is the unique mission of the Church, but her whole mission. Spouse of her Lord, she is His and exists for Him ; she serves Him in faith and love. She is not a screen between Christ and men, but the sign of Christ. Her nature is to be penetrated, to be a passage for Him ; fully transparent to His light, she effaces herself to let Him pass through. This purity, this absolute fidelity should be a matter for constant attention from men of the Church ; as sinful human beings, they will be tempted, consciously or not, to substitute themselves for the message they must bear and proclaim. The apostles preached and taught Christ Jesus without ceasing (*Acts*, V, 42). And St. Paul asserted : « We preach to you Christ Jesus. » In this sense, a Church that preached herself, and thought to be worth something on her own account, would not be the Church of Christ.

The Church is not God but « the Church of God. » The formula of faith stresses this essential shade of meaning. « Credo ecclesiam » : « I believe the Church » says the Creed. It does not say « in ecclesiam. » We believe « in God the Father... in God the Son... in God the Holy Ghost... faith is addressed to Some One, to God who manifests Himself to us ; it is the answer, the acceptance, the gift of our being to God who reveals Himself.

Paschase Radbert says rightly : « Let us not say : ' I believe in the Holy Catholic Church, ' but suppressing the word ' in ' let us say : I believe the Holy Catholic Church, like ' life everlasting ' and ' the resurrection of the body. ' » Otherwise we seem to believe in man which is not allowed. We believe in God only and in His Majesty alone... But in the Creed, the Church is presented as the first work of the Spirit, because she is the setting in which and through which I adhere and give myself to the Word who sanctifies and saves. She is the sign, the authentic one, the mirror, but the faultless one. It is in and through her that Christ loves and predestines us, for He shed His blood for her. Our personal salvation is won in that of the ecclesial community. She is the Ark of the Alliance, God's Temple, the guiding Star, Refuge of sinners, Comfort of the afflicted, Mother of all the saints.

5. *The Eternal Church.*

This presence of the Risen Christ in mystery will one day become presence in the light of glory. If on Easter Morning, the fulness of time was definitely won and inaugurated, it is not yet made manifest. The Church awaits Christ's second coming, she is journeying towards the judgment and general resurrection, she is the prophecy of this coming. The mysterious realities of her life in Christ — her faith, sacraments, the holiness of her members — are the prophetic declaration of her final accomplishment in glory.

The Church will be established in her definitive structure, she will be the heavenly Jerusalem, the eternal Church, willed and predestined by God in His Son from the beginning of the world. Gazing on this completion, the substance of our hope, we can contemplate the full dimension of the Church, her past, present and future. For this heavenly Church is no other than the one on earth, it is not a substitute, but its development and transformation in the light of the Risen Christ. When He is all in all, the mystery of His presence will vanish in glorious Reality. The earthly figure of the Church, her faith and sacraments, will pass away. The veil that hid Our Lord will fade : « We see now through a glass in a dark manner ; but then face to face... I shall know even as I am known » (*I Cor.*, XIII, 12). The signs which represented Him will recede before Him. And I heard a mighty voice, saying : « Behold the Tabernacle of God with men : and he will dwell with them. And they shall be his people... and he shall be their God... for the former things are passed away... And he that sat on the throne said : Behold I make all things new... To him that thirsts I will give of the fountain of the water of life freely » (*Apoc.*, XXI, 3-6).

The conformity of the Spouse with her Lord will then be complete. She will have lived all that Christ lived in His human flesh. During His time on earth until Calvary, the divinity of the Incarnate Word was hidden from mortal eyes ; and the Church on earth lives in mystery and is only perceptible as sign of Christ in faith. During her pilgrimage in this world she will be for it, as the Cross of Christ was, a subject for scandal and contradiction. But she is waiting with certitude for the fulfilment of her Easter, when the whole of humanity will rise again with her Head. And perhaps when that day dawns, in the appearance of her glory, we will turn back towards our past contradictions and say with the disciples : « Did not our hearts burn within us, when He spoke to us on the way, and explained to us the Scriptures. »

The Unity of the Church

by Édouard BEAUDUIN

Director of the Œuvre d'Orient, Brussels [1]

1. *The Unity of the Church Refers back to the Unity of the Three Divine Persons.*

« Father, that they may be one as we also are. As thou, Father in me and I in thee. » Christ situates the Unity of Christians directly on the level of the mystery of the Unity of His Father with Himself. The Father gives himself to the Son Who, in the movement of the Spirit, gives himself back entirely to the Father. This gift of love and consent, the Son's eternal « Yes » to his Father, in the movement of the Spirit, is the basis and very exigence of the unity of God's people, the dynamic unity by which the Church must live « That they may be one ! »

« We are all one, » says St. Hilary, « because the Father is in the Son. » In his commentary on the « Our Father, » St. Cyprian uses an excellent expression to define the Church : « de unitate Patris et Filii et Spiritus Sancti plebs adunata, » « the people assembled and unified from the very unity of the Father, Son and Holy Spirit. »

The report of the « Unity » section of the World Council of Churches at New Delhi (1961) begins with these words: « The love of the Father and the Son, in the Holy Spirit, is the source and aim of the unity which the Trinity desires for all men and the whole creation. »

It is from the unity in which He dwells with the Father and the Spirit that Christ vivifies His Church, for He is, in the humanity called to this vocation, the « sign » of the Father.

2. *The Unity of the Church founded on the Unity of Christ.*

If Christ is the « sign » of the Father, the Church is the « sign » of Christ ; She makes but one with Him, so that all may be con-

---

1. See biographical notice p. 699.

summated in unity. The Church is one with the unity of Christ,
Who lives in the unity of the Father and the Spirit. To reveal a
glimpse of this deep truth, St. Paul concentrates his thought on the
mystery of unity of Christ and the Church. « The Body of Christ
is Christ himself. The Church is Christ in so far as after His
Resurrection He is present among us and touches us here on earth. » [1]

The Church is inseparable from the Risen Christ ; She has no
other basis than Christ. More, there is intimate communion between
Him and her. Body of Christ, she is not a grouping of scattered
members possessing the same religious or moral conviction ; She
exists anteriorly to human constructions, She is given to the world,
like Christ and with Him. Paul had a particularly keen insight into
the fact of this intimate union of Christ with his Church. In his
Letters in captivity he expresses and clearly develops it ; it is found
there as the fruit of much thought, as a truth discovered and finally
grasped after a penetration — probably unique — into the depths
of a mystery, and of spiritual experience, painfully but triumphantly
gone through. On the way to Damascus he had been struck in a
second by « I am Jesus whom thou persecutest. » Become an apostle
and a missionary in the Church he then embraced with so much
ardour, a very great trial awaited him : the drama of the unity of
the Church. What did he not suffer to see the tensions and strife
that threatened to divide the Body of Christ, and separate its members ? What a degree of anguish his soul must have endured before
the eventuality of disunion. This dark night would be pierced by
the divine light which was to radiate from his last Epistles. In the
charismatic quarrels which divided the communities, he had felt
at once, and then perceived with a prophetic intuition, the absolute
exigency of the unity of the Church : for the Church is Christ, and
her unity is founded on this very identification. Christ cannot be
torn asunder ! « Now this I say that everyone of you says : I
indeed am of Paul ; and I am of Apollo ; and I of Cephas ; and
I of Christ. Is Christ divided ? Was Paul then crucified for you ?
Or were you baptized in the name of Paul ? » (I Cor., I, 12, 13).

In the conflict with the Judaeo-Christians, who wished to impose
the prescriptions of the law of Moses upon converts from paganism,
Paul with his apostle's conscience, knows no hesitation : salvation
and justification come from faith in Jesus Christ. And yet he is
equally conscious of unity and indispensable communion with the
other apostles and the Christians of Jerusalem. A break with them,
a separate church « a church of Paul » was to him an absurdity.

---

1. A. NYGREN, Corpus Christi, Lund 1943, p. 20.

It would reduce Christ's cross and the preaching of the Gospel to nothing. « I went up (to Jerusalem) according to revelation and communicated to them the gospel which I preach among the gentiles ; but apart, to them who seemed to be something — *lest perhaps I should run or had run in vain* » *(Gal.,* II, 2). So much did the Church and Christ form but one in his eyes. Christ cannot contradict Christ. [1]

3. *The Unity of the Church is Spiritual in Essence, both Visible and Invisible.*

The Church is « divine Incarnation continued. » Its nature and even unity mingle in a deep and substantial conformity with its Head. The economy of the salvation achieved through her is not different from that of the Incarnation. This takes place through Christ both fully God and fully Man : Verbum caro.

In preaching, dying, rising again, the visible Man, Jesus, really was, and showed Himself to be, the Master of things invisible. Through and in His flesh, He transforms death into life, the ephemeral into eternal. Joint action of the visible and invisible, of the human and divine, there is the whole mystery of the redemptive Incarnation, its divine and paradoxical logic. The Church, given to the world with and through Christ, continues here below, for the person and through the virtue of its Head, this work of salvation of which the Holy Spirit assures the permanence and indefectibility.

In Her as in Him the invisible and the visible cannot be dissociated ; the two elements are constituents of Her structure ; they are integral parts of Her unity. As in Christ, the visible in Her is not mere exterior appearance, variable and sociological manifestation of a mysterious reality ; but it is within Herself and Her supernatural mystery that the visible and invisible, the carnal and the divine unite to form Her unbreakable unity.

Thus the Church is one, in the two indissolubly bound elements of Her being : the invisible and the visible. On one side, there is the mysterious unity of this Church on earth, in which all those who believe in God's Word, who live by His life and are animated by His Spirit, are grouped and co-ordinated as members of one Body ; invisible community which will appear on the great day when the mystery will become plain reality, when He will present them to His Father so that « God may be all in all. » But at the

---

1. On this subject, see F. REFOULÉ, *Saint Paul et l'unité de l'Eglise,* in *Irénikon,* T. XXVIII, 1955, pp. 11-18. Dom Jacques DUPONT, *Le schisme d'après Saint Paul: L'Eglise et les églises,* T. I. Chèvetogne. 1954.

same time there is the visible and incarnate unity of this same Church, through which Christ touches our sojourning and sinful humanity, heals and sanctifies it in the faith and the sacraments of faith. It is through faith in His Word infallibly pronounced for us that we are seized, carried away, raised by Him into the Light of His Word ; it is through the sacraments, the signs that work in us the realities of faith, that we take part in the mysteries of Christ dead and risen again. Without unity of faith, communion in the sacraments of faith, the Church, and with Her, Christ, can only be torn asunder. As Christ is sign of the Father — « Who sees me, sees my Father » — so is the Church visible sign of Christ ; all breaking of this double epiphany would be a breaking of God's work itself, and according to the divine disposition, an impossibility. Paul expressed it vigorously : « One Body and one Spirit... one Lord, one faith, one baptism, one God and Father of all, who is above » all, and through all, and in us all » (Eph., IV, 4-6).

For Paul, this Church founded on Christ, with unity both visible and mystical : is the Church of the Apostles. The very movement of his thought, his whole attitude in this violent crisis, converge towards this theme : the Apostolic Church. His trials, his practical decisions, his reflections always resting on the initial intuition, become crystalized in the sentence contained in the same letter to the Ephesians : « You are... built upon the foundation of the apostles and prophets, Jesus Christ Himself being the chief corner-stone » (Eph., II, 20).

Thus the Church stands out in the unity of Her divine and human structure, in the harmonious amplitude of all Her dimensions ; she is the spiritual community of the people of God, the sanctified, united in the charity of Christ and living by His Word ; She is at the same time the community constituted on earth in which the different functions exercise in the world the ministry of Christ : sacerdotal hierarchy, preachers, faithful people, each one in their order and vocation assuring the integrity of the faith and sacraments, the spreading of the Gospel, the radiation of Christian life. Church grouping and Church grouped, Church calling and Church called to hear God's Word, one dwelling in which there is but « one Spirit... one God and Father of all... »

4. *The Unity of the Church does not Belong to the Order of Natural Realities.*

The principle of the Church's unity is essentially spiritual and supernatural, unity of faith, of sacraments of the faith, of organic communion of believers. It would be an error to force Her into uniformity of exterior and earthly expressions. Her whole strength and dynamism lies precisely in welding into one, but with a transcendent unity, respecting and accepting it, the very great diversity of the created order : peoples, races, civilizations, intellectual traditions, with their many and richly diverse behaviours and modes of expression. It would be « naturalism » to wish to reduce religious unity to an identity of natural and exterior form : one language, one liturgical form, one uniform administrative law, one invariable intellectual and theological expression, one fixed mode of feeling religious realities, with no particular accents, no original intuitions, merely an immobility and monotony regulated, which might be an exterior manifestation of unity but also the curtailing of the rich freedom of the children of God in the one Holy Spirit. « The lawful tendency to render the interior unity itself apparent, which is of supernatural foundation, must not lead to giving the exterior and natural expression of the unity of the Church the same importance as Her spiritual principles. This would be confusing sign of unity and principle of unity. There can be danger of a certain naturalism, if we doubt the unifying strength of the spiritual principles, if we demand as many exterior signs of unity as possible, as if the unity of the Church depended on them. Careful examination is needed here in order to avoid considering and giving as a principle of unity what is merely a manifestation of it, subject to variation. » [1]

5. The Sin of Division.

And yet what Paul had dreaded most of all was to appear for all the world to see ! Perhaps he had experienced at times this temptation to schism, in the throes of his disturbed conscience, but he had conquered it heroically by a greater love for Christ, so that if he is and always will be the Proclaimer of Christ to the world, he is by that fact and for the same reason, the herald of the Unity of his Church. This second aspect of his grace of election has perhaps not been sufficiently stressed ; in reality it is indissolubly connected with his basic vocation. It has been given to the Christian generation of our time, keenly alive to the wounds of division, and mysteriously filled with nostalgia for unity, to see and eagerly welcome the light which the figure of the Apostle is shedding upon our path. God is rousing us from our torpor ; we cannot escape

---

1. H. VOLK, L'unité de l'Eglise et la division du monde chrétien. Paris, 1962, p. 92, trans. by R. Marlé in : Unité de l'Eglise et tâche œcuménique.

from the appeal for unity nor the appeal of faith in the face of facts. We must tackle it. Seeing the enormous separations, and in spite of the character of fatalism which certain mental analyses take pleasure in giving them, the question arises : Has not Christ really given His Church this unity which is both visible and invisible ? According to some, did He even promise it for this world ? In that case, His great prayer for unity would only be the expression of a wish, without assurance of effect ? Would the identity between Himself and His Church be therefore devoid of real meaning ?

This is to twist the problem very badly. To say that Christ was only expressing a wish, a petition, an appeal, is a false view, as has been said earlier ; it was an injunction of visible unity, of a profound necessity inherent to the nature of the Church, in virtue of Her conformity with the Blessed Trinity. To say that Christ did not promise this unity for this earth has no sense either, since He gave this unity with all its constituent elements to the Church in very fact and the Church received it : Christ gave Himself to His Church — one Lord and Saviour ; — He gave her His Spirit — one Spirit animating the body of the faithful in one and the same faith, one and the same life ; — He made her one holy people, endowed with royal priesthood to offer the sacrifice of homage to the glory and praise of God, and to proclaim His salvation to the world ; He gave her His Word in the Holy Scripture — one Scripture ; He bestowed on her one baptism, one Eucharist ; He gave her the College of Apostles, united in faith and the priesthood to lead His Church extended throughout the world ; He gave her Peter and Peter's faith, that he might confirm his brethren. All these elements of unity, Christ has given us. We have not done what we should to develop them fully, we have been at fault, we have been blameworthy. All of us who have received these gifts have sinned. It is from these failings past and present that Christian divisions arose, it is through them that they continue. Therefore the Work of unity should begin by humility, contrition, penance.

The Church never ceases to pray for her constant purification, so that this « sign raised among the nations » may ever shine more brightly, and its lurking shadows gradually dispelled ; for the Church, being composed of sinful mankind, is not without shadows, nor beyond evil influences. « Far from being separated by law and fact from the evil world, the Church is *in* the world. The Church is a body composed of members who are grouped in the world and at the same time engaged in a process of progressive separation from the world. The world's power, alas, extends over the Church, because the Church came into the world to save it. All Christians are in the world and belong to it in the measure that sin still exercises its dominion over them, and even the best among us are not free from sin. Now although, according to the idea we have of one and the other, in their principles and future perspectives, the Church is something other than the world, for all that, the Church belongs in fact to the world and is not separated from it ; for the grace of God only partly triumphs even over religious men, and the best that can be said for us is that we have two faces, one of light and one of shadow, and *it is the latter which is seen on the outside.* So we are all something of the world for each other, although we may not be of the world. » [1]

And yet God wishes His Plan to be realized with us. He wishes man's own act and his free love to be associated with all the effects of His grace. His bounty calls for the response of His people ; its accomplishment demands our activity and can therefore be hindered or delayed by our wavering will, in a word, by our infidelity, for it comes to that. The sin of God's people is lack of fidelity, and thus the mystery of divine love operates within the mystery of iniquity. « Let a man so account of us as of the ministers of Christ and the dispensers of the mysteries of God. Here now it is required among the dispensers that a man be found faithful... » (*I Cor.,* IV, 1, 2).

We do not deserve to be what we are, because all that we are has been given us, but each one is responsible for not having been what he should have been. Therefore every time that a witness to the Gospel in the Church boasts of his quality in order to impose his truth, to the detriment of The Truth, each time that, seeking his own interest, the shepherd neglects his charge, or drives his flock before him without faith and love, each time Christians are the cause of scandal, that they betray Christ in the eyes of the world, and disfigure His image in themselves, the unity of the Church receives hard blows. The whole history of the separations and mutilations suffered by the Church on earth has its explanation and profound reason in this source of all human evils : infidelity to God's love.

It follows that there is but one way towards the full manifestation of unity : that of closer fidelity of the whole Christian people to all the gifts which God has bestowed upon His Church, that of a greater love for Christ living in all His members, in a word, of a greater charity. Charity in daily life is the bond and cement of

---

1. J.H. NEWMAN, *Parochial and Plain Sermons,* VII, 3, 35/40, quoted by H. KUNG, *Structures de l'Eglise.* Paris, 1963, p. 50.

unity. Paul had had a lightning intuition of this all at once ; he made it the fundamental pattern of his life, the most vigorous expression of his teaching. People, preachers, pastors, he summons them all to this life in Christ in charity, so that God's great plan be made manifest to all men : « That all may consummated in unity ! »

Grace and Justification

by Charles MOELLER

Professor at the Catholic University of Louvain [1]

I. FUNDAMENTAL TRUTHS

1. The first truth about grace and justification is that only God can give God. If being saved means living with God's life, becoming a sharer of the divine nature » (*II Peter*, I, 4), it goes without saying that *God alone justifies*, sanctifies. [2] The word « grace » (*charis*) signifies first of all goodness, benevolence ; the meaning of a « gift manifesting this benevolence » only comes afterwards. [3]

2. This essential truth goes together with another one, apparently in opposition to it, which is that *man consents and co-operates freely with grace.* « With fear and trembling work out your salvation. For it is God who works in you both to will and to accomplish, » says St. Paul (*Phil.*, II, 13). The paradox expressed in these words is the paradox of grace and justification. Only God saves, and at the same time, God does not save us without us. A text from the Council of Trent must be recalled here :

« The beginning of justification itself in adults must be understood as coming from the preventing grace of *God* through *Jesus-Christ*, that is from the vocation by which He calls them, without any previous merit on their part, so that those who had turned away from God by their sins, by grace rousing and helping them to turn towards justification, consent and co-operate freely with this grace, and when they are thus disposed — God touching their heart by the light of the *Holy Spirit*, (it cannot be said) either that man does nothing at all in receiving this inspiration, since he can reject it, or that he can without God's grace

---

1. See biographical note in *Lumen Vitae* X (1955), p. 51. — Address : 109, rue Van Mons, Louvain, BELGIUM.
2. It is entertaining to note that B. BARTMANN, *Précis de théologie dogmatique*, 4th. ed., t. II, 1941, p. 27, after declaring in the small print that « the cause of grace is God alone » adds « *De fide, of faith.* » A good example of the decentralization of present instruction to which we refer.
3. KITTEL, *Theol. Wörterbuch z. N.T.*, sub voce *Charis*.

turn towards justice of his own free will... » (Ch. 5, VI session, *Denzinger*, 797 (1525)).

3. A third affirmation flows from these two, concerning the *realism of our justification* : « Behold what manner of charity the Father has bestowed upon us that we should be called and should be the sons of God » (*I John*, III, 1). In a mysterious way our intimate being is changed, sanctified. It is precisely because God is truly acting within us, by His sanctifying omnipotence that we are really sanctified. It is not our personal efforts at work here, but the reality of the action of the Holy Spirit within us, when we consent to and operate with grace.

4. Then we must remember the *personal character* of grace and justification. Much of the discourse after the Last Supper recalls this fact repeatedly : « If any one love me he will keep my word. And my Father will love him, and we will come to him and will make our abode with him » (John, XIV, 23); « now this is eternal life : that they may know thee, the only true God and Jesus Christ whom thou hast sent » (John, XVII, 3). The text from the Council of Trent just quoted clearly stresses this *Trinitarian* perspective. The theme of the in-dwelling of the Trinity in the regenerated Christian has happily won back its place in the Catholic theology of grace. It is of paramount importance to explain « to what God we are converted » ; it is indispensable to stress that the God of Christians is God the Father to whom Jesus Christ leads us in the Holy Spirit.

5. Finally, the fruits of the grace of justification divide in a twofold direction : that of the *Holy Spirit within the soul,* sanctifying us interiorly, and that of the *transfiguration of the universe,* « for the expectation of the creature waits for the revelation of the sons of God » and « the creature also itself shall be delivered from the servitude of corruption, into the liberty of the glory of the children of God » (*Rom.,* VIII, 19,21). Justification is not only interior, it extends to the whole of God's creation, tending towards « new heavens and a new earth... in which justice dwells » (*II Peter,* III, 13).

II. THE VARIOUS THEOLOGIES OF JUSTIFICATION

Starting from these essential truths rooted in Biblical revelation, various theologies have developed. Usually the three principal forms are summed up in the following terms : justification is *divinization* in the perspective of the Orthodox theology ; it is « *created grace* » in the Catholic system ; it is « *extrinsic grace* » in the Reformation view, principally in Luther and Calvin.

For a long time the ruling impression was that no dialogue was possible in practice, between these three theological view-points. It even seemed that at least the Reformation theory of justification must be answered by a categorical rejection. What could be more opposed to the Catholic realism of justification than Luther's phrase « *Pecca fortiter, sed fortius crede,* » « Sin thoroughly, but believe more thoroughly still » ; or the classic imagery in many textbooks of an extrinsic (or « forensic ») justification, which covers the sinner with Christ's mantle, but leaving him — beneath this mantle — always radically a sinner, or again the typically Reformation phrase of the baptized soul remaining « *simul justus et peccator,* » « both just and sinner together. » Besides, the idea of divinization, if not entirely forgotten — how could it be without a radical impoverishment of the theology of justification ! — was at least, left a bit in the shade, on the higher shelves of the shop as for wares which are rarely wanted !

Recent studies have shown that concerning the doctrine of justification — formerly considered as one of the most inextricable knots in the relations between Reformers, Orthodox and Catholics — there is *much more agreement than disagreement*. The divergences concern much more a different theological out!ook than real opposition on fundamental points. In other words, it is more from systems proper to each of the Christian traditions that differences arise, than from a commission or negation of points of faith. [1]

1. *Grace as Divinization.*

This is the perspective most favoured in the East. [2] The starting-point of this theology is the efficacious and divinizing presence of Christ in the world and in the Church. The classic aphorism in Greek patristics asserts : « Whosoever is not assumed (by the Incarnate Christ) is not saved. » The person of Christ has, in fact, assumed human nature in its totality, for the Saviour is the *new Adam*. One of the principal arguments against Arianism (which denied the full divinity of the Word) was that if Christ is not God,

---

1. We know that H. Küng and Bouillard in their works on Barth have shown how, rightly understood, the theology of justification in the great theologian of Bâle is very near Catholic orthodoxy.

2. J. Gross, *La doctrine de la divinisation chez les Pères grecs*. Paris, 1924.

if in other words, he was only a lower god, he could not *save, that is, divinize, humanity.* [1]

This doctrine, absolutely common to the whole Christian Church, has taken a particular form in the theology of Gregory Palamas, which has had great prominence in the Orthodox tradition since the XV century. His distinction between the divine essence and the divine uncreated energies, is probably unfamiliar to us, and we know the controversies it provoked, as with the monk Barlaam. What interests us here is the meaning this distinction takes on in the theology of grace. The choice of terms « uncreated energies » stresses that God reveals Himself by acting, which excludes all « passion » from God ; but as the energies are « uncreated, » there can be no question of making them the fruit of man's merit in any way at all.

Only, this way of speaking of energies, of uncreated grace is only apparently in opposition to the Catholic terminology — which as such is not of faith — of « created grace. » As we shall see, Western theologians speak of « created » grace precisely to recall vigorously that grace is ceaselessly *created by God* within us ; man is so incapable by himself of justification that God must create this grace within him. In other words, the meaning of this term is *anti-Pelagian*, at least at the great Scholastic period.

If now we ask ourselves how the same doctrine is expressed by almost antithetic terms — *uncreated* energies, on one side, *created* grace, on the other — it must be admitted that the two theologies are answering different questions. The Eastern theologians are not seeking to explain what, in man, permits the insertion of the gift of grace ; they consider one point only : how is it that *God* who is incommunicability itself and incomprehensible, for He is a « super-essential abyss, » nevertheless communicates Himself in its essence ? The distinction of Palamas aims at this only, like his reflections on the light of Thabor. Uncreated energies for him are, if one may say so, this facet of the superessential divinity which allows Him to communicate Himself while remaining incommunicable ; but the term « uncreated » shows clearly that it is truly God who gives Himself. The Western point of view is diametrically opposed without being in contradiction. The Western theologian seeks more and more to discover what, *in man* will. permit acceptance of this « grace created by God. » This explains how gradually, this theology will express the reality of salvation given through grace, with the help of terms borrowed from Aristotle, for example, the term « *habitus*, » which was to have such success in the West, since it

---

1. L. BOUYER, *Du protestantisme à l'Eglise.* Coll. Unam sanctam. Paris, 1956.

became of current usage, without the expression : « *habitual* grace, » distinguished from « actual grace. »

As we see, the doctrine is the same on both sides : that God alone gives divine life and that we really receive it. The setting of the question differs. Within the same undivided faith, several presentations are possible, according as we consider grace *from the point of view* chiefly *of God who gives it* or *from the point of view of man who receives it* (from God).

Now these few lines from Palamas, quoted by way of illustration, will be understood better :

> « Since the Son of God, through his inconceivable love for men has not only united his divine hypostasis to our nature, and taking a living body and a soul endowed with intelligence, appeared upon earth and lived among men, but even, O wondrous miracle ! unites himself to human hypostases, and fusing himself with each believer by communion of his sacred Body, becomes concorporeal with us and makes us a temple of the whole divinity, for the plenitude of the divinity dwells corporeally in Him (*Col.*, II, 9), how does He not enlighten, by surrounding them with light by the divine brightness of His body which is then within us, the souls of those who participate in it worthily, as He enlightened even the body of the disciples on Thabor ? Then, indeed, this Body possessing the source of the light of grace was not yet fused with our bodies ; He enlightened from without those who approached worthily and sent light into their souls through their bodily eyes. But today He is fused with us, He lives within us, and naturally, enlightens our soul from within... Only one can see God... Christ. We must be united to Christ — and with what an intimate union ! — in order to see God. » [1]

It is clear that the interiority of grace is connected with its radiation on the corporeal world, as well as to its « cosmic » prolongation. The humanity of the Saviour, especially in the Eucharist, divinizes our whole person, at the same time as it makes the universe share in this grace of transfiguration. We need only remember the pages by Dostoïewski in *Les frères Karamazov*, about animal, plants and trees which are in peace because « in the Word, » to see the importance of the subject in the Orthodox theology of grace.

Thus, on condition we distinguish clearly the formulation proper to Palamas, perfectly legitimate, but which is not placed on the same level as the affirmation of faith as such, the Eastern point

---

1. This text is from a lecture by J. Meyendorf; it is reproduced in C. MOELLER and G. PHILIPS, *Grâce et œcuménisme*, coll. *Irénikon*, Chevetogne, 1957, p. 57. Reference can be made to the studies by J. MEYENDORF on Palamas, among others, the very accessible one in the coll. *Maîtres spirituels*. Paris, 1960.

of view on grace as divinization is purely and simply that of undivided faith.

2. *Created Grace.*

We must first state that this formulation is not taken, as it is,
from the Council of Trent : it merely speaks of the « infused,
inherent » character of the grace of justification, but it nowhere
imposes the terms « *habitus,* » « created grace » to faith. We are
simply at the level of theological formulas.

We have already said that the origin of this term is largely *anti-
Pelagian.* The details of this history will be found elsewhere,
remarkably analysed by Mgr. G. Philips ; [1] here we will only state
the essential and quote a few texts.

Saint Augustine was already anxious to stress that we must love
God and our neighbour *de Deo,* in the sense that it is the Holy
Spirit who « loves in us » ; it is God within us who loves our neighbour. In this sense one may speak of « uncreated grace » in St.
Augustine's thought. This idea will always be found in Western
theology ; even when there becomes question of a *habitus,* this will
always be created by God, and will permit us to love God with
the love with which God loves.

The question of a *habitus* arises over baptized children dying
before coming to the age of reason. Saint Augustine, then specially
St. Anselm and Abelard, will elaborate a theory which distinguishes
justification *habitu sed non actu.* This distinction which Innocent III
still quoted as the opinion of some, spread like wildfire ; from 1311
at the Council of Vienne it is current opinion.

What must be said here is that this term *habitus* was not applied
to the problem of grace on account of Aristotle's teaching, but first
of all on account of a very concrete case, that of baptized children.
Even if Aristotle's philosophy causes the term to become fixed, it
is not the unique, nor even the principal, source of this terminology.

When the term « created grace » appears in Alexander's Summa
the dominant idea remains that of an immediate union, in created
grace, with the Spirit Who gives it in giving himself ; they speak
of a *lumen fluens,* of a *forma transformans* working in the soul a
forma transformata. If some assert that the habitus is something previous, most point out that the habitus is the fruit of the Holy Spirit
Himself. Saint Bonaventure explains that we must admit a created
habitus in order to stress the radical powerlessness of man and to

---

1. All this section (II, 2) is a summary of the works by Mgr. G. PHILIPS,
more details of which, with references, are to be found in *Grâce et œcuménisme.*

exclude justice from works. Created grace manifests the *indigentia hominis*. Created grace is in no way then a kind of automatic possession of the human being, which would enable him somehow to do without the permanent influx of God our Saviour ; on the contrary it is ceaselessly produced by God Himself present in the soul. Placing himself at God's point of view, St. Bonaventure explains that the charity of God, in communicating itself, is operative, producing a change within man. In other words, *gratia creata* results from a continuous influence of divine light ; the soul then possesses the Spirit, or rather, is possessed by Him, « acted upon by Him. » All this is summed up is one striking formula : « to possess a habitus is to be possessed by God, *Habere est haberi.* »

In the same way Saint Thomas explains that charity « *ponit aliquid in anima*, » but points out that this *aliquid* is not a thing, nor a completed thing, but a certain reality which is not an object ; the charity of God is effective and operative ; it changes the man in whom the Spirit dwells ; from this a *habitus* results, but not in the sense of a previous reality, which would be produced by another causality than that of God Himself at the moment when He communicates Himself. In charity we are connaturalized with the Spirit; the *habitus* works in the sense of a continuous urge in the act of becoming ; it is an active attraction of God working in man ; it is a continuous trait not merely an interrupted one ; thus the *habitus* would be the wish for God, ever translating itself in the profound reality of the human being.

It can be seen that this statement diminishes nothing of the reality of what is called uncreated grace, that is, gift of the divine Persons themselves, by indwelling, in a believer's soul. The expression « created grace » only aims at stressing the complete poverty of man as regards justification, and the reality of the sanctification which God works in man, since it marks the depths of the soul, making it capable — always under God's motion — of knowing and loving God, of loving others *with* the love with which God loves.

Unfortunately, between the end of the XIII century and Luther, this vision of a *gratia creata (semper a Deo)* dwindles, in favour of a kind of substantification (*Verdinglichung*) of the *habitus* itself. Two assertions of St. Albert the Great, along with others, in the line we have just mentioned with St. Bonaventure and St. Thomas, will contribute to turn the theology of grace in this direction. The first explains that for an act to be meritorious, man must in some way, be master of it ; the second stresses that there is an infinite distance between God who gives Himself and transformed man, so that an *intermediary* is needed, created grace.

This tendency to materialize a strictly spiritual thing joins up with the opinion that sees a *previous* disposition in the habitus ; it accords also with the statement which insists more on the actualization of the gift of grace than on the ontological transformation it performs.

Luther did not grasp the real meaning of created grace. He held the celebrated opinion of Peter the Lombard, who identified grace with the Holy Spirit Himself. We have just seen that this perspective is in no way denied by the partisans of the formula of created grace ; on the contrary since for both St. Bonaventure and St. Thomas, this grace is created by God, who works unceasingly within us to unite us to Him. Unfortunately, this perfectly clear view became obscured at the time of Luther. The danger of substantification was no illusion. That is why he opposed, in the name of anti-Pelagianism, this new notion, whereas, we have just seen, it was explicitly in an anti-Pelagian perspective that the formula had been elaborated ! The tragedy of the history of the Reformation is there : it opposed a Middle Ages in a state of decomposition, drowned in adventitious speculations, much more than the great tradition of the monastic and Scholastic Middle Ages.

This brief sketch allows a few conclusions to be drawn concerning the presentation of the doctrine of grace in instruction and catechesis.

— We must *banish the dualism between created grace and the doctrine of indwelling.*

— We must keep a series of valuable aspects : the *efficiency of the charity of God,* which really achieves in man a capacity created (by God) to know and love Him ; that is a philosophical way of saying the same thing as what Biblical phraseology calls a « new creature. »

— We must insist that this transformation is *lasting,* for the habitus is an intentionality of knowledge and love ; to grow in grace is to be more and more « activated by the Holy Spirit. »

— We must safeguard the idea of *immediacy* in the *habitus* ; this is not a being interposed between man and God ; we must make use of grace, not enjoy it. In other words, we should not find complacency in God's gifts, but continually find God Himself in them, through these gifts ; if we must not use (*uti*) God, we must enjoy (*frui*) Him. This doctrine, classic with St. Thomas, shows very clearly that we must tend towards God Himself, and that grace within us is simply this disposition animated ceaselessly by God, thanks to which we come out of ourself to attain God, to cross the desert and strain towards vision of the divine Face.

— We must stress the *vitalism* of the habitus : we never dispose of God but of the possibility (ceaselessly created by God) of making an act of charity towards God, in function of His active and continual presence.

— Finally, in this perspective, *merit* is better understood : it is not a thing, allowing us to obtain something else, for it simply is the reality of man, in the depth of his soul, become « *worthy of.* » It is the *personal character* that must be stressed here : a man merits because he *is.* It is not an acquisition, but the fruit of the whole man acting under God's motion. Thus we can understand that, in rewarding our merits God crowns His own gifts. This subject, classic since St. Augustine, links up quite naturally with the theology of grace properly understood ; which is itself continued by the theology of the gifts of the Holy Spirit. Life at the level of the gifts produces a more habitual sensibility to the *actual* motions of the Spirit.

— We must *then* develop certain essential traits especially the *personalism of the relations* between the soul and God ; the created *habitus* is simply an *active receptivity,* of which, on the plane of more philosophical formulation, the idea of *participation* would be a felicitous approximation.

It seems then that properly understood the terminology of created grace, of the *habitus* of grace does not imperil the essential truths on the gift of God, but the reverse. But one may wonder whether the expression « *state* » of grace, still much used in both teaching and preaching does not offer more inconveniences than advantages. The term « *state* » signifies the reality of the transformation worked by God in the human being ; but anyone can see how misunderstanding is easy. Too many Christians still think of the life of grace within them as some mysterious thing, which must not be lost, and if lost, must be found again as soon as possible. But, as Bernanos remarked, faith is not lost like an umbrella. Grace is a network of active relations within us with God. If it is quite true that the sacrament of Confession restores us to friendship with God, this sacrament is still too often misunderstood, and confused with the recovery of a lost object !

3. *Extrinsic Grace.*

Reformation theology insists on the extrinsic, « forensic » character of justification. This formula, as has been said, has long been taken to mean a kind of purely exterior justification, leaving the soul in its state of sin, this being no longer imputed to it.

This explanation disregards an all-important fact, that the Reformation tradition has *two* terms, *justification* and *sanctification*, for the whole life of grace, whereas since Trent, only *one* term, justification, expresses one *and* the other. For the Reformers, grace has three aspects : justification, sanctification, redemption. Justification and regeneration are *inseparable*, as Calvin states for example : « We cannot apprehend this justification unless we also have sanctification in Jesus Christ who contains both inseparably. Now we cannot possess Him without his sanctification since He cannot be torn asunder. » [1] Of course, we must not confuse justification and sanctification : the first comes from God ; the expression « extrinsic » only seeks to signify the gratuity of God's act and its eschatological character, but it certainly does not signify that sanctification, through the Holy Spirit, is adventitious, secondary. On the contrary, the union of God with man, the principle of all Christian life, has for *immediate* consequence sanctification ; our whole life becomes the Spirit's field of action. The gift of the Spirit is creative, vivifying, efficacious in the man who renounces himself and lets God work within him.

There is nothing substantially different here from Catholic thought. What differs, as we have said, is the terminology. Some of the Fathers at Trent wanted the decree to contain the idea of « first justification » and « second justification, » from a desire, among other motives, to speak more explicitly of this two-fold aspect of justification, as it appears in Reformation thought, and also in authentic Catholic theology. This distinction was not retained in the Council's texts. It none the less remains that there is a typical case of ecumenical dialogue here. The basic orthodoxy of the Reformers' view on this point is beginning to be recognized by all theologians. But this is far from being the case in the domain of current catechesis ; here it too often allows it to be understood that for the Reformers there is a kind of extrinsicality of justification, even going so far as to insinuate a kind of « immoralism » or distrust of a « holy life. »

Apart from the difference of accent — Calvin putting it on God's action in its perpetual renewal, Catholics stressing the results in man of the action of God — the Reform also admits the realism of justification-sanctification. The special mark of the Reform is a spirit of *joyful gratuity,* of increasing readiness before the Spirit's creative role. Sanctification is real, therefore it is interior ; justification and sanctification are inseparable, like complementary aspects,

---

1. CALVIN, *Institution chrétienne,* éd. Budé, t. II, p. 317.

one exterior, the other interior of one act. We are far away from silly caricatures now. We need only draw attention to the reality of a holy life among Reformers, [1] to realize the gravity of the error of adhering to the antiquated polemical categories.

« Sola fide, sola gratia, soli Deo gloria (man is justified by faith alone, grace alone, for the glory of God alone) is a formulation of a particular evangelical statement. Only the thrice repeated « sola » can give rise, in controversy, to an exclusion, and thus run the risk of an unilateral presentation. But, as we have seen, this exclusivism is nonexistent in the great Reformation tradition ; the formula simply means that without faith, grace, nothing is accomplished. [2]

It is well to remember, in concluding this section, that in the beginning, the term « Protestant » did not mean « one who protests against » but « one who testifies in favour of... » according to the real meaning of the Latin verb « protestari » ; the term « Catholicism » also should never mean « what is anti-Protestant » but what is *universal*, what is qualified to integrate in the unity of undivided faith the various riches of theological, liturgical, canonical and spiritual traditions.

III. CONCLUDING REFLECTIONS

1. Ecumenical dialogue is *indivisible*. We must beware of confining it to a series of two-sided comparisons, Catholicism-Orthodoxy, Catholicism-Protestantism, Protestantism-Orthodoxy, etc. This would enclose us in a succession of blind alleys. We must keep in mind, *ceaselessly and simultaneously*, the Orthodox, Reform, Catholic and Anglican points of view. On our present subject, the Reformation links up with the Western tradition earlier than the nominalistic current of the XVI century ; if at that epoch, Catholicism had preserved real contact with the Eastern tradition, so strongly attached to the divinization of the Christian, Luther's attempt would probably not have been strengthened by the schism; Luther would have more easily discovered that the deep realism of Christian sanctification

---

1. Cfr L. BOUYER, *Du protestantisme...* the whole of part I, pp. 1-144, illustrates the point in masterly fashion.

2. It need hardly be said that none of these precisions, although elementary, appear in the volumes on the Reformation in the *Histoire de l'Eglise* by DANIEL-ROPS; these two volumes are particularly badly directed, for if a whole series of material details are exact, the depth of the problem facing the Catholic Church in the XVI century escapes the author all together. We warmly recommend catechists and teachers not to use these books when talking to their pupils of the Reformation.

and justification simply did not endanger the gratuity of the divine action, but the reverse. Also, if the tradition of the Christian East had maintained contact with Western tradition, it might have escaped the danger of not considering sufficiently what happens *within man* when penetrated by the Spirit. Divinization, created grace, do not oppose but complete each other, but through two different formulations ; just as what the Reformation declares by « extrinsic grace » merely recalls that « without Christ we can do nothing, » and that all comes from God.

2. As to *content*, Orthodox thought is very like ours ; but there is a world of difference between Eastern and Western perspective when it comes to *categories of thought*. By contrast, there are often great differences of content between Catholic thought and the Reformers, but their categories of thought are similar ; over grace, for example, discussion immediately places itself within St. Augustine's terminology. Hence the facility of discussion between Reformers and Catholics, but hence also the dead-lock they soon reach.

3. Three aspects should be especially brought out in the matter we have been considering : stress of the *personal character* of justification, marking the *Christocentric* aspect also, will safeguard both the realism of interior justification and its *cosmic efficiency* in the transfiguration of the world, towards the new heaven and the new earth. Justification is Christ, who saves our intimate being in purifying it, and delivers the universe from the servitude of corruption. The grace of justification directs us, with the universe for which God has made us responsible, towards the Kingdom, this Kingdom which is already present ; that is why « we are children of God. » This Kingdom which has not yet come ; that is why « we are saved in hope. » Grace is received and waited for, in the joyful straining forward which unites, in hope, tribulation and joy.